THE
WINNING
DIFFERENCE

HOW TO GET WHAT YOU
WANT, NEED, AND DESERVE

Other Books by Jane Hight
(Formerly Jane Hight McMurry)

The Dance Steps of Life

The Etiquette Advantage

Etiquette for the Christ School Gentleman

Readers Theatre for Senior Citizens

Success is a Team Effort

Navigating the Lipstick Jungle

THE WINNING DIFFERENCE

HOW TO GET WHAT YOU WANT, NEED, AND DESERVE

JANE HIGHT

STELLAR PUBLISHING

Text copyright © 2024 by Jane Hight

Published by Stellar Publishing
All rights reserved.

All rights reserved under International and Pan-American Copyright Conventions. Reproduction or translation of any part of this work beyond that permitted by Section 107 or 108 of the 1976 United States Copyright Act without the permission of the copyright owner is unlawful. No part of the book may be reproduced in any form or by any means including photocopying, electronic mechanical, recording, or by any information storage and retrieval system, without permission in writing from the copyright owner.

FIRST EDITION 2024

Library of Congress Cataloging-in-Publication Data

Hight, Jane.

The Winning Difference: How to Get What You Want, Need, and Deserve / Jane Hight.

Includes bibliographical references and index.

ISBN Paperback: 978-0-9849660-3-5

1. Business
2. Self-Actualization
3. Personal Development
4. Success

Library of Congress Control Number: 2022942708

Summary: A step-by-step guide teaching how to win in business, sports, and entertainment.

Printed in the United States of America

10 9 8 7 6 5 4 3 2 1

Book design by Andy Meaden, Oxfordshire, England meadencreative.com

*In thanksgiving and memory of my parents,
Joan Williams Hight and Henry Wesley Hight, Sr.
who made the winning difference for me.*

*For
Auggie, Cora, Wells, Mary Jane, Hart,
Beau, Harriet Joan, and Veta*

And for
everyone who wants to know what they need beyond
education, technical skills, and talent to win.

Acknowledgements

Thank you to Joan and Henry Hight Sr., and the following athletes, celebrities, and CEOs who through their performance examples and explanations shared the actions that made the difference in their achievement of peak performance in conversations, interviews, media appearances, books and an array of print and broadcast media: Michael Phelps, Sugar Ray Leonard, Sara Blakely, Carlos Santana, Anna Paquin, Michael Jordan, Madeline Albright, Arnold Palmer, Ben Affleck, Muhammad Ali, The Beatles, Chad Dickerson, Bon Jovi, Tico Torres, Barbara and Jack Nicklaus, Kelly Slater, Stuart Scott, Tim Brown, Carli Lloyd, Pharrell Williams, Brian Baumgartner, Barbara Walters, Carol Meyrowitz, Jennifer Lawrence, Warren Buffett, Bill Gates, Arthur Ashe, Steve Azar, Amanda Beard, Joshua Bell, Bobby Bones, Al Borland, George Brett, Mark Bryan, Brandi Chastain, Chevy Chase, Misty Copeland, Joan Cronan, John Daly, Patrick Davis, Ellen DeGeneres, Jim Valvano, Admiral Patrick Driscoll, General Robert E. Milstead, Jr., Wayne Dyer, Julius Erving, Helen Hayes, Thomas Gugler, Oprah, Wayne Gretzky, Tim Hardaway, Carla Harris, LeBron James, Lolo Jones, Rob Kaufmann, Joe Morgan, Tom Welling, Kevin Nealon, Ahmad Rashad, John Rassias, Jerry Rice, The Right Reverend Sidney Sanders, Alan Thicke, Michael Waltrip, Sam Walton, Lady Gaga, and others.

Special thanks to Dar Kendrick, Ph.D., Jeri Bills, DDS, Win McMurry White, Belinda Judkins Allen, Virginia Callaway, and Terri Haywood who edited this book and to Allison McMurry Cordell, Steve Nelson, Frank Dworsky, CFP®, and Richard Earl Morgan, M.D.

Contents

Preface
    Playbook For Peak Performance 13

Introduction 15

Chapter One
    Toppermost Of The Poppermost:
    How To Create A Strategy For Rock Star Results 21

Chapter Two
    D.R.A.T. (Don't Remain A Tadpole):
    How To Leap To The Gilded Lily Pad 51

Chapter Three
    Don't Be An Asshole:
    How To Attract, Develop, And Maintain Winning
    Relationships 89

Chapter Four
    Open The Window And Shout:
    How To Package And Promote To Reach The Top
    Of The Charts 147

Chapter Five
    You Don't Ask, You Don't Get:
    How To Talk Your Way To The Top 201

Chapter Six
    Understand One Word:
    How To Use Technology For Peak Performance 215

Chapter Seven
    Wave A Wand:
    How To Conjure Hollywood Magic 237

Chapter Eight
    The L.A.S.T. Result:
    How To Turn Problems Into Super Star Solutions 245

Chapter Nine
> *Pay To Play:*
> *How To Take Championship Actions* 259

Chapter Ten
> *Booyah!*
> *How To Be Memorable And Live On Forever* 279

Afterword
> *The Biggest Difference* 297

Notes 305

Index 311

Bibliography 323

About the Author 343

Preface

Playbook For Peak Performance

Why do some people with the same educational backgrounds and technical skills as others make it to the top while the rest do not? What actions make the winning difference for the most successful people on the planet? What do they do to beat the competition in business, healthcare, sports, and entertainment? What are their secrets? How do winners win?

If you want to achieve peak performance, find out what actions world-class achievers took and take the same actions. *The Winning Difference* removes guesswork revealing their secrets and explains exactly what they did and how they did it so you can win.

Fusing research with fascinating stories of some of the greatest winners of all time to reveal the actions they took to win, this book will make the difference in your life if you take the same actions no matter who you are, where you are from, who your parents are, where you went to school, or what past mistakes you made.

It is the only book to reveal the actions of many of the Greatest Of All Time (G.O.A.T.) winners by disclosing not just *what* they did to win but to *fully explain how* they won so you will know exactly how to take the same actions to achieve your own brand of super success in your field.

*If you don't have time to do it right,
when will you have the time to do it over?*

– John Wooden

Introduction

*I was once a child with a dream looking up to the stars.
Now I'm an adult in a spaceship
looking down to our beautiful Earth.*

– Richard Branson
First Person to Blast Off in Space in His Own Spaceship

Michael Phelps' laughter seemed inappropriate and came out of the blue when he, my daughter Win, and I were driving to my home near Wrightsville Beach, North Carolina. After all, I was talking and Michael was my guest. He might be the most decorated Olympian in history but my time on earth is as valuable to me as his is to him, and I'd spent a chunk of my time getting ready for his visit, taking care to make him feel welcome, and introducing him to friends at the beach club where he'd spent the day. I was in the middle of relating a story about one of the people he'd met who I'd just said is "one of the nicest people in the world" when the laughing started.

"What's so funny?" I asked Michael.

"Do you know how many of the 'nicest people in the world' you've introduced me to today? So many that I've lost count!"

The three of us laughed through two stoplights. Win laughed so hard tears rolled down her face. She giggled, "Mom, you say that all the time."

I laughed at myself realizing for the first time that I do say that about many people I know. When I finally stopped laughing, I said, "Gee, you know you're right, Michael. I do know a lot of the nicest people in the world. Most of the people in the world are nice, but I also know people who are not. Life is too short to waste your time or mine with ones who are not."

"By A Hundredth," the name of Phelps' thoroughbred race horse — honored the fraction of a second, quicker than a flash of lightning, that resulted in his winning his seventh gold medal in Beijing. You may not appreciate one one-hundredth of a second as much as Phelps, but perhaps like Phelps you value time.

Michael Phelps told me a secret. He had to. Phelps had retired from swimming and spent the past year enjoying a social life and activities that he'd never had time to experience. His secret was that he had recently enrolled in the Olympic performance enhancement drug-testing program required of all athletes six months before they compete in events and a WADA (World Anti-Doping Agency) agent might knock on my door at any time during his visit to test him.

Many journalists had already begun to speculate on a Phelps' come back saying that because of his age in 2016 that it would be a shame if Michael competed and did not win as it would tarnish some of the shine on his medals. Michael knew better. The shame for the most decorated Olympian in history would be if he wanted to compete but chose not to and later looked back with regret when it would be too late to try. A-List G.O.A.T. (Greatest Of All Time) mentality is different from B-List and C-List mentality. Elite achievers know there is no shame in trying when you are able and have the desire to pursue personal and professional goals. The shame is living in fear of failure and not pursuing dreams. They approach goals with an attitude of achieving them but they expect inevitable failures along the path. They are as vulnerable as you and I. They fail hundreds of times before they win. People who make it to the top of every field understand that growth results from previous failure. That's why they do not fear failing while those not on the A-List do.

> *Fear defeats more people*
> *than any other one thing in the world.*
>
> – Ralph Waldo Emerson

Michael failed many times before winning 18 Olympic medals — a record that would likely have prevailed for eternity. He would not have lost his 18 medals if he had chosen not to compete in all future competitions. He knew he would win regardless because of the growth that results from the pursuit of new goals. You grow when you take risks that include inevitable, periodic losing. Success occurs when you have the courage to pay the price. Tennis legend Billie Jean King said in an interview with the *New York Times,* "Play as long as you can, because someday you can't play, even if you want to. If you're willing to pay the price, just keep going."[1] Excellence costs time and is paid for with growing pains caused by periodic, inevitable failures. The good news is that if you have higher goals you'll get higher results.

> *Do the thing you fear,*
> *and the death of fear is certain.*
>
> – Ralph Waldo Emerson

A reporter asked Michael Phelps what music he listened to on his headphones before he walked onto the pool deck to break a world record in Barcelona. Phelps told the reporter it was from the music group *Eminem.* The next reporter asked Italian swimmer Massi Rosolino, whom Phelps had just beaten, what he would do to try to beat Phelps the next time they race. Rosolino answered, "The first thing I'm going to do is buy that CD. Then I will listen to all the songs to see if one of them can make me swim that fast." As a reaction, Phelps scribbled a note to five time gold medalist Australian swimmer Ian "Thorpedo" Thorpe who was sitting beside him. The note read, "It's not about the CD."[2]

Phelps won because of the time he'd spent taking the actions he needed to take in order to win. Phelps later said, "I think goals should never be easy, they should force you to work, even if they are uncomfortable all the time. If you want to be the best, you have to do things that other people aren't willing to do."[3]

> *The price of inaction is greater
> than the cost of making a mistake.*
>
> – Meg Whitman,
> Previous President and CEO of Hewlett Packard Enterprise and Former eBay CEO Quoting Meister Eckhart to CNN's Poppy Harlow

Phelps had another secret. He customarily only shared his goals with his inner circle. On the TV program, *Undeniable*, he showed host Joe Buck a goal sheet on which he'd written his goal at age 11, "winning a gold medal." Phelps had scratched it out because at the time he thought it was unrealistic. However, on the back of the sheet he had revised his goal writing, "I would like to make the Olympics," and then included time targets for three events. "That's about right," Phelps told Buck. "It's really the motto I live by today. Dream. Plan. Reach. You come up with a dream, you figure out how you're going to get there and you go for it. What's the worst that happens? You fail? Great. Get up and do it again. It's that easy."[4] "If you put a limit on anything, you put a limit on how far you can go."[5]

> *The greater danger for most of us
> lies not in setting our aim too high and falling short
> but in setting our aim too low, and achieving our mark.*
>
> – Michaelangelo

Phelps followed his plan and proved the naysayers wrong. He added four gold medals and one silver medal in the 2016 Summer Olympics in Rio to rack up 28 total Olympic medals. Eight days after the 2016 Olympics he shared via a *Sports*

Illustrated Facebook post why he'd chosen to compete again. "Being able to come back and do what I did is something I'll remember for the rest of my life. I didn't want to have a 'what if,' and being able to come back and finish how I did is the absolute best way and only way for me to go out on top. That was the cherry on the top of the cake."[6]

> *I have lived a long life and had many troubles,*
> *most of which never happened.*
> – Mark Twain

If you want to win, you have to dream, plan, invest time and pay full price for top results. Phelps' decision to un-retire showed the world that he was not afraid to continue where he left off because he knew he could "keep going." You may not own any shiny medals or many material possessions, but just like Phelps you own your time and you can invest it in acquiring skills that will help you pay the price it costs to achieve your dreams without wasting time. The real competition in life is not only overcoming fear to pay the price of success but choosing how you spend your time without allowing others to rob you of your time — and your dreams. Life doesn't wait. You can't get time back — not even one one-hundredth of a second. This book is the "what if" game changer that will save you time and teach you what to do and how to win now while there is time so later when "you can't play, even if you want to," you won't scratch your head wondering why you didn't win and what you could have done that would have made the winning difference.

> *Failure is an inevitable condition of success.*
> – J. Robert Oppenheimer
> Manhattan Project Mastermind and Father of the Atomic Bomb

If one does not know to which port one is sailing,
no wind is favorable.

– Lucius Annaeus Seneca

Chapter One

Toppermost Of The Poppermost: How To Create A Strategy For Rock Star Results

"Where are we going fellas?" John Lennon asked.
"To the top Johnny," sang out
Paul, George, and Ringo.
"Where's that fellas?"
"To the toppermost of the poppermost!"

Trash talking boxer Muhammad Ali did something different to become "The Greatest" boxer in history. It wasn't just trash talking and it wasn't just boxing. The Beatles did something different to become known as "the greatest rock band" in history. It wasn't just 10,000 theoretical hours of practice and it wasn't just their music. *"What made the winning difference?"* I wondered as a young student listening to The Beatles many miles from home and later when I was older and met Ali when he came to dedicate a building on the Durham College campus where I taught. Whatever it was, it remained hidden and conducted in private. It was not formally taught in any educational institution where I had the privilege to study. My time spent in ivory towers, fueled by these early fascinators, yielded only interesting theories, ideas, and suppositions. I craved to know exactly — *exactly what and exactly how* A-Listers like the G.O.A.T. boxer and the G.O.A.T. band achieved superstardom. Only by examining what these and other A-Listers had done out of the public eye that had made the difference in their winning would I be able to definitively know and be able to strategically teach others in the classes and programs I present what they truly need to know to achieve peak performance. Determined, I knew I had to dive deeper to find the treasure only epic winners could bring to the surface. I set about studying their lives, scrutinizing media interviews, and finally doing the one thing that made the difference in learning the answer — unabashedly asking winners face-to-face from diverse fields, "What made the winning difference?" I discovered that winning is a learnable skill. You can learn to win at anything.

This book takes the guesswork out of what legendary winners did to achieve glory by shining a spotlight on what they did in private. You'll learn exactly how to take the same actions to achieve your own brand of super success. The stories of many of the most successful people on the planet — legendary athletes, CEOs, award winning journalists, healthcare providers, academy award winners, globally successful musicians, and more reveal the actions that made the difference. The goal of this step-by-step playbook for peak performance is to teach you the actions peak performers take and to teach you step-by-step how to take the same actions.

To set the stage, I'd like for you to see what I saw that sparked my curiosity and ultimately led me on the hunt to uncover the secret actions they took out of the limelight that resulted in winning. The stories debunk many myths about winning to reveal that legendary winners are people just like you who took actions you also can take to win.

Cassius Marcellus Clay, Jr. knew what he wanted early in life. "I'm going to 'whup' that thief," he snarled to police officer Joe Martin when his bicycle was stolen in the rundown part of his hometown Louisville, Kentucky. The cop told Clay to stop being angry and advised young Cassius if he wanted to fight anybody he'd first better learn to box. Clay set about learning to fight in Martin's basement gym so if anyone ever stole his bike again he would have the skills he needed to win. Weighing only 98 pounds, Clay soon won his first fight in a split decision. Afterwards he said, "I am the greatest. I will be champion of the world. I am the greatest." The twelve-year-old believed in himself and set a goal for himself. He was always focused, saying a few years later, "Clay is a slave name. I didn't choose it and I don't want it. I am Muhammad Ali — it means beloved of God — and I insist people use it when they speak to me. I know where I'm going and I know the truth, and I don't have to be what you want me to be. I'm free to be what I want."[1] Ali wanted to be "the greatest." He believed he was. In time, the world agreed.

> *I don't want to be the next Mark Spitz,*
> *I want to be the first Michael Phelps.*
>
> – Michael Phelps

Across the ocean from Ali there was a group of poor young men in England with enormous odds against them who were also on the rise to meteoric success. Like Ali, they were unwilling to compromise their individuality or personal values to reach their goals. They traveled to the United States to promote their band. The American tour involved photo-ops including a stop at the Miami training camp of Sonny Liston, the current heavyweight champion of the world. Liston, according to *Time* magazine writer Robert Lipsyte, refused to pose with the mop-topped "little sissies" so their manager took them to pose with Liston's competition — the second best fighter, Muhammad Ali, who was predicted to lose 7–1 in the upcoming fight against Liston. When Ali walked into the dressing room to meet them he said, "Hello there Beatles. We oughta do some road shows together. We'll get rich." At the end of the shoot Ali said, "Man, you guys are the greatest. The whole world is shook up about you!"[2]

A week later, Ali beat Liston to become one of the youngest heavyweight champions of all time, and The Beatles music soared to the top of the *Billboard* charts. The boxer and the band so significantly eclipsed boxing and music that they revolutionized politics, society, modern culture, sports, music, and art.

Muhammad Ali became one of the most recognizable faces on the planet. He was known not only for being the only person to win the heavyweight championship three times, but for standing up for his convictions including political activism during the Vietnam War and the Civil Rights era. He was a philanthropist, a showman, and a genius at turning sporting events into spectacles.

On the surface, the legendary success of Ali and The Beatles seems to be the result of overnight magic. In reality no one rises and stays on the top without taking sustained actions.

My curiosity about the success of The Beatles began when I moved 4000 miles from the small southern town where I was born. I was a young student at Oxford University where I was fascinated that The Beatles' music was as popular with my classmates from other countries as it was with my former classmates in my small North Carolina town. Decades later, The Beatles' music continues to be played as much in my small hometown as it is anywhere on planet Earth and into the universe thanks to NASA who beamed their song "Across the Universe" into space on its 50th anniversary. Beatles' songs were streamed 50 million times in the first 48 hours after they became available to listen to on the internet for the first time.[3] Today, over four decades since The Beatles ceased to be a group, a Beatles' song is played somewhere in the world every fifteen seconds.[4]

According to The Pew Research Center, The Beatles' music is the fourth highest selling in every age group 16–64.[5] The Beatles or their heirs make more money each month than most people will earn in a lifetime. Unless you live under a rock, you know The Beatles. And likely you know the names of all four members of The Beatles — first and last. Can you do that for any other music group? They became masters at doing what would make the winning difference in order to sell their music, their products, and their ideas. Consider this, they sold over four times as much music as any other band — nineteen #1 albums, over a billion records and tapes. They became the most disruptive force in the history of pop culture significantly influencing popular art, literature, movies, fashion and politics by doing what made the difference.

Popular thought when The Beatles burst onto the world stage was that they were an overnight success, the result of nothing short of magic. Truth is, they were not an overnight hit. The Beatles took multiple sustained actions that made the winning difference in addition to performing live an estimated twelve hundred times — the supposed 10,000 hours rule — before they experienced legendary success. However, as you'll see in this book, no one rises and stays on the A-List without taking sustained actions. Other theories credit their investment of 10,000 hours and life conditions as the fuel of success while others believe that they were successful because they had fewer obstacles than competing rock bands. I didn't think so. It was time to peel the onion. I began with the notion that there were fewer odds against John, Paul, George and Ringo.

For starters, not a single one of The Beatles had any formal education. They were from low socio-economic backgrounds, lacked money, played poor quality instruments, and had no support or encouragement from family. They were constantly in trouble. They got into fights. They had no agent. They were refused a contract by every recording studio. They initially were poor, struggling, naughty boys failing to reach their goal to make a lot of money as musicians until they took actions that propelled the sale of their music.

John Lennon said the following about what the early days were like for The Beatles until they took actions that transformed them into one of the most successful money-making groups of all time:

> I would say to the others when they were depressed or we were all depressed and we'd think the band was going nowhere, and there was this shitty deal, shitty dressing room. I'd say, 'Where are we going, fellas?' And they'd go, 'To the top Johnny,' in pseudo-American voices. And I'd say, 'Where's that, fellas?' And they'd say, 'To the toppermost of the poppermost.' And I'd say, 'Right.' And we'd all sort of cheer up." When I was a Beatle I thought we were the best fucking group in the goddamn world and believing that is what made us what we were. It was just a matter of time before everyone else caught on.[6]

Once you make a decision,
the universe conspires to make it happen.

– Ralph Waldo Emerson

The Beatles lacked support and were depressingly aware of numerous obstacles. John Lennon's Aunt Mimi who raised him told him, "The guitar's all very well, John, but you'll never make a living out of it."[7] Paul McCartney was so poor that he once used a piano string for his guitar when he could not afford a guitar string. Ringo was sickly. George Harrison failed his high school exams.

If you want to increase your success rate,
double your failure rate ... That's where
you'll find success — on the far side of failure.

– Thomas J. Watson, Sr.
Founder of IBM

There are people who will always come up with reasons why you can't do what you want to do just as they did for John, Paul, George and Ringo. Ignore them.

> *If you end up with a boring miserable life*
> *because you listened to your mom, your dad,*
> *your teacher, your priest or some guy on television*
> *telling you how to do your shit,*
> *then you deserve it.*
>
> – Frank Zappa

The Beatles had no silver spoon and no luck. They had no rabbit foot, no lucky star, no fairy godmother, no trust in a que sera sera positive "everything will work out" attitude, or voodoo. Visualizing their success as the "best fucking group in the goddamn world"[8] and practicing 10,000 hours were important, but alone were not enough. The wheels were falling off the dream. George Harrison said about The Beatles' tour to Germany:

> It was a pretty pathetic tour. By the end of it we were broke, had no money, were all cold and freezing and you know just miserable and that was it and we came back to Liverpool and nothing happened really. We were like orphans really. Our shoes were full of holes and our trousers were a mess and we didn't have uniforms. We were crummy and the band was horrible. We were an embarrassment. We didn't have amplifiers or anything.[9]

> *Shallow men believe in luck.*
> *Strong men believe in cause and effect.*
>
> – Ralph Waldo Emerson

What made the difference for The Beatles I reasoned had to be something more because everyone who visualizes, practices 10,000 hours and is from a certain background does not make the A-List. Popular theory is that "the secret" to success is visualizing what you want. Hogwash. Winners who make the A-List prove winning requires more.

The Beatles success began to take off with the entrance of a "Fifth Beatle," a manager named Brian Epstein, who directed the actions every individual member took to overcome obstacles so they could sell their music. Taking the actions you'll learn in this book resulted in the plain, common, ordinary, struggling, naughty boys becoming The Fab Four — one of the highest functioning, globally successful G.O.A.T. teams of all time — without compromising their ideals. In this book you'll learn the path forward so you can turn your dreams into reality by doing the same. You'll learn through stories and actions of The Beatles and iconic legends in every field. You can accomplish your goals the same way when you know not simply what winners do that you also can do, but by knowing exactly how to take the actions using this step-by-step guide that explains what you need to know and do to reach the pinnacle of success.

Life for The Beatles, Muhammad Ali, and for every A-Lister you'll read about in this book is just as it is for you — full of the inescapable dull and ugly. People you love will die. People you don't expect to disappoint you will disappoint you. You can do the very best you or anyone else can possibly do, but your best efforts sometimes cannot stop the free will of other human beings who will intentionally or unintentionally hurt or take advantage of you. Life changes for all of us in hundreds of unexpected ways we encounter on our individual human paths. Sometimes change is painful; sometimes change is joyful. Pain and joy are normal parts of life. Expect both because whether you like it or not, no matter who you are — Michael Phelps or Oprah — you're going to get both. Life is like this, how it's meant to be, and happiness would mean nothing if life were not this way. You are not going to escape pain although many people try to dull it or stop it by using drugs and or alcohol. The reality is that it is impossible to selectively numb pain without also numbing joy. When you use drugs or alcohol to numb pain, you also numb yourself to the joys of life. It is impossible to selectively medicate feelings.

This book is a unique guide teaching how to proactively deal with life no matter what your current situation is in life and how to react when challenges and opportunities occur — without a silver spoon, a rabbit's foot, or medication. It's about what a monk sitting under a shady tree in Chiang Mai, Thailand told me makes the biggest difference in his life — "knowing the actions to take to make the difference and learning to control the actions." You get to choose the actions you alone will take. This book is about the actions champions take that you can take — regardless of who you are or where you live, whether it's in Indiana or India — that will make the difference in your life if you want to reach peak performance in any field whether it's boxing, music, the military, or selling motorcycles.

Top global achievers in business take the same actions elite sports figures and celebrities take. It's the reason many A-List businesses partner with famous athletes and celebrities to facilitate brand awareness and increase sales. They start with vision, measurable goals with timelines, strategies, and then take the necessary actions to reach their goals to rise to the top.

Luck is what happens when preparation meets opportunity.

– Lucius Annaeus Seneca

Hero MotoCorp Ltd, formerly Hero Honda, is a motorcycle and scooter manufacturer based in New Delhi, India. When Vice chairman, CEO, and managing director Pawan Munjal became CEO in 1995 he determined to steadily go global with a goal to grow not only the Hero brand but also its sales. In 2001 Hero became the world's largest two-wheeler manufacturer and has continued on top. When I met Munjal in 2015 at Albany in The Bahamas, he said his company intended to go into 50 global markets in the next couple of years and to take annual production volumes to 12 million by the year 2020. Hero had just signed a four-year contract with Tiger Woods because according to Munjal, "Taking the brand out there into new markets where Hero is not a known brand, we believe that Tiger's brand, Tiger's recognition, Tiger's attributes, will also lift and make the brand Hero as recognizable as Tiger."[10]

When asked about the synergies in the Hero brand and the synergies in Tiger Woods' brand that complement each other, Munjal answered, "I'll just make it simple. I'll use one word. It's all about quality. What Hero MotoCorp do, his job, me and my job, going for the topmost quality in whatever we do. I think that's the biggest synergy. There are many other things, but that's the biggest one." According to Munjal, "Hero represents on top of everything, excellence."[11] Tiger Woods added, "Mr. Munjal just put it perfectly. I think it's quality and it's excellence and I think it's growth."[12]

> *How do you go from where you are to where you want to be?*
> *I think you have to have enthusiasm for life.*
> *You have to have a dream, a goal.*
> *You have to be willing to work for it.*
>
> – Jim Valvano

The first action you must take to achieve your goal despite whatever is going on in your life, whether your goal is to be a rock star, a business titan, a professional athlete, an admiral, or a celebrity is to build a rock solid foundation. Your body would collapse without bones. So will your goal — no matter what it is. You will accomplish the foundational bones your goal needs to maximize results by performing *in order* the steps described in this chapter. The omission of a single step or doing steps in a different order is a big reason many people do not reach their goals. Omitting a step or changing the order of steps is like thinking you can reach a person by phone if you omit one of the numbers or by dialing all of the right numbers but in the wrong order. It won't work. All the numbers in the correct order are required to reach the person you seek to connect with via telephone. Similarly, reaching your goals requires doing all of what you must do *in the right order*. The highest degree of professional success, as you will see, comes from following ordered steps. The Beatles reached the pinnacle of success with Brian Epstein's guidance. They dreamed, visualized aloud, and wrote down individual and group goals — often in songs. They wrote down timelines on blackboards and on the backs of envelopes. They practiced in jam sessions. They took action every day no matter where they were. It's tempting to want to jump ahead but top results just don't happen this way — not for The Beatles, Barbara Walters, Sam Walton, Michael Jordan, Carlos Santana or for any of the distinguished winners you'll read about in this book.

> *If what you learn leads to knowledge, you become a fool; but if what you learn leads to action, you become wealthy.*
>
> – Jim Rohn
> Entrepreneur, Author and Mentor to Brian Tracy, Tony Robbins, Mark Victor Hanson and Jack Canfield
> (*Chicken Soup* Book Series) and Many Others

How To Set A Goal You Will Reach

A barber lathers a man before he shaves him.

– Dale Carnegie
Author of *How to Win Friends and Influence People*

Eight Steps to Achieve Your Goals

1. *Visualize the success you want.* Achieving whatever it is you want begins with your dream. Dreams are easy and do not require time, money, or effort — only imagination. Dreams can go on forever and get bigger and bigger without ever coming true. Dreams without a deadline have no value unless they inspire goals. Goals, not dreams, come true when they are properly set and acted upon. Goals that are properly set and acted upon will change you and your life. One of the greatest secrets to winning is to determine what you love to do and want to do and then to use your energy to devise a plan for the actions you need to take to accomplish what you want.

The man with no imagination has no wings.

– Muhammad Ali

Mark Bryan's vision was a successful career in music. He was a freshman at the University of South Carolina when he heard Darius Rucker singing in the shower. Together they formed the rock band Hootie & The Blowfish that today enjoys platinum album status, selling over 21 million albums in the United States alone.

"What made the difference in your success?" I asked Bryan on a trip to South Carolina.

"The thing that made the difference for me was the never-ending spirit to play music for the rest of my life. I knew that whatever I would do would be based around music. Even at age 48 I have like five jobs and they're all based around music and I kinda always knew it would be that way. Having that spirit and that drive is what helped me succeed."[13]

Carli Lloyd, two-time Olympic Soccer Gold medalist, is famous for scoring the hat-trick (three goals in a game by the same player) resulting in the U.S.A.'s 5–2 victory over Japan during the 2015 FIFA Women's World Cup final. She said in a *CBS This Morning* interview after the win, "I think for starters if you have a dream, it's definitely achievable through hard work, through dedication, sacrifice, everything. We have been those little girls screaming and jumping up and down when they see us. We've had dreams of our own, we've had struggles, we've been cut from teams and we've still all managed to get here to this point."[14]

> *Logic will get you from A to B.*
> *Imagination will take you everywhere.*
> – Albert Einstein

Sam Walton recalled when he had the idea in 1962 for Walmart, "Most folks ... were pretty skeptical of the whole concept." One skeptic, David Glass, fourteen years later had to eat his words, "It was the worst retail store I had ever seen." Glass later became CEO of Walmart and is the owner of the major league baseball team the Kansas City Royals. Walton believed in his idea and said, "I knew we were on to something. I knew in my bones it was going to work .... Ours is a story about entrepreneurship, and risk, and hard work, and knowing where you want to go and being willing to do what it takes to get there. It's a story about believing in your idea even when some folks don't, and about sticking to your guns."[15]

> *A clear vision is instrumental*
> *to the success of every goal.*

My daughter, Win, met "Rudy" Ruettiger, the University of Notre Dame football player whose story was the subject of the American sports film, *Rudy*. For those not familiar with Rudy's story, Rudy overcame enormous obstacles, including poor grades, limited talent, modest social finesse, and small physical stature to achieve his goal of playing football at Notre Dame. Win asked Rudy what made the difference for him. "The thing that made the difference was never giving up. And having a crystal-clear vision. And not telling others who are naysayers."[16] Rudy understood that what we say to ourselves is as important as what we say or don't say to others — and what others say to us.

Ideas are fragile so be careful not to share your ideas until you are ready to move forward because people — including those who love you most — often shoot down ideas in an effort to protect you from failure. They will tell you why they believe an idea is poor and won't work and that can rob you of the confidence you need to actualize your vision. Trust yourself. Tell people who can help you move your idea forward — not people who are merely able to validate you or your idea.

> *Be careful who you vent to.*
> *A listening ear is also a running mouth.*
>
> – African American Proverb

NBA All Star, Tim Hardaway, retired No. 10 for the Miami Heat, told me the following about the importance of believing in yourself:

> People telling me that I can't do, trying to put doubt in my mind, saying I can't be a point guard, saying I can't run a team, never having confidence in me. You gotta always have confidence in yourself in order to do anything in life — to be a doctor, a lawyer, a garbage man, a mechanic or whatever you're going

to do in life, you gotta have confidence in yourself that you can do whatever it is you want to do. When people put doubts in your mind or try to put doubts in your mind, or always be negative towards you, you gotta believe in yourself and rise to the occasion. You gotta show them. I believed in myself when others did not. That's what made the biggest difference and made me who I am today. Focus on what you believe in.[17]

Walt Disney kept going even after a newspaper editor fired him saying that Disney "… lacked imagination and had no good ideas." Disney believed in himself and his ideas later saying, "If you can dream it, you can do it. Always remember that this whole thing was started with a dream and a mouse."[18] Disney World was built in 366 days from the first shovel to the first ticket sold. Disney dreamed and Disney ACTED because dreaming alone is not enough. You must add action. Like Disney, you must have 100% clarity of your desired outcome before taking action and believe in yourself regardless of what others think.

In the song "Imagine" John Lennon sings,

You may say I'm a dreamer
But I'm not the only one
I hope someday you'll join us
And the world will live as one.

Be careful not to limit thoughts that will limit your goals. If you think small thoughts you will get small results. Thoughts that are unlimited result in unlimited experiences. Big thoughts make a difference.

You can't outwit fate by trying to stand on the sidelines and place little side bets about the outcome of life. Either you wade in and risk everything to play the game, or you don't play at all. And if you don't play, you can't win."

– Judith McNaught
Author and First Female Executive Producer at a CBS Radio Station

Michael Phelps didn't listen to high profile naysayers who were national and international sports journalists who proclaimed him too old to compete in the 2016 Olympics. Phelps' style is to power on to meet goals he, not others, sets for himself. Phelps' response, "You can't put a limit on anything. The more you dream the farther you get."[19]

I met Michael Phelps for the first time at Michael Jordan's golf tournament in Las Vegas where we sat at a large round table with several of Jordan's guests who gathered for drinks in the clubhouse at Shadow Creek Golf Club. Michael sat beside me. When he rose to leave, he bent down to shake my hand and said, "It was nice to meet you. I will see you again." He paused as he held my hand and with an intense expression and penetrating stare said, "I will see you again." He paused again, stared and repeated, "And I will see you again." Not long afterwards he was a guest in my home.

One of the nicest unspoiled walks I've ever taken was with Sean Foley at Arnold Palmer's Bay Hill Invitational in Orlando. Foley is golf's hottest coach and has been golf whisperer to Tiger Woods, Sean O'Hair, Stephen Ames, Justin Rose, Lee Westwood, and Hunter Mahan. Foley shared in a *Golf Digest* interview that legendary basketball coach Phil Jackson's use of Zen meditation as a means of training inspired his own work with Tiger Woods.[20] I share admiration for Jackson whom I reference in leadership and team-building programs I present. Jackson was the perfect starting point for our conversation.

Foley, dressed in a royal blue sweater with a high-speed

video camera slung in a bag over his shoulder, talked about the "head game" of golf. I confess, sometimes I got lost trying to follow his details about neuro-linguistic programming, kinesthetic sub-modalities and how the mind affects winning physical performance, but I kept walking and trying my best to keep up with his thought process. He talked as he calmly watched the players he coaches from outside the ropes. In fact, even though the game's etiquette is to shush when players drive and putt, Foley only lowered his voice and slightly paused. He showed no emotion when one of his players made a good or a poor shot, maintaining a steady stride and confident cadence as he kept walking and watching — casting his eye back and forth between the action on the course and me. His mind was focused on the final goal. The holes, with good and inevitable less good shots, were simply highs and lows along the path to the goal.

Foley is exceedingly polite. His conversation reminded me of Phil Jackson's in his book *Sacred Hoops*, but unlike Jackson, Foley talked more about how people learn, how they think — and how winners can practice to affect winning results. He said his favorite books are *See and Feel The Inside Move the Outside* and *The Art and Zen of Learning Golf* by Michael Hebron. The main takeaway from our walk is that while physical preparation in sports is essential, it is not enough to sustain repeated victories.[21] Visualizing the success you want in sports and in business contributes to making the difference in winning top results.

The good news is that you do not need to achieve mastery level understanding of neuro-linguistic programming and kinesthetic sub-modalities in order to visualize the success you prepare to win. If you want to be like *The Great One*, Canadian ice hockey player Wayne Gretzky, do what he said he does that makes the difference, "I skate to where the puck is going to be, not where it has been." And when you get to the place of the puck, take a whack at it because like Gretzky said, "You'll always miss 100 percent of the shots you do not take."

> *You expect yourself to show up and win every weekend. There's no point in showin' up if you're not plannin' on winnin'.*
>
> – Jess Lockwood
> Youngest World's Number One Bull Rider

> *Never look where you're going.*
> *Always look where you want to go.*
>
> – Bob Ernst
> Former Men and Women's Rowing Coach
> During 42-Year Association with the University of Washington and
> Four-Time Coach of U.S. Olympic Women's Rowing Teams

2. *Define your journey in writing.* Don't attempt to accomplish any goal without taking a moment to write down in twenty-five words or less exactly what you want to accomplish. *A faint pen is more powerful than the keenest mind.* Be clear. Be concise. Be exact. Simple clarity is incredibly powerful. The act of writing down your goal will send a message to the subconscious part of your mind to prime it to discover the path you should take to reach your goal. Michael Phelps writes in his book, *No Limits*, "Every year since I have been swimming competitively, I have set goals for myself in writing … Pretty soon after I made my first goal sheet, I hit every one of the times to a tenth of a second. Precisely. Exactly. It's like I have an innate body clock. I don't know how or why I was able to do this. I just could, and often still can."[22]

> *What gets written gets done.*
>
> – Frank Dworsky
> Top Financial Advisor

Almost everyone has dreams, but according to Franklin Covey, only 5% of people set goals even though people who set goals and write them down have a 95% greater chance of attaining goals than people who do not write them down.

The Beatles not only wrote down the different goals they set in life, they sang them. "Money That's What I Want" was one of their first songs. Goals that become reality begin single, simple, and measurable. For example, Bill Gates' vision for Microsoft was to "Put a computer on every desk."[23]

3. *Know what's in it for YOU* — not what's in it for the people with whom you live or work. World-class achievers own their goals. Everyone you'll read about in this book did. Ali knew his goal at age twelve and what was in it for him. The Beatles knew exactly what was in it for them if they reached their goal (to be bigger than Elvis and make a lot of money) — they would get a lot of girls.

4. *Take a personal inventory* of your current skills, experiences, background, abilities, and education. Clearly and succinctly define yourself as who you are now. Consider where you are with regards to product knowledge and education and how that affects your current success. Note weaknesses and acquire the degree of competency you need in weak areas to reach your goals.

Sonya Carson who had only a third grade education, married at the age of thirteen and had children. She divorced after dicovering her husband had another family. She raised her sons in Detroit tenement housing and rode a bus to clean houses for the wealthy to support her family. She noticed what was different in the homes where she worked from the homes where she lived. Books.

Her son, Ben, was at the bottom of his fifth-grade class. She determined that books made the difference so she began requiring that two books be read each week. Ben Carson went to the top of his class in the sixth-grade and went on to earn a scholarship to Yale. He became Director of Pediatric

Neurosurgery at Johns Hopkins Hospital when he was thirty-three years old — not only one of the youngest in the world to achieve that position but also the first black person to hold a leading position at a renowned medical center. He was awarded the nation's highest civilian honor, the Presidential Medal of Freedom, in 2008. In 2016, President Donald Trump announced Carson as his choice for Secretary of the Department of Housing and Urban Development. Reading books made the difference.

Carson said in an interview when inducted into the Academy of Achievement:

> There is no such thing as an average human being. If you have a normal brain, you are superior.... My mother was a person who would never accept an excuse from my brother or myself. It didn't matter what the situation was. If you came with an excuse, she would always say, 'Do you have a brain?' And if the answer was "yes," then you had a way to get around it. Maybe you should use the brain. That was her point. After a while it became clear to us that no excuse was acceptable, so we became pretty creative.... Once I recognized that I had the ability to pretty much map out my own future based on the choices that I made and the degree of energy that I put into it, life was wonderful at that point. I used to hate my life up until that point because I hated being poor. I hated the environment. But, once I came to that realization, I didn't hate it anymore. It's sort of like if I said to you, 'Put your foot in that ice bucket.' You would hate to do that, but if you knew you could take it right back out, it wouldn't be such a chore. So, I saw my situation then as being temporary, knowing that I had full power to change it and that completely changed my outlook.[24]

> *Your present circumstances don't determine where you can go; they merely determine where you start.*
>
> – Nido Quebein
> President of High Point University

5. *Determine the skills you are missing* to reach your goals. List them on paper. Build on your strengths in areas where you have talent but when you are weak in an area, identify people who have competencies you lack and ask them to help you reach your goals. Create a written plan of action including what you need to reach your goal. If you want to reach the top, take the actions described in this book. Make a plan.

You can change a plan — but only when you have one! No one plans to be average. Average is the result of no plan. If you want to be average, do what average people do — *the 95% who do not write down their goals and make a plan to achieve them.* You've probably heard before that "if you fail to plan, you plan to fail." If you want to get what you want, need, and deserve, you must plan to have it. Your plan needs to include resources, equipment, additional education, training, and mentors.

Include people who can help you accomplish your goals and people who have the strengths you lack. List people with skills you need. You will need an advisor, a mentor, and a sponsor. A mentor will save you time because it can be time consuming to learn all you need from books. In case you're thinking that it might feel uncomfortable to involve others, consider that asking for help is less embarrassing than failing by yourself.

> *Failure we can do alone. Success always takes help.*
>
> – Simon Sinek
> Founder of the Optimism Company, Author, and Motivational Speaker

A sponsor can help you the most because he will advocate for you to get what you want and argue on your behalf for opportunities.

My mom was my sponsor. When I finished graduate school, my then husband and I took an extended celebration trip across the USA. I'd sent out resumes and was hoping for interviews, but I would not be home to receive job offers or requests for interviews in the mail.

My mom agreed to drive to my home in Chapel Hill once a week to check my mail. One week she opened a letter inviting me to come for an interview at Durham College — that very day. She got in her car, drove to Durham, and interviewed for me. I got the job! It is great to have a sponsor who will go to bat for you and toot your horn when you're not around to speak for yourself. I learned firsthand that a sponsor can most certainly make the difference.

Help others first get what they need. Remember, "To have a friend, be a friend." What goes around comes around. If you freely give to others first, others will give to you what you need and want.

6. *Determine the steps needed to reach your goal* once you establish a plan for where you want to go. Obstacles will arise that will throw you if you don't have a clear goal with a defined plan.

"Don't let anything throw you off the goal you set for yourself"[25] is the advice of 103-year-old Judge George N. Leighton who as a young African American lawyer in Chicago was neither allowed to join the American Bar Association nor allowed to rent office space in most downtown buildings. Despite racial discrimination and many other obstacles, Leighton became a federal judge, professor of law, civil rights leader, and a legal legend. Leighton said goals can be attained through "study, the love of learning, and high standards of personal performance at all times, in all things, and in all ways."[26]

> *Our great weakness lies in giving up.*
> *The most certain way to succeed is*
> *always to try just one more time.*
>
> – Thomas Edison

Forbes Magazine calls nationally syndicated iHeart radio star Bobby Bones "the most powerful man in country music."[27] Bones is the center of a growing media empire heard weekdays in 153 markets by over 9.2 million listeners. I met Bones on a visit to Arkansas while doing research on Sam Walton. Bones was with his producer Eddie Garcia, the other member of their hilarious two-man band called *The Raging Idiots*. Bones is instantly likeable. I learned a little about Bobby Bones then and more when I returned home and read about his life.

> *It is what it is but it will be what you make it.*
>
> – Coach Pat Summitt
> NACWAA and NACDA Athletic Director of the Year,
> Sports Hall of Fame Administrator of the Year, and
> Women's Basketball Coaches Association Leadership Award Winner

Life didn't start out easy for Bobby Bones. He was born in rural Arkansas in a town of 800 people mostly employed by the local sawmill. His alcoholic and meth addicted mom was 15 when Bones was born and while his father lived within a few miles, he never knew him. He says he was called "the head lice kid, the poor kid" in school.[28] He studied, tuned out people who degraded him, didn't drink or use drugs, and determined to be a success with his heart set on being a radio broadcaster. Bones said in an interview with a writer for *The Tennessean*, "I remember thinking, 'I don't want to end up having kids that are as sad as I am right now.' It was never an option. I was convinced, and I still am convinced, if I take a drink, I'll be an alcoholic. Everything I do, I do one hundred percent. I have no moderation inside me."[29]

Bones says that focusing on what he wanted to do made the difference. In an episode broadcast on December 28, 2016 available on YouTube regarding what it means to fail, he says, "If you fail, never give up because F.A.I.L. means 'First Attempt In Learning.' End is the end. In fact, E.N.D. means 'Effort Never Dies.' If you get NO as an answer, remember N.O. means 'Next Opportunity.' So let's be positive."[30] Bones' book, *Fail Until You Don't: Fight, Grind, Repeat* is an inspiring read about the common denominator (failure) of super successful people who get back up when they fail.

> *You were born to win, but to be the winner you were born to be you must plan to win and prepare to win. Then and only then can you legitimately expect to win.*
>
> – Zig Ziglar
> American Author, Salesman, and Motivational Speaker

7. *Determine a time frame and a deadline* for accomplishing your goal with a specific outcome. Write it down. Unlike dreams, goals are not imaginary so base your goals on what you can actually accomplish if you act on your plan according to your plan.

Warren Buffett and Bill Gates first met at a dinner party hosted by Gates' mother who asked her dinner guests what they believed was the most important factor in their success. Buffet and Gates gave the same one-word answer, "Focus." Warren Buffett added, "The difference between successful people and very successful people is that very successful people say 'no' to almost everything."[31] Saying "no" frees up time to focus on goals without being sidetracked by distractions and creates the time you need to focus on your goals.

> *There's a reason a thoroughbred wears blinders.*

Tightly focus forward on your goal instead of diluting your thoughts with multiple thoughts and actions as that will slow you down and prevent you from reaching your goal. Don't look backwards or ask negative questions like, "Why didn't I win the game, the job, or the gig?" There is truth in the sayings, "Where focus goes, energy flows," and "You can't chase two rabbits at the same time." Consciously choose where you focus. What you focus on directs and shapes your whole life.

Peter Carlisle, sports agent for Michael Phelps, practices what Buffet preaches as much as Phelps. His agency, Octagon, receives about 300 calls a day requesting Phelps' endorsement of products. In an interview with Anderson Cooper on *60 Minutes*, Carlisle said that offers from companies that don't fit in with Phelps' lifestyle are rejected — even big ones like one for five million dollars that was offered during the interview.[32]

When talking to Phelps about the many places he'd seen when traveling to swim meets around the world, I asked what he'd seen that he liked the most. He said, "I see the same thing every place I travel — the black line on the bottom of the pool."[33]

Focus is often unrecognized and misinterpreted. Phelps' sinister looking expression, "PhelpsFace," made when wearing headphones and his hood up when his 2012 South African rival Chad le Clos shadowboxed in front of him immediately before a race at the 2016 Rio Olympics became the meme of the internet. Comments abounded such as, "Phelps or Anakin Skywalker?" and "When you're the real Slim Shady but someone else stood up." In actuality, Phelps was unfazed and not mean-mugging le Clos as viewers thought. Instead Phelps was getting in his own zone listening to rap singer Future's song, "Stick Talk." NBC reporter Michelle Tafoya asked Phelps what he was thinking in that pre-race moment. "Nothing, honestly," said Phelps, "I was trying not to really even look at him. He does his thing, I do my thing. I was watching the heat in front of me."[34]

Disciplined focus is critical. Legendary Navy "Air Warrior"

Rear Admiral Patrick Driscoll, former Deputy Commander and Chief of Staff for the U.S. Pacific Fleet and past Commanding Officer of the Blue Angels, said the number one thing that made the difference reaching his career goal was staying focused on his goal. He said he turned down military opportunities that did not align with his career objectives even though they offered higher pay and would have been easier on his family.[35]

Cyril Northcote Parkinson coined what is known as Parkinson's Law, "Work expands so as to fill the time available for its completion."[36] Deadlines are vital. NOW spelled backwards is WON.

> *Perhaps the most valuable result of all education is*
> *the ability to make yourself do the thing you have to do,*
> *when it ought to be done, whether you like it or not;*
> *it is the first lesson that ought to be learned;*
> *and however early a man's training begins,*
> *it is probably the last lesson that he learns thoroughly.*
>
> – Thomas Henry Huxley
> English Biologist and Writer

Advice from a Sanskrit text is as valuable today as it was centuries ago: "Whenever there is a decision to be made, make it as wisely as possible and forget it for the moment of absolute truth may never arise." Remember these words of wisdom in every aspect of your life. Don't even waste time over what to order in a restaurant when you could be enjoying the company of your dinner partners. If you don't know what to order, ask your waiter for advice or narrow your choice and then let your waiter choose. The goal you want is good food and for it to satisfy you. Most day-to-day decisions are not life or death decisions. Taking too much time to make unimportant decisions will rob you of precious time you can choose to spend on what you value. Do the hardest, most important, and dreaded tasks first so you can focus on what you want to do.

I'm so fast that last night I cut off the light in my bedroom and was in bed before the room was dark.

– Muhammad Ali

Manage your time and find balance in your life by using the 80/20 rule of time management known as the Pareto Principle. Italian economist Vilfredo Pareto observed in 1897 that 20% of a person's efforts produce 80% of the results.

Simply put, the 80/20 rule states that the relationship between input and output is rarely, if ever, balanced. When applied to work, it means that approximately 20% of your efforts produce 80% of the results. Learning to recognize and then focus on that 20% is the key to making the most effective use of your time. Use the 80/20 rule to cut time wasters from your life so you will have the time you determine you need to reach your goal by the deadline you impose.

8. *Take action.* Good things don't come to those who wait. You have to go get what you want. You cannot just sit inside your cave and expect what you want, need, and deserve to appear. You must go out to find it, earn it, get it, and bring it home. You have to know what you want, make a plan to get it, get off the couch and make it happen because life doesn't give a damn about what you like or want. It's your responsibility to do what you need to do to get what you want. Decisive deliberate action is the cost you pay for your goal to come true. Like my mama always said, "All good things come to those who waiteth, if they worketh like hell while they waiteth." Goals produce results when you act on your plan every single day!

Nothing happens until something moves.

– Albert Einstein

Justin Timberlake showed video of traumatic and triumphant moments of ex-Denver Bronco Peyton Manning, former Los Angeles Laker Kobe Bryant, and Olympic gold medalist and soccer player Abby Wambach before presenting the co-winners of the 2016 ESPN ESPY Icon Award (Excellence in Sports Performance Yearly). The video included Manning's neck injury, Bryant's medical setbacks, and Wambach's head injury when she had her head stapled during a game in order to return to play. When Kobe accepted the award, he summed up what the trio had in common:

> We are not on this stage just because of talent or ability. We are up here because of 4-ams, 2-a-days, or 5-a-days. We're up here because we had a dream and let nothing stand in our way. If anything tried to bring us down we used it to make us stronger. We were never satisfied, never finished, and will never be retired.[37]

Bryant finished by quoting his high school English teacher, "Rest at the end, not in the middle," saying his next dream is to be honored for inspiring a new generation to have a dream, sacrifice for it, and never ever rest in the middle.[38]

Taking persistent actions that match the goal you've determined is vital. Do not doubt yourself. Do not give up. You will get knocked down. Get back up. Keep your focus on the "toppermost of the poppermost."

It's not finished until it's done.
It's not done until it's done right.

– Richard Head
Father of Coach Pat Summitt

*There are no limitations if you broaden your horizons.
If you don't succeed you haven't failed because
you cannot fail if you've tried your hardest.*

– Carl Lewis
Winner of Nine Gold Medals and One Silver Medal
at Four Consecutive Olympic Games

*A winner is someone who recognizes his God-given talents,
works his tail off to develop them into skills,
and uses these skills to accomplish his goals.*

– Larry Bird
American Former NBA All-Star and Three-Time MVP Award Winner

Chapter Two

D.R.A.T. (Don't Remain A Tadpole): How To Leap To The Gilded Lily Pad

Don't you ever let a soul in the world tell you that you can't be exactly who you are.

– Lady Gaga

Chaing Mai, located in the northern kingdom of Thailand, is the laid-back home of Buddhist temples and omnipresent monks wearing orange robes. I traveled there to ride an elephant in the nearby jungle, but found myself so intoxicated by its exotic tranquility that I stayed longer to understand what it was about this special place that makes life here peaceful. Monks sit under shady trees late in the afternoon at the temple of Wat Suan Dok and welcome visitors to talk — a chance for curious people like me to ask questions and a chance for monks to practice English and learn about life outside the temple.

My monk was as curious about me as I was about him. Somehow our conversation turned to lotuses, tadpoles, and frogs with the monk explaining the symbolism of the nine stages of lotus flowers. For Buddhists, the lotus represents rebirth and the belief that all growth begins in muddy water. The lotus made me think of frogs, so I brought up the topic of tadpoles. Together we discussed the vital importance of mud for rooting, incubation, and growth as necessary for lotus, tadpoles, and people. "Indeed," he said, "No mud, no lotus."

Hmmm, I added, "The start begins at the bottom where

tadpoles must change into frogs and then risk leaping if they want to land on the fully opened petals of mature lily pads. Drat!"

"What means 'drat'?" asked the monk. "Don't Remain A Tadpole!" I laughed. "You can't remain a tadpole if you want to reach the top of the lily pad. Like tadpoles we must grow from the darkness of the mud, undergo uncomfortable change, leave what is familiar, and risk taking a leap!"

It occurred to me sitting under that tree that if there is anything I'd learned from winners it is that they endure periodic inevitable failures taking risks for growth before they leap to the gilded bloom of ultimate success. Muddy periods that include trials, tribulations, and suffering are precisely like the monk said — initially necessary to attain future enlightenment/growth/success.

Sara Blakely, the CEO of SPANX, was accustomed to the darkness of failure long before she leapt to the top to become the world's youngest and first female self-made billionaire. She didn't make the grades to get into law school so she sold fax machines from the trunk of her car. She was not discouraged by this disappointment. One day when she didn't like the way she looked in a tight pair of white pants, she had an idea for a solution. Despite not having taken a business class, despite not having experience in fashion or retail, and despite not having a trust fund, she decided to try her hand at a new business — not bothered by the possibility that her actions might not work out. She developed SPANX from her living room in Atlanta. In a *60 Minutes*' interview with Allison Langdon, Blakely explained what she learned from her father:

> Don't fear failure. My father would ask my brother and me at the dinner table every night what we had failed at. 'Guys, what did you fail at this week?' And if we did not have something to tell him he

would be disappointed. And I remember distinctly coming home and saying, 'Dad, I tried out for this and I was horrible' and he'd high five me. He'd say, 'Way to go.' And I didn't realize it at the time but what he was doing was reframing my definition of failure. My definition of failure is not trying versus the outcome.[1]

Langdon then asked Blakely, "What's the greatest lesson you've learned in life?"

"To be willing to fail. To just keep trying. The greatest lesson is that there is a hidden blessing in everything that you consider a failure and if you are willing to see it and train yourself then life really opens up for you."[2] Blakely is proof of that. Your outcome is the outcome of the actions you try.

> *F.E.A.R. has two meanings —*
> *__F__orget __E__verything __A__nd __R__un or*
> *__F__ace __E__verything __A__nd __R__ise. The choice is yours.*
>
> – Zig Ziglar

Richard Branson, an English businessman, investor, and founder of the Virgin Group that comprises more than 400 companies, tweeted about failure, "I have failed so many times that I couldn't list them all. But it is because of those failures that I have enjoyed success."

> *The test of success is not*
> *what you do when you are on top.*
> *Success is how high you bounce when you hit bottom.*
>
> – General George S. Patton

Margaret Mitchell's manuscript *Gone with the Wind* was rejected thirty-eight times. More recently, twelve publishers rejected destitute and nearly homeless single mother J.K. Rowling's *Harry Potter* manuscript. A year later, one publisher gave her a chance but told her to get a day job since she had little chance of making money in children's books. Rowling says, "Failure taught me things about myself that I could have learned no other way. I discovered that I had a strong will, and more discipline than I had suspected. You might never fail on the scale I did, but some failure in life is inevitable."[3]

> *It is impossible to live without failing at something, unless you live so cautiously that you might as well not have lived at all — in which case, you fail by default.*
>
> – J.K. Rowling,
> Author of *Harry Potter* Series and the
> First Person to Become a Billionaire from Writing

In 1984 Steve Jobs was fired from Apple — the company he founded. In his 2005 commencement address to Stanford University students he said the following about being fired. "I didn't see it then, but it turned out that getting fired at Apple was the best thing that could have ever happened to me. The heaviness of being successful was replaced by the lightness of being a beginner again, less sure about everything. It freed me to enter one of the most creative periods of my life."[4]

> *No pressure, no diamonds. No grit, no pearls.*
>
> – Thomas Carlyle
> British Historian, Essayist, and Philosopher

Ben Affleck acknowledged in his 2013 Academy Awards acceptance speech for Best Picture the depths to which his career plummeted after winning a screenplay Oscar fifteen years earlier for *Good Will Hunting*. "You have to work harder than you think you possibly can, you can't hold grudges. It's hard, but you can't hold grudges. And it doesn't matter how you get knocked down in life, because that's going to happen. All that matters is that you gotta get up."[5]

Jennifer Lawrence, that very same night at the Academy Awards, physically fell while ascending the stairs to accept her Oscar for Best Actress. She momentarily hung her head in her hands after tripping on her voluminous floor length Dior dress. Her fellow *Silver Linings Playbook* co-star Bradley Cooper and her *X-Men: First Class* co-star Hugh Jackman rushed to help her. Lawrence declined help, picked herself up, and continued up the steps to accept the award. Success like learning to walk, talk, read, and everything else in life can be defined by getting up one more time — literally and figuratively.

> *Never explain. Never complain. Just get up.*
>
> – Benjamin Disraeli
> British Prime Minister

America's favorite dad, *Growing Pains'* Alan Thicke, wasn't always popular. One of his first jobs was hosting a late night talk show, *Thicke of the Night.* Ratings were dismal and criticism harsh. Thicke was hurt saying, "I know some people say, 'It doesn't matter what they say as long as they're talking about you.' Those people have never been written about the way I have. It hurts." He used failure to inspire him to move forward. "You don't want to leave that on your tombstone," he told the *Los Angeles Times.* "You don't want to become a trivia question: 'Who was the guy who hosted the show with the biggest hype and the lowest ratings in the history of the free world?'"[6] Thicke chose to move forward believing in himself and his work. He composed TV theme songs for several popular shows including *Diff'rent Strokes, The Facts of Life, and Wheel of Fortune.* He produced a variety of television shows, hosted a wide range of TV events, acted in movies and landed the starring role in *Growing Pains.*

*If you say can't,
you're restricting what you can do or ever will do.
You can use your imagination to do whatever you want.*

– Bob Bowman
Olympic Swim Coach

The winning secret for many top-ranked business and healthcare organizations is to implement a blameless policy in which the organization does not blame any person or group for inevitable failures. The blamelessness policy is the opposite from the bad apple policy typical of average organizations that punish, shame, blame, or fire individuals who make mistakes. The bad apple policy creates a stymied culture in which employees avoid risks, fear failure, and cover up failures. In contrast, organizations with a blameless policy embrace inevitable failures as learning opportunities. They believe doing so unleashes creativity so employees are not afraid of taking risks integral to optimal growth. They reward instead of punish employees who make mistakes so employees will describe what went wrong and why and then discuss what can be done differently to prevent the same thing from happening in the future.

Chad Dickerson is the CEO of Brooklyn-based Etsy, an e-commerce website focused on handmade and vintage items and supplies that operates in the tradition of a craft fair. Etsy sellers can sell their goods for as little as twenty cents per item. One of the first things Dickerson did when he became CEO was to institute a culture of blamelessness he calls a "blameless postmortem." Since the inception of this policy, Etsy has delivered sensational results including new mobile products to accelerate sales growth. Investors rewarded Etsy with a new $40 million investment and a $688 million valuation. What made the difference? According to Dickerson, "One of the things I allowed people to do is make mistakes more freely. The best way to learn to ride a bike is to ride the bike and fall down. We have a ground rule that the purpose of a postmortem is to find out what happened and how to make it better, not to find a person to blame. What we've seen is a company that is learning and moving faster."[7]

Nothing's impossible. You can attain your dreams.
We've all had failures. There's nothing wrong with failing.
There's something wrong with quitting.
Just get back up and keep going.

– John Mack
2003 Horatio Alger Award Winner, Former CEO &
Chairman of the Board Morgan Stanley and CEO Credit Suisse

The difference for successful people and successful businesses that reach excellence is not their failures but that they got up the last time they got knocked down. The actions that make the difference in reaching mediocrity and excellence are minute. To illustrate this point, think about the difference between very hot water and boiling water. At 211° water is hot. At 212° it boils. One degree makes the difference. A small extra degree of uncomplicated effective actions make a difference in the achievement of excellence. Actions shape what you achieve.

The average margin of victory between winning and losing is a small degree — frequently less than a second in every Olympic competition. Michael Phelps' closest victory margin was a mere five hundredths of a second! The average margin of victory for the last twenty-five years in all major golf tournaments is fewer than three strokes. You are responsible for your results. Take the extra action. Persevere one step at a time. Turn up the heat as little as one degree to maximize your results.

I've failed over and over and over again in my life.
And that is why I succeed.

– Michael Jordan

Persevere. Procrastination is the thief of time and power. Weak people procrastinate because they are afraid of rejection, failure, fear that they will create more problems than they will solve, or because they have distaste for a task. You are just like everyone else. You are just as good as everyone else. Remember the African American expression, "Make a way out of no way" if you are in a situation so dire that you feel there is no exit. There is always a way. The only person who can stop you is yourself.

Cosmonaut Sergey Ryazanskiy, the world's first scientist to become a spacecraft commander, shared that he had periods when he was devastated when people around him told him he had absolutely no chance to fly and that he needed to surrender. "What made the difference for you?" I asked. Ryazanskiy answered:

> I always asked myself one question. 'Did I perform everything that I am able to do or is there something else that I did not try to achieve my goal?' Always I was able to find something else that I can do to increase my chances. It took me ten years but finally I fly to space. [8]

Ryazanskiy took the Olympic torch of the Sochi Winter Olympics into outer space on his first space flight. His second flight was one of the longest in the history of Soviet and Russian cosmonautics. During his career, he logged 306 days in space and accomplished four spacewalks totaling 27 hours 39 minutes.

Oprah Winfrey interviewed Marianne Williamson, author of *A Return to Love*. In the interview, Oprah reads her favorite passage from the book:[9]

> Our deepest fear is not that we are inadequate. Our deepest fear is that we are powerful beyond measure. It is our light, not our darkness, that most frightens us. We ask ourselves, Who am I to

be brilliant, gorgeous, talented, fabulous? Actually, who are you not to be? You are a child of God. Your playing small doesn't serve the world. There's nothing enlightened about shrinking so that other people won't feel insecure around you. We are all meant to shine, as children do ... If we wait for the world's permission for us to shine, we will never receive it.[10]

Asking for permission is empowering others to make a decision for you. People by nature love power. They will seize your power if you give it to them.

You are no better and no worse than anyone else. You are good enough — as good as anyone else, even when you are afraid of the obstacles in your path. Remember, everyone faces obstacles. You have the same power as everyone else as you face inevitable challenges equipped with the skills in this book to turn obstacles into objectives for positive growth. It will make the difference if you give yourself permission to shine every day in full pursuit of your goals despite obstacles and naysayers. The ability to learn and to grow is not fixed. You are meant to shine your way through the dark spots of life. The sky is always blue — even when it is covered with gray clouds. It's life and you are on this earth to live it the best way you can every minute of every day. The actions in this book will help you reach your full potential so you can shine your brightest.

To accomplish a dream you must have a goal and you must give yourself permission to go for it today. You must not be afraid to take action today. Waiting for the future will not work. What you get tomorrow is the result of the actions you take today. You are the only person who can do what is needed to achieve what you want, need, and deserve. Taking action on written goals gives the necessary wings to the dreams you visualize.

If you haven't heard of Patrick Davis you've probably heard his music. Artists including Lady Antebellum, Jewel, Jimmy Buffett, Darius Rucker and many others record the Nashville songwriter's songs. When asked, "What made the difference in your success?" Davis answered, "The thing that helped me the most in my journey has been figuring out that what was really important was deciding what success was to me — and what my version of success was. If you follow someone else's dream it's not going to work out so you kinda have to figure out what it means for yourself to be successful. If you do that chances are you're gonna succeed."[11]

To achieve the results you want, to maximize results, you must take complete charge of your destiny. You must write your own script for the life you want without letting anyone write it for you. Others can walk with you through life but you have to walk all the steps by yourself if you want to win what you want. Listen to yourself. Tune in to those you trust. Like Rudy Ruettiger, "Don't tell the naysayers." Listen to your inner voice. Other people have their own ideas and their own goals. BEWARE: other people like John Lennon's Aunt Mimi will frequently tell you what they think your goals should be. They mean well, you can consider what they say, but if you do not agree, do not let them sabotage your goals. If you don't determine your goals, somebody else will, and guess what they have planned for you? Not much.

Stupidity well packaged can sound like wisdom.

– Burton Malkiel
Author of *A Random Walk Down Wall Street*

Plan you own unique success. Don't live your life to please others. You get one life. Every person gets one life. One life – only one life. This is *your one life*. Don't give your one life and what you want to do with it to anyone. Tune out everyone who lacks faith in you. Politely thank people for their advice, but unless you agree with their plan for your life do not accept the goals others want to assign to you. Determine your own goals and follow your goals — not the goals others have for you unless you share the same goals. There is no need to explain yourself because people only understand from their level of perception. People treat you based on how you value yourself. If you don't value yourself, who will? Demonstrate respect for yourself, your ideas, your goals — your life.

Success does not happen in a comfort zone where life is always safe. The true day you are on the road to the success you want is the day you turn your back on what is safe, comfortable, and what others often call common sense.

One hot summer's day my father, Henry W. Hight, Sr., who was a small town politician in North Carolina, went to visit a constituent who farmed out in the country in Vance County. According to my dad, when he got to the farmer's house he found the farmer on his wide wooden front porch rocking in a chair with his moaning hound dog stretched out in front of him.

"What's wrong with your dog?" asked dad.

"He's probably stretched out over a nail jutting up out of the porch. When it hurts enough, I reckon he'll move," answered the farmer.

My dad believed that most people are like the farmer's dog when it comes to exerting action — comfortable enough not to be in the best shape they could be and willing to settle because they are modestly getting their needs met. Comfortable enough results in average results. When people want excellent results, they have to take uncomfortable actions that require a shift in position. Instead of wasting time moaning on the porch like that hound dog, move to action and you'll find yourself getting results.

It will not be easy and you will experience inevitable failures that are part of the process required for success. Luckily, what Zig Ziglar said is true, "Failure is an event, not a person."

Imagine that in order to have a great life you have to cross a dangerous jungle. You can stay safe where you are and have an ordinary life, or you can risk crossing the jungle and have a terrific life.

– Ray Dalio
Billionaire Founder of Bridgewater Associates —
World's Largest Hedge Fund

People want to be told what to do so badly they'll listen to anyone.

– Don Draper
AMC TV *Mad Men*

You'll have to continually pick yourself up and keep going. Losers don't trust in themselves or their abilities so they believe they have to know everything in advance which is virtually impossible. Meanwhile they do nothing. Winners win because they are positive with a "ready, aim, fire" attitude. Losers do not take action because they think that they should not do anything until they've identified every possible problem and know exactly what to do about it. None of us can ever know it all. Losers never take action and so they always lose. Winners see opportunities and jump on them while the losers are still preparing.

The biggest opponents to the success you want will be between your internal and external files of information in your mind, including your fears, your doubts, and your insecurities fueled by people who "want to protect you" or secretly want you to fail. These doubters will tell you that you're not ready, or that you can't, or that you shouldn't follow your dreams because they don't believe you will succeed for whatever reasons they choose.

When you shut out those voices and listen to your own mind telling you that you can achieve what you want, then you're ready to get out of your comfort zone to begin the work you need to do to achieve your goals. You must be willing to be a little uncomfortable today so you can achieve what you want. Michael Phelps says about naysayers:

> So many people along the way, whatever it is you aspire to do, will tell you it can't be done. But all it takes is imagination. You dream. You plan. You reach. There will be obstacles. There will be doubters. There will be mistakes. But with hard work, with belief, with confidence and trust in yourself and those around you, there are no limits ... My mum and I joke that I had a middle school teacher who said I'd never be successful.[12]

We are not stamped at birth Winner, Loser, Winner, Loser. We get to choose our mindsets and our actions ultimately stamping ourselves as Winners or Losers. You get to decide whether to be a Winner or a Loser despite what your parents, teachers, or so-called friends tell you about yourself and your ability to win. You know yourself better than anyone else. Listen to yourself and take the actions you need to win.

During my research, one of the biggest differences I observed in winners and losers is that winners are people who are willing to act in spite of fear. Losers let fear stop them. The biggest mistake most people make is waiting for the feeling of fear to subside or disappear before they are willing to act. These people usually wait forever. It's not that winners have no fear or get rid of fear before they act. Winners have fear, they have doubts, they have worries. They just don't let these feelings stop them. Losers have fears, doubts, and worries and let those feelings stop them.

Courage to act in spite of fear defines victors. "Ulysses don't scare worth a damn," declared one soldier of small-framed General Ulysses S. Grant during the American Civil War. What the soldier and no one else knew about Grant until he wrote his memoirs from his deathbed was the valuable lesson he'd learned about the importance of acting with courage despite fear when he received orders to move against Confederate Colonel Thomas Harris. Grant wrote:

> At the time of which I now write we had no transportation and the country about Salt River was sparsely settled, so that it took some days to collect teams and drivers enough to move the camp and garrison equipage of a regiment nearly a thousand strong, together with a week's supply of provision and some ammunition. While preparations for the move were going on I felt quite comfortable; but when we got on the road and found every house deserted I was anything but easy. In the twenty-five miles we had to march we did not see a person, old or young, male or female, except two horsemen who were on a road that crossed ours. As soon as they saw us they decamped as fast as their horses could carry them. I kept my men in the ranks and forbade their entering any of the deserted houses or taking anything from them. We halted at night on the road and proceeded the next morning at an early hour. Harris had been encamped in a creek bottom for the sake of being near water. The hills on either side of the creek extend to a considerable height, possibly more than a hundred feet. As we approached the brow of the hill from which it was expected we could see Harris' camp, and possibly find his men ready formed to meet us, my heart kept getting higher and higher until it felt to me as though it was in my throat. I would have given anything then to have been back in Illinois, but I had not the moral courage to halt and consider what to do; I kept right on. When we reached a point from which the valley

below was in full view I halted. The place where Harris had been encamped a few days before was still there and the marks of a recent encampment were plainly visible, but the troops were gone. My heart resumed its place. It occurred to me at once that Harris had been as much afraid of me as I had been of him. This was a view of the question I had never taken before; but it was one I never forgot afterwards. From that event to the close of the war, I never experienced trepidation upon confronting an enemy, though I always felt more or less anxiety. I never forgot that he had as much reason to fear my forces as I had his. The lesson was valuable.[13]

Everyone you meet is afraid of something, loves something, has lost something and the bravest among us have fear but seem calm on the surface. Herman Melville described Ulysses Grant, "As calm as the cyclone's core." Grant's goal was to win every battle. He kept right on formulating plans and taking action despite fear — even as bullets whizzed by his head. His direct and utterly clear orders to tackle cyclones he, his officers, and men could easily follow were vital to his success. Abraham Lincoln said about him, "When it is time for action, Grant makes things git." Colonel James Rusling described Grant as a man who could "dare great things, hold on mightily, and toil terribly ... he knew exactly what he wanted, and why, and when." He was unafraid of taking calculated risks. "If his plan goes wrong he is never disconcerted but promptly devises a new one," said William T. Sherman.[14]

> *Every great batter works on the theory that the pitcher is more afraid of him than he is of the pitcher.*
>
> – Ty Cobb
> Arguably Baseball's Greatest Player of All Time

The difference in winners and losers is not just to dream of winning but to create a clear plan for winning and then to "git" on with doing what is needed without delay despite any fear.

> *Don't let weeds grow around your dreams.*
>
> – H. Jackson Brown, Jr.
> Author of *Life's Little Instruction Book*

It's *your* life. You can let other people write the script for your life and follow the story line they write for you, or you can choose what is your right — to write and follow your own script for the life you want for yourself. Use your backbone to stand up for yourself and your goals. Put self-approval before social-approval. You have as much right as anyone else to achieve what you want. This book teaches how you can be in control to win what you want.

> *Success is going from failure to failure without losing enthusiasm.*
>
> – Winston Churchill
> British Prime Minister Who Led Britain to Victory in World War II

Train people how to treat you if they are not treating you the way you want to be treated. Do this by consistently using words to describe yourself the way you want others to see you and with behavior congruent with what you say. Stand up for yourself. Set boundaries. Live your life — the way *you* choose.

Yogi Berra, baseball great and philosopher known for his comically wise sayings, accurately said, "When you get to the fork in the road, take it." Remember you and you alone are responsible for your destiny — not your parents, your company, or the government. Seemingly insurmountable obstacles will not hold you back if you know the steps required to find or to create the circumstances that will lead to the success you want. "The world is a banquet, but most poor suckers are starving to death,"[15] says Auntie Mame in the classic comedic book and film, *Auntie Mame*. The world will serve up the feast you want, need, and deserve when you have the skills and use them to take control of your destiny. The good news is that YOU can learn to get what you want by applying actions to get what you want, need, and deserve. WINNING IS LEARNABLE.

Misty Copeland, the first African American woman to be promoted to principal dancer in the American Ballet Theatre grew up pretty much homeless and often lived in a motel with her single mother and siblings. Food was scarce. She stumbled across classical ballet late for a dancer — not until she was a teenager on a visit to the Boys and Girls Club in Los Angeles. The example she wants to set for others who might feel that the odds are too great against them, "That you can dream big. It doesn't matter what you look like, where you come from, what your background is."[16] Her book, *Life in Motion: An Unlikely Ballerina*, is an inspiring read for anyone who doubts his or her ability to succeed.

Be Sold On Yourself

Before you can sell yourself to anyone you must first be sold on yourself. Self-confidence is sexy to others. If you don't have it, you'll lose out to people who are self-confident. Winners know this. They are self-confident because they do whatever it takes to be accomplished or knowledgeable about their product, service, or skill. They are not "all talk and no action." They have a plan and take action. They do not waste time.

Muhammad Ali is considered the greatest heavyweight boxer in history, but his success was not due to being the biggest, strongest or most muscular. Ali was the grand master of mind games. He totally understood the importance of being totally sold on yourself — valuing yourself, and realizing that you train others how to treat you. He believed in himself even when he was an underdog. Prior to his fight with Sonny Liston who was favored 7–1, Ali prophesied to the press, "I'm gonna whoop him like I'm his daddy." In an interview later he told CNN's Nick Charles that despite his bravado, "I was scared to death. I just acted like I wasn't."[17]

Throughout his career, Muhammad Ali so thoroughly believed in himself that he shamelessly promoted himself at a time when most fighters let their managers promote them. Clay knew what he wanted to achieve saying, "I can do this, and I do it. Confidence. Confidence. I am the greatest!" He set out to prove it. And he proved that he was: 56 fights, 51 wins — only 5 losses, and 37 knockouts. Ali valued himself and in doing this showed people how to treat him. "Float like a butterfly, sting like a bee, I am the greatest — Muhammad Ali."

It's the repetition of affirmations that leads to belief. And once that belief becomes a deep conviction things begin to happen.

– Muhammad Ali

The world responds to you based on the signals you send about your value. You have to act *as if*. Everyone is in the process of becoming whatever it is we each want to become. Acting *as if* is not about being delusional. Acting *as if* is about giving yourself permission to be what you have the capacity to be. Richard Branson put it this way, "If someone offers you an amazing opportunity and you're not sure you can do it, say yes — then learn how to do it later."[18]

Whenever you are asked if you can do a job, tell 'em, "Certainly I can!" Then get busy and find out how to do it.

– Theodore Roosevelt

Muhammad Ali strode into the Muhammad Ali Health

and Physical Education Building at Durham College for the dedication of the new building. Blocked by massive men protecting "The Greatest," people craned their necks to see him. I was lucky. As a faculty member, I landed a front row seat. Ali ascended the stage. Staring out at the student body, Ali stood still, smiled, and raised his hands. The deafening roar stopped. His message lifted and inspired students — including the most disadvantaged in the nation. Growing up poor like most of these students and graduating at the bottom of his class ranking 376 out of 391, Ali did not let poverty or a poor academic record stop him from being known as he always knew he was, "The Greatest." He did what made the difference in his ultimate success — he didn't listen to naysayers, he believed in himself, he promoted himself, and he took charge of his destiny taking action on his goals. His message that day — every person is of value and every person, no matter what their background, can do what will make the difference in their own lives and the lives of others.

If they can make penicillin out of moldy bread, they can sure make something out of you.

— Muhammad Ali

The feeling of not being good enough at some point in our lives is natural as we compare ourselves to others and evaluate our worth in the world. In reality we can never measure up equally to anyone because each of us is unique. Bullies, bosses, mean girls, siblings, immature classmates, insensitive teachers, coaches, parents are only some of the people who either knowingly or unknowingly can contribute to feelings of unworthiness that become part of our programming. This programming results in self-talk about our ability/inability, worthiness/unworthiness, and anxiety about what other people will say and what other people will think if we try to achieve our dreams and possibly fail. Ignore disempowering negative internal self-talk and external negative talk telling you that you can't do something. Focusing on negative talk will cause you to find roadblocks instead of finding the path to your goals. Be aware of your focus. Refocus if you are not on the course you want.

> *Often the difference between a successful person and a failure is not one has better abilities or ideas, but the courage that one has to bet on one's ideas, to take a calculated risk — and to act.*
>
> – Andre Malraux
> French Minister of Cultural Affairs and Winner of Le Prix Goncourt

The good news is you are in control and you get to choose what to do with comments people make that can build you up or bring you down if you let them. My father offered a liberating message when he told me, "One third of the people you know like you, one third of the people you know don't like you, and one third of the people you know don't care. Do what you like because the one third who like you will continue to like you and the other two thirds don't matter."[19]

Stefani Joanne Angelina Germanotta, better known as Lady Gaga, was bullied as a child for being unique. Her college classmates created a Facebook group called, "Stefani Germanotta, you will never be famous." She dropped out of school to pursue music. A lot of people wouldn't give her the time of day when she began her career. In an interview with Jocelyn Vena for *MTV News,* Lady Gaga said, "Some people didn't get it. Some people still don't get it. I read reviews sometimes and I'm like, 'Wow, that guy really doesn't f---ing like me.' Like, they really don't get it, but that's cool." Lady Gaga elaborated that before her songs became radio staples, she was hard-pressed to convince anyone to play them on the radio. "The real struggle is that they didn't want to play my music on the radio. We fought and we fought and I played every club. I had chicken dinner with every program director I could get my hands on."[20]

Lady Gaga persevered and now towers over the pop culture landscape as a music icon, fashion icon, and gender equality icon. When she accepted the Oscar for best original song she said:

> If you have a dream, fight for it. There's a discipline for passion, it's not about how many times you are rejected or you fall down or you're beaten up, it's about how many times you stand up and are brave and you keep on going.[21]

Her success is due to more than talent — nothing is more common than unsuccessful musicians with only talent, unless it is unsuccessful men and women with only education. She is inimitable — authentic and original in every way. Her success is due to a combination of talent, crystal clear vision for what she wants, persistent action on clear plans to reach goals, and doing what is right for her even though everyone does not like her music, fashion, or style.

You can reprogram yourself much as Sara Blakely did when she was at a low place in her life when people close to her died and her parents separated when she was sixteen years old. Her father suggested she listen to Dr. Wayne Dyer's motivational lecture *How to Be a No-Limit Person*. Blakely said she listened to the cassette tapes so much that she actually memorized them — in essence reprogramming her self-esteem.

> *Whether you think you can or whether you think you can't, you're right.*
>
> – Henry Ford

Be aware of self-limiting programming that you unintentionally let yourself believe about yourself. Make a willful effort to reprogram your belief in yourself because self-limiting programming will hold you back. Erasing what's been intentionally and unintentionally programmed on your personal hard drive is impossible without a lobotomy, but you can choose to overwrite self-defeating programming with positive programming to make the difference in your ability to achieve your goals.

> *There is an expiry date on blaming your parents for steering you in the wrong direction; the moment you are old enough to take the wheel, responsibility lies with you.*
>
> – J.K. Rowling

> *Life's under no obligation to give us what we expect.*
>
> – Margaret Mitchell

Self-esteem will atrophy if you don't practice it every day. Well-organized modesty, putting it in its right place, is good, but just be sure not to let it subdue self-confidence that makes a big difference in the mind game of success.

> *Never apologize for your accomplishments, your hard work and where it has gotten you. Own all of who you are.*
>
> – Carla Harris
> Senior Client Advisor at Morgan Stanley and Chair of National Women's Council

Michael Phelps chose to let negative comments motivate him instead of beat him. As a child, Phelps had big ears and a lisp. He was teased and bullied. He chose not to be brought down by negative comments. He stayed focused on his goal. When someone beat him in a race, he placed his competitor's picture on his locker. When Phelps read that legendary Australian swimmer and five-time Olympic gold medalist Ian Thorpe said it was "highly unlikely for Phelps to win eight gold medals at the 2008 Summer Olympics in Beijing," Phelps taped the quote to his locker at his training pool where he saw it every day. He used the negativity to motivate himself, to prove naysayers wrong, and went on in his career to win not eight but twenty-three gold medals in addition to three silver and two bronze medals for a total of twenty-eight Olympic medals — more than anyone in Olympic history.[22]

The truth is other people are too busy thinking about their own lives to be concerned about your life. It is time to let go of whatever those people said or did to you. Get over it. You are good enough. Your life is YOUR LIFE. Don't let other people control how you choose to live your life. Muhammad Ali said, "I don't have to be what you want me to be. I'm free to be what I want."[23] You are too.

It isn't the mountains ahead to climb that wears you down. It's the pebble in your shoe.

– Muhammad Ali

It's about having the courage to fail. Not breaking when you are broken. It's doing what they say you can't. It's not about the shoes. It's about what you do in them. It's about being who you were born to be.

– Michael Jordan

One of the "baddest" boys in tennis, seventeen-time Grand Slam champion John McEnroe, visited my hometown, Wilmington, NC, to play an exhibition match with Todd Martin during the Azalea Festival Tennis Challenge. While McEnroe was in town he reconnected with a local doctor, Larry Linett, who is one of the few people who can boast of beating McEnroe. The two played multiple times, including four times in the juniors when growing up in New York. Linett won three times.

Linett remembers those matches saying, "John, even back then, had a pretty good temper .... All our matches were knock-down-drag-out matches. I mean never was an easy match in the four."[24]

McEnroe remembered it differently in an interview with local ABC affiliate television station WAAY 3:

> He (Linett) didn't seem to have a great forehand, a great serve, great volley, so I called my parents up. I said, 'Don't worry about this. I got it under control. And I lost 6–0, 6–2. I learned some of the things that you believe are not going to come true until you work at it, and I needed to work on my all-around game. But he definitely inspired me, made me think I gotta get it together a little more, and it worked out for me.[25]

At times you might perhaps feel unprepared to take on high-powered competition or feel as Linett did that there is never an easy match. Even so, do not delay taking action because you feel that you are not ready. In the words of two-time winner of the Daytona 500 Michael Waltrip, "You are never really ready to go to the races, I have learned. It's just time to go."[26] GO! Perfect timing is usually fiction.

Waltrip's advice is spot-on. "Job Requirements are Mostly Fiction and You Should Ignore Them" advises a *Quartz* article citing *The Harvard Business Review* and an oft quoted internal report by Hewlett Packard as the reason many people don't apply for jobs. "In job searches, people frequently look at the listed requirements, see a gap, and move on, fearing rejection and not wanting to waste the employer's time and their own. They're making a big mistake, and potentially holding back their careers. A job posting doesn't describe a real person. It describes a fictional (an often unrealistic) ideal that companies don't really expect to find."[27] It's true, people who win top jobs and achieve excellence, like Waltrip who wins big races, have the chutzpah to enter the races even though they may think they "are never really ready to go to the races."

Sara Blakely wasn't "ready to go to the races" either by business school standards when she got a meeting at Neiman Marcus to sell SPANX. She tossed the prototypes for her body shapers that lacked fancy packaging into a beat-up red backpack and rushed over to make the sale. Blakely executed her idea for SPANX without knowing anything about women's undergarments, patenting a new product, manufacturing, website development, online commerce and much more. She researched to learn what she needed and hired people who could help her. Believe in yourself. Pursue your goals. If you wait until you have everything you think you need you will likely never reach your goal. Like Waltrip said, "It's just time to go."

> *They said, 'Give it up.'*
> *I didn't pay any attention ...*
> *I did not listen to the 'No.'*
> *I used that attitude as a blueprint*
> *for the rest of my life.*
>
> — Arnold Schwartzenegger
> Body Builder, Actor, Politician

Sports Illustrated magazine lists NBA basketball player Julius Erving, aka Dr. J, as one of the most important athletes of all time.[28] Dr. J leaned forward to answer when I asked what made the difference for him:

> Innovation is the one thing that made the difference to me. I was doing things no one else was doing. Willingness to take calculated risks, being innovative, being creative, the willingness to risk failure by being innovative doing what no one else had done or was doing made the difference for me.

Being innovative helped me be part of a team that didn't win all of the games, but won most of the games. The willingness to risk doing something different made the difference.[29]

I never failed once.
It just happened to be a 2,000 step process.
— Thomas Edison

It's a common reaction to be afraid to risk failure. Athletes, celebrities, and CEOs who've won A-List results have all taken risks — and they've all experienced failures. What they've realized is that every failure brings the gift of experience. The gift is the knowledge of how to do something differently and better the next time. If you need a risk management tool to determine the extent to which you should take a risk, Nido Quebin offers one. Quebin, President of High Point University and one of the highest-paid leaders of a college or university in the United States, is former chairman of Great Harvest Bread Company, serves on the Executive Committee and Boards of companies including Truist (a Fortune 500 company with over $500 billion in assets), La-Z-Boy Corporation (one of the world's largest and most recognized furniture retailers), and Dots Stores (a chain of fashion boutiques with more than 400 locations across the USA). Quebin asks himself three questions as a risk management tool for every decision he makes that has inherent risk:

1. What's the best thing that can happen as the result of taking this risk?
2. What's the most likely thing that can happen as the result of taking this risk?
3. What's the worst thing that can happen as a result of taking this risk?

He says,

- If the most likely thing to happen will get me closer to my goals and if I'm willing to live with the worst thing that can happen, I march onwards.
- If the most likely thing to happen will not get me closer to my goals, it's futile for me to be discussing this risk. I move on.
- If I am not willing to deal with the worst thing that can happen, I must run away as fast as I can.

You are free to make whatever choice you want, but you are not free from the consequences of the choice.[30]

The willingness to get out of your comfort zone is important to success in every field. Actor and director, Tom Welling, best known for his twelve season stint as Clark Kent/Superman in the TV series *Smallville*, admitted to me over deep-dish stuffed pizza at Giordano's in Chicago that it was his willingness to abandon a comfortable job as a model and move to Los Angeles to audition for jobs as an actor that made the difference to his success.[31] As the saying goes, "It's like monkey bars — you have to let go to move forward."

In case you might be thinking that the only people who should take risks are people like Welling who are 6' tall and drop-dead gorgeous Superman types, consider Nick Vujicic.

You can have a "ridiculously good life" even if you are born without arms or legs and people beat you down or make fun of you if you are willing to be innovative to achieve the success you want. Nick Vujicic is someone you need to know about if you have trouble being sold on yourself. Take a moment to watch an interview with Vujicic posted on YouTube. Take your pick: *Oprah, 60 Minutes* and all major TV network news programs have interviews with him posted on YouTube. I will tell you briefly about him, but seeing Vujicic in action is something you need to see for yourself.

Vujicic is an Australian man born with normal mental abilities but without limbs — no arms and no legs. He does have feet. Vujicic was bullied, had low self-esteem, and contemplated suicide. His life changed once he accepted his challenges and figured out how to overcome obstacles. He writes with two toes on his left foot and a special grip that slides onto his big toe. He uses a computer and can type up to 43 words per minute using the "heel and toe" method. Vujicic can throw tennis balls, play drum pedals, get a glass of water, comb his hair, brush his teeth, answer the phone, and shave. He enjoys swimming, skydiving, playing golf and soccer. He is married to a beautiful woman, has two children, and is a highly successful author and motivational speaker. He lives a "ridiculously good life" which is the subtitle of his book, *Life Without Limits*. You can too once you believe in yourself, know what you can do — and do it.

Everything is hard before it is easy.

– Goethe
German Poet, Novelist, Playwright, and Scientist

Joe Morgan has never waited for things to happen. No, sir. Joe Morgan has always made things happen. To be a star, to stay a star, I think you've got to have a certain air of arrogance about you, a cockiness, a swagger on the field that says, 'I can do this, and you can't stop me.'

– Joe Morgan
Ten-Time All-Star, Five-Time Gold Glove Winner,
Baseball Hall of Famer and ESPN Commentator

> *If you want to be the best you have to do the things*
> *that other people aren't willing to do.*
> *It didn't matter if you were sick.*
> *You got out of bed to do whatever you can*
> *to take one step forward to reaching your goal.*
>
> – Michael Phelps

Successful people willing to do whatever it takes to accomplish their goals with excellent results are found in every field — music, sports, politics, healthcare, and business. The Beatles, Michael Phelps, Vujicic, and the world's number one retail salesman Joe Girard, all had obstacles, set goals, and were willing to do whatever it took to achieve their goals. The Beatles started out playing on the back of a pickup truck, on John's Aunt Mimi's front porch, and in seedy bars. Before Michael Phelps won a single gold medal he demonstrated willingness to do whatever it took by practicing over six years and racking up 12,480 miles in the pool — that's like swimming the full length of the Great Wall of China three times. Joe Girard was from a deplorable ghetto in Detroit. He stuttered because his father beat him, told him he was "a no good bum," and damaged his self-confidence. Girard says he achieved his selling goals by learning his profession, embracing the notion that he could do what he knew to do, and doing it every day. He is known for having a positive, self-confident, can-do attitude and a daily plan. His motto: "If it's to be, it's up to me. He can who thinks he can."[32]

> *Here's how I'm going to beat you.*
> *I'm going to outwork you.*
> *That's it. That's all there is to it.*
>
> – Coach Pat Summitt

Legendary University of Tennessee women's head coach Pat Summit went to bed sick after losing at the NCAA

Women's Final Four Basketball Tournament for the fifth time in a seven-year stretch. Summitt shuffled around in her pajamas for two days blaming herself saying, "You should have done something different." In 2013 she shared that commitment makes the difference and that devoting sustained focused attention translates on and off the court: "Commitment is all about risk and also about the tedium and willingness required to persevere through problems without quitting and without demoralization ... the only thing we failed to do was win one more game. As hard as I took our losses, there was dignity in them. We were willing to fail ... I went from feeling like we would never win, to feeling like you couldn't ever count us out again."[33] She was not counted out again appearing in every NCAA tournament from 1982 until her retirement when she held the record for winning more games (1,098) than any other college coach – male or female – in basketball history.

Duke University's Coach Mike Krzyzewski followed Summitt holding the record for the most wins in college basketball history until 2024 when Stanford University's Tara VanDerveer eclipsed his record. Krzyzewski demonstrated the importance of being sold on yourself and sharing mutual trust with teammates in order to perform at the highest level during the final time out and final play of the 1992 NCAA Regional Championship basketball tournament. The University of Kentucky was leading Duke with 2.1 seconds left on the clock. The lack of time made hope for a Duke victory seem totally impossible. Everyone watched in disbelief when Duke won. TV networks re-played the final 2.1 seconds of the game over and over trying to figure out what had happened. A transcript of Coach K's conversation with his players Grant Hill and Christian Laettner solves the mystery and illustrates the importance of being sold on yourself as well as the importance of getting a commitment from others that they can do what you ask by a specific time.

Coach K to Grant Hill: "I want you to throw the inbound pass to Laettner who will be at the top of the key — 75 feet away. We need a three-quarter-court pass. Grant, can you make the pass?"

"Yea, Coach. I can do it." (Coach K got commitment.)

Coach K to Laettner: "Christian, you're going to flash from the left corner to the top of the key. Christian, can you catch it?"

Laettner nodded that he could. (Coach K didn't get a strong enough commitment, and didn't let Laettner off the hook.)

Coach K pushed harder, and got his commitment.

Laettner: "If Grant can throw it, I can catch it and hit the shot."

Hill threw the pass. Laettner hit the shot.[34]

Religions and philosophies for centuries have put forth that thoughts shape destiny. The popular book *The Secret* by Rhonda Byrne focuses on the ancient philosophy that what you plant in your life and mind will come to pass because your subconscious mind will lead you to take the actions you need to succeed. Conversely, if you tell yourself you will fail — you will fail. Either way you choose to think, you will be right.

The first year my daughter, Win, played in Michael Jordan's charity golf tournament she made a hole-in-one during the practice round on one of the course's most difficult holes. The hole is so challenging a car dealership agreed to award a new car to anyone who aced the hole during the tournament. Before the first tournament round, Jordan told her that he'd heard she had an ace in the practice round and asked,

"Are you going to make another hole-in-one this week?"

"I don't know," she responded.

"Then you won't," Jordan said.

She didn't make a hole-in-one during tournament play.

Michael Jordan's belief that you have to expect things of yourself before you can do them is important insight into his belief that you have to anticipate the future with a confident mindset that precedes your competence. Jordan boasted at the welcome dinner on Thursday night to his guests that he would win his tournament. He did not win but was unflappable Sunday afternoon when Vince Coleman and Ozzie Smith did. Jordan had learned the winners' way for handling defeat when results don't meet expectations from his UNC coach, Dean Smith. Sports psychologist, Dr. Bob Rotella, shares what Jordan told a group about Smith's lesson in his book, *How Champions Think*.

Once when Jordan returned to the University of North Carolina for a visit during the NBA off-season, he told Coach Smith that his Chicago Bull's teammates' cavalier attitude towards losing bothered him so much that he would stay in the shower for an hour replaying everything that went wrong in a game and sometimes sit by his locker with a towel over his head thinking about mistakes while his teammates would shower and leave. Smith told him:

> Don't give more than ten or twenty minutes thinking about a bad performance. That's long enough to learn everything that can be learned. After that, think about playing great basketball in the next game — or do something else and not think about basketball at all. If all you do is keep reliving your mistakes, you're going to destroy yourself.[35]

Words that run through the mind repetitiously inevitably become reality. If you feed the computer in your head with garbage about yourself telling yourself you won't make your goal, including a hole-in-one, you won't. Your subconscious mind does not know the difference between something real and something imagined. It only knows what you tell it.

Take risks now and do something bold. You won't regret it.
– Elon Musk
Founder, Chairman, CEO of SpaceX,
Product Architect and Former Chair of Tesla

The subconscious mind works to prove that anything you say to yourself is right. Jordan knew that an important key to winning is what you tell your mind about what you can achieve. You must believe in yourself. You must commit to yourself. If you are not completely sold on yourself you likely will not achieve your goals on the various courts of your life despite your education and technical training. This way of thinking is often kept secret by winners who choose instead to outwardly appear modest in order not to appear cocky, arrogant, or offensive. However, the first person referred to as a G.O.A.T. and the most well known global icon of all time was forever vocal about his belief that he was "The Greatest." Muhammad Ali shared the following about being "The Greatest":

> I said that even before I knew I was. I figured that if I said it enough, I would convince the world that I was really the greatest. To be a great champion you must believe you are the best. If you're not, pretend you are ... It ain't bragging if it's true.[36]

Shlomo Breznitz and Collins Hemingway, authors of the book *Maximum Brainpower* explain it this way:

> ... the brain does not want the body to expend its

resources unless we have a reasonable chance of success. Our physical strength is not accessible to us if the brain does not believe in the outcome, because the worst possible thing for humans to do is to expend all of our resources and fail. If we do not believe we can make it, we will not get the resources we need to make it. The moment we believe, the gates are opened, and a flood of energy is unleashed. Both hope and despair are self-fulfilling prophecies.[37]

To affirm a goal, *write it down as if it already exists and say it repeatedly*, sincerely believing it has already been accomplished. Write down your affirmation several times a day and place your affirmation where you will see it — on the refrigerator, on your mirror, by your bed, etc. Your conscious action will direct your subconscious mind to determine and direct the actions to achieve what you will.

> *Imagination is more important than knowledge.*
> – Albert Eistein

Lolo Jones, one of the fastest women on the planet, sat beside me at a rooftop party following the ESPYS in Los Angeles. Lolo radiates positivity even though she has failed to win an Olympic medal, received a lot of criticism, and has plenty of haters. How does she deal with losing, the opinions of others, and keep going? When asked by journalist Gayle King, Lolo said she takes joy in small victories and believes:

> How you leave something is how you enter the next. You don't want to carry the negativity forward ... look at the good side ... you must stay positive ... opinions mean nothing to me. At the end of the day, I just have to know that what I have done is not altered by what they think of me. It comes by how

hard I have worked and by what I have achieved. Anyone is going to face criticism when they are going after a goal. Somebody starting a business, their thing is like, 'Ah you're not going to be able to do that.' You have to be able to tell yourself, 'I can do this.' And look at where you started from. Take joy in the small things and you get where you are at.[38]

> *The only way to avoid criticism is to say nothing, do nothing, be nothing.*
>
> – Aristotle

Plant in your mind the success you want. It is critical because your mind is just like the earth. It will yield what you plant. If you seed your mind with negative thoughts by telling yourself you aren't good enough, smart enough, talented enough, etc., you will kill your dreams. Plant positive thoughts for success in your mind to yield the results you want.

Lennie Rosenbluth was the 1957 basketball player who with his University of North Carolina Tar Heel team took down Wilt Chamberlain's University of Kansas Jayhawks in triple overtime to win the NCAA championship by one point 54–53. One point — just one point, made the difference in Rosenbluth's life, the lives of his teammates, Carolina basketball, and the Atlantic Coast Conference as a major player in the NCAA. Here's what Rosenbluth told me made the one point possible that made all the difference:

> Confidence is the best word. Confidence in my ability and having a team willing to go the extra. Play to the best of your ability in most of the 40 minutes. Go the extra little bit every minute. I was captain of the team and used to have weekly meetings with players. I'd ask them, 'Is there any reason why we

shouldn't win?' There wasn't. We believed. We never gave up. You get that mentality and you win. Once you have that in your head it happens. And it did. We believed in it so much that we did.

The other thing that made the difference was we had a team but we didn't have any players. We all knew what to do and where to go and we didn't get in anybody's way. We had good ball players. A lot of teams might have one player. We had four who you could go to and who wanted the ball.

You don't hear anything when you're playing a game. If you hear anything you won't have a good team. You are on the floor. If you are a player watching, you won't be a good player. You have a job to do and doing what you have to do. You don't hear the crowd at all. It's the mentality we are not going to lose. We won. That's how you win and what made the difference. My teammate Tommy Kearns said about the final point that made the difference, 'One point changed our lives and Carolina basketball.'[39]

In basketball, you can be the greatest player in the world and lose every game, because a team will always beat an individual.

– Bill Walton
Winner of Three-Time National College Player of the Year Leading UCLA in 88-Game Winning Streak, NBA Finals Most Valuable Player Award, Naismith Memorial Basketball Hall of Famer

The margin of victory for A-Listers is often just a point. Don't remain a tadpole. Fuel your launch to the lily pad with confidence by taking calculated risks that include opportunities for growth often first disguised as failures.

*The fight is won or lost far away from witnesses
behind the lines, in the gym, and out on the road,
long before I dance under those lights.
... I'm experienced now, professional.
Jaws been broke,
been knocked down a couple of times, I'm bad!
Been chopping trees. I done something new for this fight.
I done wrestled with an alligator.
That's right. I have wrestled with an alligator.
I done tussled with a whale.
I done handcuffed lightning,
thrown thunder in jail. That's bad!
Only last week I murdered a rock,
injured a stone, hospitalized a brick!
I'm so mean I make medicine sick!*

– Muhammad Ali

*My parents taught me a long time ago that you win
in life with people, and that's important,
because if you hang with winners,
you stand a great chance of being a winner.*

– Coach Pat Summitt

Chapter Three

Don't Be An Asshole: How To Attract, Develop, And Maintain Winning Relationships

> *Business is never so healthy as when, like a chicken, it must do a certain amount of scratching around for what it gets.*
>
> – Henry Ford

Singapore is the regional hub for many international companies including Apple, Citigroup, Cisco, Microsoft, IBM, and Johnson & Johnson. Hundreds of languages are spoken there. Travel guides say, "The lifeblood of Singapore is the river." In reality, relationships are its lifeblood. The river's existence is not enough to create the success it enjoys today as a first-world oasis in the middle of third-world countries. Its increase in business growth is the result of strategic planning begun in the 1970s and lots of what Henry Ford called "scratching around" to attract foreign direct investment (FDI) to fuel growth. This chapter will teach you how to "scratch around" to increase your business whether it is in Asia, Australia, or Alabama, because successful and prosperous people know people in addition to knowledge and facts. The ability to connect, convey, and convince people is essential.

People do business with people they like. They like people with whom they have fun and share experiences. According to Brian Tracy, "Eighty percent of life's satisfaction comes from meaningful relationships" and the five words that really matter are "the quality of your relationships."[1] Take time to have fun with people in your network. Enjoy your network. Prize the power of connections your network will reap that not only enrich personal life but propel professional success.

The basics for developing relationships with people all over the world are the same — caring about others. Caring begins with giving. Because regional and international customs vary, take time to learn how to show you care in the manner appreciated by people who live outside of your hometown. It will accelerate top results.

The night before the 2014 Daytona 500 I was seated at dinner beside two-time Daytona 500 champion Michael Waltrip and Rob Kauffman, the successful international business investor and billionaire founder of Fortress Investment Group who salvaged Michael Waltrip Racing when cash-strapped Waltrip was on the brink of abandoning his dream. Michael Waltrip Racing owes its survival to a relationship forged by a mutual friend in each of their networks. The mutual friend, Charlotte businessman Johnny Harris, knew Kaufmann, a former auto-mechanic turned banker who shared Waltrip's love of racing. When Waltrip called Harris for help with financing, Harris thought of Kaufmann whom he correctly believed would be the perfect business partner.

I asked Waltrip when I first met him a few weeks earlier what made the difference in his success. Quick as a wink he said:

> Not being an asshole. Winning the Daytona 500 and what made the difference in my winning is the relationships I took the time to make. I was nice to people and being nice to people helped me to build the relationships that made me win. Not being an asshole made the difference. Some people who

are smart, talented, and good in something get by because they are smart, talented and good. I'm a good driver, but there are lots of good drivers. Being nice to people helped me to build relationships that made the difference in my success. The people who helped me were willing to work hard for me because I was nice to them. They did the extra things that helped me to win. The relationships I developed because I was nice to people made the difference. I am as nice to the people in the pit as I am to everyone else.[2]

Waltrip says when talking about Kaufmann, "Without him there would be no Michael Waltrip Racing. Us hitting it off and sharing the same goals and dreams for the team, now seven years later, we're the best of friends."[3]

Include others and make them feel a part of your team even if it's just an invitation to lunch at a local diner. Simple validating gestures make others feel accepted and valued. Extending kindness works like magic and costs nothing. Your inner magic, which you may not have realized you possess, works wonders when you release it. It not only makes the other person feel better about himself but also makes you feel better about yourself. Voila! Doors that you never imagined would open will open and remain open to you.

Kindness. Noun.
Loaning someone your strength
instead of reminding them of their weakness.

Not being an asshole begins with remembering that most people do the best they know how to do. You'll always be able to find something a person does that you won't like. Instead of criticizing what you don't like, look for what you do like and compliment. It will work like magic. People like praise and will work harder for your compliments than they will for your criticism.

How To Give Compliments

Giving sincere compliments or repeating second-hand compliments that you've heard about a person promotes good will and is a friendly way to begin a conversation. Compliments make others feel good and can be made directly, indirectly, privately, and in front of others. Give compliments whenever you honestly can. The bonus of second-hand compliments given behind the backs of others shows you value others, while talking negatively about anyone detracts from you and will cost you personally and professionally. Be careful what you share. People tend to associate good as well as bad news with the messenger often disliking those who share negative news and views.

The nature of bad news infects the teller.
– William Shakespeare

Compliment with sincerity. Be careful not to overdo. If you like a person's clothing, simply tell why you like it with a simple phrase like, "What a beautiful sweater." Avoid going on and on about the color, style, weave, etc. which could make for boring conversation. Adding a comment such as, "That sweater is better looking than the red one you wore yesterday," detracts from the compliment.

Compliment indirectly. Indirect compliments let the person know that you admire or value something about him without directly saying so. An opportunity to give indirect compliments often arises when you want assistance. For example, "This sweater is bulkier than the ones I usually wear. You know so much about fashion, I'd really appreciate your opinion."

Secondhand compliments are an indirect way to make others feel good and let's them know you recognize their value. For example, "Harriet told me you were instrumental to our company winning the new contract in yesterday's meeting."

Compliment with discretion. Giving compliments in the presence of others must be done with sensitivity to others who are present. Giving a compliment to one person without complimenting others who are present may be interpreted as an insult to the others. For example, if you single out one person in front of others to express your like of something the person did well or if you point out something you like about one person without complimenting every individual in the group, the others who are present may feel that you are implying that you don't like, appreciate, or value something similar about them or their actions.

Receiving compliments. Treat compliments you receive the same as you treat receiving gifts. Let the giver know that you appreciate the gift of a compliment. In the United States it is appropriate to say, "Thank you, I'm glad you like it," "What a nice thing to say," or "I appreciate that," "Thank you for noticing." Responding to a compliment about your work or efforts by minimizing or denying it with a remark such as, "It was nothing," insinuates that the person has made a mistake. Instead, politely take the credit and say, "Thank you for noticing." If you receive a compliment about your clothing such as a sweater, instead of saying, "This faded sweater is an old hand-me-down that has a hole under the arm, etc." which would make the compliment giver feel that you don't respect or value the compliment, instead say, "Thank you." The universal custom of receiving compliments is to return a compliment of goodwill with a gesture of gracious appreciation. Europeans receive compliments without words by giving a friendly smile. Asians acknowledge compliments with a gracious bow.

David Gregory, former host of NBC's *Meet the Press*, in an interview, discussed getting fired. He said what he could have done better is the way he treated people and that if he'd treated people differently they might have been rooting for him a little more.[4]

Legendary, larger than life professional golfer "Long John Daly" enjoys cult-like popularity. Daly went from "zero to hero" when he won his first PGA Championship getting to play as the ninth alternate. Daly told me, "All relationships made the difference to me — the good ones and the bad ones."[5]

You learn from every interaction but positive relationships and especially "networking with the right people and taking calculated risks is what made the difference in my success," says Charles "Chuck" Simonton, M.D., cardio thoracic surgeon, Chief Medical Officer and developer of Abbott Vascular's revolutionary dissolving stent.[6] General Robert E. "Boomer" Milstead, Jr. put it this way when he spoke about the difference relationships made to his rise in rank. "No one gets to the top without other people."[7]

> *You can judge the quality of your life*
> *by the quality of your relationships.*
>
> – Joseph Robinette "Joe" Biden, Jr.
> 46th President of the United States

It's amazing how many people in business are jerks to people like janitors and administrative assistants and afterwards wonder why they didn't make a sale or get a promotion. Administrative assistants can open doors for you by putting your calls through, finding time on the calendar of the people you want to talk to, or they can slam the door shut.

> *The excellent person manages himself.*
> *He will not allow the environment to manage him.*
>
> – Rex Resurreccion
> Author of *Called To Excel*

It's important to know where to look and how to cultivate a strong network of developed relationships that can help you reach your goals. Like Waltrip, you won't always know where to look. That's why you need to be nice to everyone and know how to build your network so you can have a diverse enthusiastic group able to help you reach your goals and connect you to people they may know who share your interests — whether it's in the pit changing your car's oil and tires or connecting you with someone to finance the equipment you need to reach your goals. In this chapter we're going to discuss what you need to do to attract, develop, and maintain the relationships you need to reach your goals.

Joining clubs with a focus that interests you is one of the best ways to meet people and form relationships that can help you develop your network. Identify and join clubs in your community with missions you want to support. Many clubs are international, such as Executive Women International, Rotary International, Kiwanis International, Business and Professional Women, Lions Club International, and Zonta International. Your involvement will require an investment of your time, but you will be a better person for the investment. Attend meetings with the attitude that you will give before you get. Consider how you can be of assistance to the people you meet. You will reap the rewards of fellowship, friendship, and contacts that will enhance your personal and professional life.

Don't overlook your church, your alumni association, and opportunities to meet people at museum events or art openings. Don't limit yourself to who you talk to at these events by only gravitating to people you already know. Connect with everyone — young, old, men, and women.

Power is in numbers, but only if you take the time to develop the connection into a relationship. Powerful networking takes time and is worth the investment. Your networking goal at meetings and events should not be to talk to as many people as possible, but to leave with one to five personal connections where you've taken the time to learn more about these individuals. You never know when you will meet someone who can help you reach your goals.

Don't settle for interacting with the people who are the easiest to access. You need to reach outside your comfort zone because there you will find a wealth of new connections that will add power to your success.

Always be on the look out for new groups in new places. Be active. Visit different places and try new activities. You never know who you will meet at a yoga class or community event. Invest your time in everyone including people you think you will never see again because you never know the doors a new person can open for you or you for them. Why for them? We are all in this world together to make the world a good place. Help others whenever you can.

> *If you go looking for a friend,*
> *you're going to find they're scarce.*
> *If you go out to be a friend,*
> *you'll find them everywhere.*
>
> – Zig Ziglar

In an ideal and fair world, you would reach your goal as a direct result of your talents, abilities, and the quality of your products, services, and ideas. However, the world is neither ideal nor fair. In reality, it is often not what you know but who you know that is important. Further, it's an interesting fact that much of a person's success is frequently not due to a primary connection but to one that is once or many times removed. In other words, someone you know knows someone who knows someone who can help you. You need connections to reach top success.

According to Richard Wiseman, Ph.D., a professor at the

University of Hertfordshire in England, the greater your network, the more opportunities you have. His research shows that the average person knows approximately 300 people by first name. He concludes that if you go to an event and meet someone new you will be "only two handshakes away from 300 times 300 people. That's 90,000 new possibilities for a new opportunity just by saying hello."[8] If the yoga class or museum opening you attend attracts 50 people, you're just a couple of introductions away from millions of people who may be able to help you achieve your goal. If no one introduces you, you must introduce yourself. "Lucky people create, notice, and act upon the chance opportunities in their lives."[9]

Introduce yourself to someone you would like to meet by smiling and saying, *"Hello, My name is John Doe. I haven't had the pleasure of meeting you."*

As you begin to build your network you'll find yourself invited to business and social events. Your first responsibility when you are invited to any event is to respond. Respond to every event to which you are invited. If you're invited by telephone you can respond by telephone. If you are invited via formal invitation, respond with a formal reply. Failure to respond to an invitation shows lack of respect.

Social interaction is often the reason for business events. Many participants experience anxiety at the thought of facing a room full of people whether or not they know the people attending. Business and social events are places to connect with many people — not a place to have deep, meaningful conversations with just a few. Most conversations run their course in seven to eight minutes so while you might connect with more people, you'll likely have time for only seven to eight conversations per hour.

You need to master the fundamental skills so you can maximize your effectiveness for business opportunities. Entering a room correctly, making good introductions, and engaging in good conversation will help you attract, develop, and maintain business.

Wear a nametag when tags are available. Wear yours on the upper right shoulder so those you meet can easily see. People shake hands right hand to right hand so the natural direction of the eyes is to the right shoulder. If possible, add one or two words about yourself below your name (company, town, etc.) This conversation bait will help others know you and can be a springboard for conversation.

Enter the meeting space with purpose and be in charge of yourself. Most people walk into the work place, a business, or social event without prior planning for successful interaction. Walk through the doorway and then step to the side out of the traffic path. Pause and look around the room. Look for key people you must speak to such as the host, an honored visitor, or a high-ranking official. Few people will notice you do this, but if they do, so much the better because this is the correct way to enter a room.

Look approachable, maintain good posture, and wear a pleasant facial expression. Lower your volume when entering the room with others with whom you may already be engaged in conversation. Noisy conversationalists send the subliminal message that they have low self-esteem or are seeking attention.

Confidence is quiet. Insecurity is loud.

If there is a receiving line, go through it early. If you arrive on time you will not have to waste time standing in a long receiving line to greet your host and any guests of honor who should be greeted when you first arrive. A receiving line is a courtesy established to make saying hello easy to those you must greet. It's poor manners not to go through the line.

Do not eat or drink until you've greeted the hosts even if you don't know them. A woman traditionally precedes her male escort through a receiving line. It is correct for the woman to introduce herself. If you bring a guest to the event, precede your guest and introduce your guest to the host who in turn introduces you to the guest of honor. Men precede women through receiving lines only if the event takes place at The White House, an all-male campus, or a military event when the man is enlisted and the woman is not.

You will need to find the guest of honor, your boss, and your host when there is no receiving line. Wait for a break in conversation when you approach a guest of honor surrounded by many people. Say, "Excuse me, I would like to introduce myself and to say hello." Be careful not to monopolize the guest of honor or the boss who is generally in high demand. Greet the host and any honored guests traditionally with a firm web-to-web handshake. *(NOTE: this centuries old custom is evolving since the Coronavirus pandemic. Nonverbal communication including handshakes and evolving gestures is discussed in Chapter Four).* Tell the guest of honor that you are delighted to be at the event and to meet him. You do not need to engage in lengthy conversation because other guests will be waiting to say hello. Arriving on time is also beneficial because you can make maximum use of building and maintaining your network at the event.

> *Manners require time,*
> *and nothing is more vulgar than haste.*
> – Ralph Waldo Emerson

The reason for business events is meeting and greeting, so eat last — or before you go! You will look like a cow chewing cud if you stand around grazing. If and when you eat, get a plate and start at the beginning of the buffet table. Do not overload your plate. Find a table after you've served your plate. Sit down to eat. If you want seconds from the buffet, get a clean plate and start back at the beginning of the buffet line without cutting in front of others for the specific food you want to replenish. Look for a service table to place your dirty plate if no waiter is available to clear your plate. A service table is a side table that is completely empty and is usually off to the side of a room.

When you arrive at a table with guests who are seated, speak to everyone seated. Walk around the table to introduce yourself to people you do not know. This will distinguish you as someone who knows what to do. You'll be recognized as a leader when you do this. Be sure to give your first and last names and offer a small amount of conversation bait to the guests at your table. Accompany the beginning of your conversation with a gesture of greeting — traditionally with a firm web-to-web handshake while looking a person in his eyes or using an evolving alternative gesture.

Be the one who goes first.
The world rewards those who go first —
not those who wait for others to do so.
Say hello first. Introduce yourself first.
Help a stranger first.

Rise to greet men and women who arrive at your table after you are seated. Rising in your grandmother's day was an act primarily done by men to show respect to women and to men while corseted women, once perceived to be the weaker sex, remained seated. Today, men and women who are polished, savvy, and want to be treated equally in the workplace rise to show respect to everyone.

A host who carefully plans seating arrangements may indicate the seats for guests by using place cards. Do not switch the cards. Sit in the seat a place card indicates for you to sit.

Good guests are not boorish. They participate in event activities. Learn to dance if you don't already know how to dance. Nobody cares if you don't dance well. Get up, dance, sway, and have fun. Laugh at yourself and others will laugh with you and love you for not taking yourself too seriously.

At the conclusion of an event, find your host to say, "Thank you." Add to your thanks the mention of at least one thing you especially enjoyed. For example, "Thank you so much for including me. The fabulous band made dancing so much fun!"

Build the right relationships with the right people and nurture them over time and you'll always have a leg up on the competition.

– Paul May
CEO BuzzStream

What To Say That Makes The Difference

The most important part of meeting and greeting is called the introduction. Social introductions differ from business introductions. Social introductions are based on gender with deference shown to the woman while business introductions are based on rank. The exception to the hard and fast rules of both social and business protocol occurs when introductions involve members of the clergy, ambassadors, chiefs of state, and royalty. In these instances, those officials are accorded the most respect and a woman should be introduced to them. For example, "Bishop Michael Curry, I'd like to introduce to you Dr. Madeline Moss."

Proper introductions always include first and last names. In addition, they often include the use of honorifics — those titles that indicate membership in professional areas or marital status. Examples are Dr., Mr., Mrs., Miss, Ms., Professor,

President, Judge, Ambassador, Bishop, etc. Titles such as Senator, General, and Judge are for life. You may choose to omit the honorific when making an introduction but not the first and last names. If you use an honorific for one person, it is good to use an honorific for the other person involved in the introduction. For example, two people could be introduced correctly by saying, "Judge Hanna Sharp, I'd like to introduce to you Dr. Martha Roberts." Alternatively, you might introduce the two women by saying, "Hanna Sharp, I'd like to introduce to you Martha Roberts."

Address people in purely business settings the same way you address them in business/social settings. For example, if you call your boss "Mr." at the office, continue this habit even if the invitation you received referred to him by first name. Your spouse should address your boss and your boss' spouse with a title and last name if that is your usual business custom.

Add conversation bait to help people make conversation. Bait included in the introduction above might include information about the type of cases Judge Sharp hears, and the type of medicine Dr. Roberts practices, where each is from, their hobbies, or how the introducer knows each person. Here's how Angelo Dundee, Muhammad Ali's famous trainer, remembers fifteen-year-old Ali introducing himself over the telephone when he was staying in a hotel in Louisville: "This is Cassius Clay, the Golden Gloves champion of Louisville, Kentucky. I'm going to be the heavyweight champion of the world. I'm in the lobby. Can I come up?"[10] Ali didn't wait for anyone to introduce him. He provided bait, he asked directly and specifically for what he wanted. He was invited up.

A person introducing him/herself does not generally include a personal title but indicates a professional designation with conversation bait. For example, Dr. Roberts might introduce herself in the following way. "Hello, I'm Martha Roberts, an orthopedist from Atlanta." The correct reply would be, "Hello

Dr. Roberts. I'm Hanna Sharp from Savannah. I'm a judge holding court in this district." Dr. Roberts might choose to say, "Please call me Martha." Judge Sharp might choose to say, "Please call me Hanna."

The mixing of the social and business worlds is inevitable so it is smart to know the correct way to introduce people in a variety of settings and situations. But first, if you come upon a friend and a group of people you don't know, make the first move — introduce yourself.

Social Introductions

Introducing Yourself

Stand up. Look the person in his eyes, extend your right hand for a firm web-to-web handshake or use an evolving alternative gesture such as placing your hand over your heart accompanied by a slight bow, say your first and last names and something about yourself. For example, "Hello, I'm Jane Hight from Wilmington, North Carolina, the keynote speaker for the convention."

Make each person feel important by providing important information about each person as you make the introduction. Disclosing the interests, special talents, hometowns or even the schools of the people introduced will give a basis for small talk. For example, say, "Cora Cordell, I'd like to introduce to you my friend from the Swiss Bank office in Zurich, Natasha Gimals. Cora is an Olympic alpine skier and has a fun hobby — magic!" An introduction such as this can result in several avenues of conversation — the Olympics, skiing, Switzerland, banking, and magic.

Five Rules For Making Proper Social Introductions

1) *Introduce less important persons to more important persons.* Say the older, more important, or female's name first followed by one of the following phrases: "I'd like to present to you," "I would like to introduce to you," "I would like for you to meet," or simply, "This is" followed by the name of the person being introduced. For example, "Governor Goodman, I'd like to introduce to you Gordon Upshaw who is a new graduate of MIT. He is a software designer from Chicago."

2) *Introduce a man to a woman.* Introduce a man to a woman when they are the same age. Do this by first saying the woman's name. For example, "Sarah Lewtas, I'd like to introduce to you my friend, George Harris, a radio host and author from Sarasota. George, Sarah is a chef from Seattle.

3) *Introduce a younger person to an older person.* Do this by first saying the older person's name. Use the honorific to show respect. For example, "Mrs. Allen, I'd like to introduce to you my neighbor from Henderson, Mary Jane Cordell. Mary Jane, this is Mrs. Allen. Our fathers were friends in Vance County."

4) *Introduce a new friend to a group.* Do this by first saying the new friend's name. For example, "Wells White, I'd like you to meet my friends." Say the names of the members in the group or have your friends introduce themselves to your friend.

5) *Introduce a nonfamily member to a family member.* Nonfamily members regardless of age are given precedence except a child who introduces a mother or father.

Business Introductions

Three Rules For Making Proper Business Introductions

1) *Introduce a junior member to a senior member of the same company.* Do this by saying the senior member's name first.

2) *Introduce a person from your own company to a person outside of the company* even if the person from your own company is the CEO. A client or future client is always shown deference.

3) *Provide information to make conversation easy.*

Mention the interests, special talents, hometowns or even the schools of the people introduced. This will give a basis for small talk. For example, say, "Beau White, I'd like to introduce to you the friend I met at the Maryland convention, Auggie Cordell, who is a wildlife writer from Annapolis." An introduction such as this can result in several avenues of conversation — wildlife, writing, convention, the historic coastal city of Annapolis!

A foolproof method for making both business and social introductions correctly is to use the following formula. Say the name of the person accorded the most respect first, followed by the phrase "to you," followed by the name of the person introduced. Just remember, flubbing up is forgivable, failing to make an introduction is not.

Responding To Introductions

- Do not reply with a simple "Hi" or "Hello."
- Stand up, extend your hand (or alternative gesture), smile, lean towards the person and say, "Hello ___. How do you do?" Some people prefer to say the phrase, "It's nice to meet you." Even though the traditional response is, "How do you

do?" it is helpful to conversation when you personalize what you say.
- Phrases asking, "How do you do? How are you today?" etc., are pleasantries — not inquiries intended to pry into your personal health or affairs because no one, except maybe your mother, really cares. Respond with a succinct pleasantry such as, "Fine thank you, I hope you are well." This response does you a favor. It does not invite a personal treatise about the other person's health or state of affairs.
- When you meet someone you have heard about say, "I've heard good things about you," instead of "I've heard a lot about you."
- Always repeat the person's name.
- Immediately ask the person to repeat a name if you didn't hear the name clearly or are not sure how to pronounce it.

Techniques for Remembering Names

Validate people calling them by name and coming to a complete stop when you speak to them. The act of stopping to speak gives people a special moment that demonstrates that you value them enough to fully recognize them. You do not have to stop for long — a pause as brief as three seconds during which you give full attention looking the person in his eyes will show you value the person. You do not have to engage in conversation. You can say something as simple as, "I just want to stop and say hello. I hope all is going well for you." Rushing past others and only quickly glancing and speaking to them while you are walking makes what you say seem obligatory and insincere.

Make a concerted effort to remember the names of people you meet. Do this by first paying attention to the new name when it is said during the introduction. Listen carefully to the name and if you do not hear it clearly ask the person to repeat the name. It is helpful to ask for the spelling of a unique sounding name. For example, you might say, "Hello, Dr. Miars. Do you spell your name M-i-a-r-s or M-e-y-e-r-s?" This will provide another opportunity for your brain to remember the name when the correct spelling is heard.

Repeat the name aloud in your first response to the introduction and during the conversation. In addition, silently repeating the name will assist you with remembering the name.

Other techniques that are helpful in remembering names are thinking of someone else you know with the same name or remembering the name with a word association. For example, a person might remember the name of a woman named Mrs. Strause by associating her name with the strawberry printed dress she is wearing. This system is not without danger. Someone I knew used this technique when he met Mrs. Strause wearing her strawberry print dress and two months later greeted her saying, "Hello Mrs. Strawberry." Perhaps he would have had better luck if he had associated her name by imagining straws coming out of her ears but then there is the possibility of saying, "Hello Mrs. Hay" if one is not careful with the association.

At some point, everyone forgets a name. It is possible to let the person know that you remember him even when you admit that you have forgotten his name and ask for it again. Begin the conversation by reintroducing yourself to the person whose name you have temporarily forgotten. For example, "Hello, I'm Harriet Joan Cordell. I believe we met at the technical conference in California." More often than not, the person will be grateful as he too may have forgotten your name and will readily supply his name. If the person does not reply with his name after I have refreshed his memory of my name, I say, "Please tell me your name again" or "I really want to remember your name. Would you please repeat it?" Asking for the person's name again demonstrates interest in the individual and shows that you are human.

Conversation That Makes The Difference

Business people who have good conversational skills are more likely to succeed even though they may not be better educated, smarter, or better looking. Studies conducted as early as the 1930s by the Carnegie Institute of Technology have revealed that in all fields only 15% of one's financial success in life is due to technical knowledge, while "skill in human engineering" (skill in communicating with people) is the factor responsible for the remaining 85% of financial success.[11] John D. Rockefeller knew this. He said, "The ability to get along with people is as purchasable a commodity as sugar and coffee, and I pay more for that ability than any under the sun."[12] He knew that the marketplace is fiercely competitive and that product knowledge and hard work are not enough to win clients and new contracts — or keep the ones a business has. To outclass the competition and exceed bottom line goals often requires an essential business tool not found in every company. Rockefeller's success and the success of the businesses he ran were the result of individuals with excellent people skills.

A study conducted by The United States Bureau of Hiring and Training Management Practices surveyed 3000 employers throughout the United States. The employers were asked to identify the top two skills sought in hiring new people. The survey required ranking in order of importance: previous work experience, recommendations by previous employers, positive attitude, experience in occupational field, good communication skills, and degree of education. The top two skills determined by this survey were a positive attitude and good communication skills. The Pew Research Center now indicates that up to 90% of your success in life is due to your people skills.[13] Fortunately, people skills can be learned.

> *Networking is an essential part of building wealth.*
> — Armstrong Williams
> American Political Commentator, Entrepreneur, Author and Talk Show Host

Mixing and mingling at the highest level is easy with a little advance preparation. Plan for success by positioning yourself around people who can make a difference in your life. Do this often. Wake up every morning and ask yourself, "Who can I meet today who will make a difference in my success?" In fact, go a step further, write it in big, **bold letters** and tape it on your bathroom mirror.

Also consider who can help you meet your goals. Is it a prospective customer? A client? A colleague with contacts? Key members of an association who may become prospects?

Don't settle for interacting with the people who are the easiest to access. You need to reach outside your comfort zone where you will find new connections that will help you get what you want, need, and deserve.

When I was a young woman, I moved a thousand miles from my home in Chapel Hill, North Carolina to Hanover, New Hampshire. I knew no one in my new town. Lucky for me, a woman named Linda Nicks, who formerly lived in the house I moved into, knew how to help me navigate my new environment. In addition to the fresh flowers she had picked from the meadow behind our house and left on the mantel above our fireplace, she left a list of people in the area who could help me. Beside each name she wrote the person's telephone number and a short note about the person. For example, next to one man's name she wrote that he had a snow plow, would plow our driveway, was handy at fixing just about anything, and had a wife and a daughter who sewed, cleaned, etc. It made it easy for me to call on them to introduce myself. I had a place to begin conversation.

Years later, I moved back to North Carolina. As fate would have it, the same woman who had no ties to the South had moved to the same new town to which I moved! She brought me cookies and invited me to the opening of the local hospital's Hospitality House where I would meet new people. This time instead of giving me a handwritten list to help me, she personally prepared me for the people I would meet and then introduced me to them. Here's what she did.

Linda picked me up early in order to get a parking space smack dab in front of the Hospitality House. She told me a little about each person as he or she walked into the building. When we finally went inside, I found mingling easy and fun. I remember many people from that day, but I especially remember what my friend told me about Maryann Robison. "That woman can move mountains." Maryann could get things done in our community better than anyone else not only because she was nice to everyone, but because she was a pro at navigating the community to accomplish her goals. Maryann's daughter-in-law, Margaret, now carries the torch raising huge sums of money for the community college and local charities, primarily the result of her stellar skills at navigating local business.

Be a prepared guest with good conversation. Ask your host or meeting planner the names of guests before an event. Asking demonstrates your interest in guests and your commitment to do your part to make their event a success. For this reason, hosts and event planners are usually happy to share their guest lists. Identifying people you will encounter will help you to recollect what you know about guests you have previously met so you can follow up with earlier conversations. To prepare for conversation with new people on the list, ask other people to share what they know about the guests you will meet for the first time, Google search names of guests, and visit networking sites like LinkedIn that include subscribers' photos, schools, employment history, special skills and interests.

I visited a golf club whose members are from throughout the United States. On Friday evenings the club offers a popular event called "The Gathering" for members to gather for fellowship, cocktails, and an elegant buffet supper. After a round of golf at the club, my friend, a successful businessman, went into the secretary's office and asked for a printed list of the names of people with reservations who would be attending that evening's "Gathering." The secretary obliged. We took the list back to my friend's home. My friend mixed me a drink, got his membership book from a drawer, sat down in a rocking chair beside me on his porch overlooking the 6th green and went over the list telling me about each person who would be attending — name, city where each member was from, spouse's name, etc. He'd written notes in his book including information he'd learned about the members during rounds of golf and social activities. The review was good for both of us — his memory was refreshed in preparation for follow-up on previous conversations and I was equipped with ideas for conversation with new people. "Prior preparation prevents poor performance."

Do what you can to learn about people before you meet. My daughter, Win, was invited to a dinner party at the home of Barbara and Jack Nicklaus in Palm Beach Gardens, Florida. She was the date of a guest and assumed that the Nicklauses would only know her date. Win shares the following about the Nicklaus' ability to make others welcome in their home:

> I had the pleasure to be a guest at the Nicklaus' home. I would estimate there were at least 100 people in attendance. Everyone who came through the door was greeted in a receiving line first by

Barbara and then by Jack. It was the perfect way for them to welcome their guests and they couldn't have been more gracious.

Barbara and Jack had done their homework on everyone who walked through the door. While I'm sure they did know many of those visiting their home that day, they took the time to learn about those they did not. It was my first time meeting them, but Barbara immediately made me feel welcome by conversing with me about my life in a way that showed she had taken time to research and learn about me. Pretty spectacular.[14]

You can do the same as Barbara and Jack Nicklaus. Ensure the interest of your potential conversation partners by learning enough about their backgrounds, interests, and occupations so that you can intelligently discuss subjects important to them. Know some of the insider lingo particular to their interests and businesses. For example, a speaker planning a conversational encounter with a sports fan and alumni of the University of North Carolina at Chapel Hill during basketball season could easily learn from the sports page of a regional newspaper the names of key players and that the Carolina team is referred to as "The Tar Heels." In addition, a local sports page reveals important rivalries and often hot issues that are on the minds of fans. Good conversation is enhanced by the introduction of topics that can kindle a conversational bonfire.

Read at least one newspaper a day so you can initiate or participate in current event discussions. Survey every section — sports, leisure, international, entertainment, travel, and business. Even a cursory glance at the different sections will be of use to you later as you converse with people you do not know. Take time to periodically digest each section and to become aware of the vocabulary particular to different topics. Plan to interact with people out of town by browsing the websites of that town's newspaper and business magazines.

Read at least one book from the *New York Times'* Best Seller List. Read reviews for all of them. Your memory will help you with conversation when you prepare in advance with diverse reading and experiences.

> *Chance favors the prepared mind.*
> – Louis Pasteur

Prepare for conversation with people you have never met by consciously sampling a variety of activities and entertainments in your leisure. The vocabulary you pick up from a onetime experience (scuba diving, horseback riding, going to the opera) can serendipitously provide the responsive cord that connects you to a new business associate. Steve Jobs in his commencement address to Stanford University graduates told a personal story about taking a calligraphy class that seemed irrelevant at the time but that the design skills he learned were later baked into the first Apple computer. You never know what will be useful ahead of time. "You can't connect the dots looking forward; you can only connect them looking backwards. So you have to trust that the dots will somehow connect in your future," said Jobs.[15] In order to have dots to connect in business and in your relationships you need to be willing to try new things. Collect dots.

Read the trade journals of potential conversation partners who function in a particular industry. These journals will help you to identify the hot issues concerning the industry as well as supply you with the vocabulary you need to sound like an insider. When Michael Waltrip invited me to the Daytona 500 he knew I knew nothing about NASCAR. He said, "I'm going to send you some homework." He promptly sent me a copy of his book, *In The Blink of An Eye*. It made a big difference in my

Daytona experience from the moment I arrived. Waltrip had invited my daughter and me to dinner the night before the race. Seated beside me was Rob Kaufmann. I immediately knew who he was. Conversation was easy because I'd read about racing and Kaufmann in Waltrip's book.

If all else fails, use Eleanor Roosevelt's technique. Eleanor Roosevelt had a reputation for her ability to talk to everyone including the most challenging conversation partners. A fabled story is about a reporter who once asked her how she always seemed to be able to talk to anyone. She said, "Sometimes I have to use the alphabet." The startled reporter asked her to explain. "Well, I start with the letter 'A.' For example, I might say, 'Nice crop of apples this year. What is your favorite variety of apple?' I never give up on anyone even if I have to go through the whole alphabet. One time I got all the way to the letter T."

Follow up on the last conversation you had with guests. For example, "You were planning a trip to Africa the last time I saw you. Tell me about the part of your trip that was the most exciting?" Ask open-ended questions that require more than a simple yes or no response.

Start conversations in business and social settings by using an indirect approach. Asking direct personal questions turns off potential business and social contacts as you are viewed as intrusive and nosy. Avoid questions such as:

- "Where do you live?"
- "What school did you attend?"
- "How do you know so and so?"
- "Where did you get …?"
- "How much did it cost?"
- "What church do you attend?"
- "Are you married?"
- "Do you have children?"
- "Who are you voting for?"

Avoid asking, "What do your parents do?" This question is a turn-off because it makes the asker seem to be determining the value of the person. Do ask questions that focus on current topics of interest and subjects so broad that your questions will not be viewed as invasive.

The question, "What do you do?" is a question that is bothersome to many conversationalists. The risk of offending is most likely with two groups of people. First, people who are not proud of their jobs, and second, people who are not employed. The second category includes people who may be fortunate enough not to need to work and do not wish to discuss that privilege. Ask the question, "What do you do?" only when you sense that the individual will be amenable to answering it and that he will enjoy talking about his work. The best phrase to use when you are not sure is, "What do you enjoy doing?" The person who enjoys his work will gladly discuss his job and the person who does not work or like his job is free to direct conversation to whatever he likes best.

Ask general questions, ones relevant to the occasion, or the reason for the person's participation in the event you are both attending instead of talking about yourself, your health or the other person's health. Good comments and questions are:

- "Thank you for ___." (your business, your help, your time, etc.)
- "I'm not sure, but I will find out." (It's ok if you don't know the answer. Be honest and find help.)
- "What do you enjoy doing in your free time?"
- "What else can I do for you?" (Go the extra mile … there is less competition there.)
- "What is most convenient for you?"
- "How may I serve you?"
- "How may I help you?"
- "How did I do?"

Make people feel welcome and comfortable. The two most important words — "Thank you." The single most important word — "Yes." Positive relationships result from a positive attitude. Remember, people don't care about your ailments and troubles so spare them. What people care about is how they feel when they are around you. Your optimism will make them feel good and it will also help you feel good and that will help you to win in your relationships. Let people know how much you care about them because they won't care about you until they know how much you care about them. Off-color jokes make others feel uncomfortable. Avoid them. Giving too much information about anything — your children and grandchildren who may mean the world to you — is generally boring to others. Focus your conversation on the other person, his family — and not on your own. Don't ever make the mistake of focusing on yourself and being anything but an optimist.

Read the body language of the key people you observe when you enter a room. Determine which key people are currently the easiest to approach. The easiest to approach are people standing alone who are feeling awkward who will appreciate your attention and groups of three or more. Dyads with closed body language standing with their heads close together and their backs turned are generally more difficult to enter than triads. When you approach a group, stand on the fringe of the conversation space with one foot slightly forward if a small space is open. Participants will typically open the space to let you join them. Listen to the conversation to grasp the topic. Enter the group of people you do not know by waiting for a break in conversation and then coupling a self-introduction with a comment. For example, you might encounter a group discussing the upcoming NCAA (National Collegiate Athletic Association) tournament. When a break occurs, you might say, "Hello, I'm (first and last names). I was listening to ESPN radio on my way here and they reported that Duke's point guard fell during practice and is injured." Most groups welcome a new breath of conversational life.

Welcome newcomers to your group by slightly opening the space between you and the group when you notice someone who wants to join your group.

Body language at every business and social affair should be professional. Remember, the only acceptable form of professional touch is the handshake — a universal nonverbal business communication custom of goodwill that abruptly stopped during the Coronavirus pandemic. Many believe the handshake will resurface when social distancing is no longer necessary to remain healthy. Regardless, business and social events are not the place to demonstrate romantic affection for anyone.

The average conversation lasts seven to eight minutes so you'll likely have time to meet only seven or eight people per hour. Make it your goal to optimize those encounters. This does not mean avoiding your coworkers. Acknowledge them and include them in conversations.

Putting yourself in host mode will help you feel like you belong. Help others when you spot an opportunity. Consider offering to help your host pass hors d'oeuvres if you are a guest in someone's home for a small party. Every group will open to welcome you!

Small Talk
That Makes The Difference

One of my favorite stories is about a young psychologist from Los Angeles who took a month off from his practice to fly back and forth every day from Los Angeles to New York. He booked the middle seat of a three-seat row for every flight because he wanted to have conversations with the people seated on either side of him. His plan was to completely focus on being interested in his seatmates. He asked good questions and let his fellow passengers speak. At the end of each flight, he suggested they exchange contact information so they might stay in touch. A week after each flight, he had researchers telephone each of his seatmates. All remembered him, said they liked him, and how interesting he was. However, none of them knew his occupation or if he were married (because he never told them). The moral of the story — be interested rather than interesting if you want to be thought of as an interesting person.

How can you get people to be interested in you, to care about you, and want to have a relationship with you? Ask your conversation partner two follow-up questions when he shares a story or information. Saying three simple words will quickly show that you are listening and interested in what he is saying. "Tell me more." These three words empower relationships because they demonstrate focus on the speaker. Three bonus words further let the speaker know you are interested, "What happened next?" When people know you care about what they say, they will be interested in you and want to have a relationship with you.

There is no such thing as small talk. It's the foundation for all big talk. Knowing how to make small talk will help you establish rapport when you're networking, speaking with a new prospect, warming up a customer before selling or upselling, or asking for a referral. The mere sound of a person's voice offers clues to the person's physical and emotional condition. Listening to the person's voice during small talk will help you determine if the person sounds healthy or sick, happy or sad, confident or anxious. Use information gleaned from small talk topics to transition to deeper conversation.

Small talk conversation stagnates when cliché topics like the weather and food are exhausted. Sometimes the body language of conversation partners indicates a willingness to terminate or continue the conversation. If the body language is open, and the facial expression shows interest, the savvy conversationalist knows what to listen for and how to steer the conversation to deeper talk. Transitioning from small talk is easy for the good listener. He listens for a topical cue (a word or reference) to direct talk in a deeper direction. For instance, the good listener might hear his conversation partner say, "This food tastes like the food in France." The alert listener might pick up on the word France and respond, "Have you been to France? I've always wanted to travel there to sample regional food and wine." The conversation then begins to take on new life. Even though the person who asked the question about France may not have a deep interest in France, chances are good that the conversation partner does and for that person the small talk is no longer small.

The conversationalist transitioning from small talk to deeper conversation often reflects back an understanding of his communication partner's message and feelings. For example, the conversation about France may digress to conversation about a trip to a castle in the Loire Valley where the person took cooking classes taught by a famous chef. "Wow, it must have been exciting to visit that area of France. I can tell that you have more than a passing interest in good food," the attentive listener may respond.

Using empathizers (short, simple supportive statements) demonstrates understanding important to establishing rapport in relationships so that conversation can continue beyond small talk. Listen for what is emotionally significant to your conversation partner and let him know that you understand what is significant to him. This is more important than any clever remark you might venture to make. Why? Because in a new relationship people generally feel that the least interesting things about themselves are more important than the most fascinating things about people they do not know. Use phrases like:

- "I can understand why you feel …"
- "I can see you really understand …"
- "I appreciate why you …"
- "It's obvious you really worked hard for …"

These phrases are also useful in relationships that have developed and become meaningful. These same empathizers then demonstrate sincere interest in the other person that may be greater than the interest in one's self. The use of the pronoun "you" can positively be used to shift the focus of the conversation to the other person. Remember, people subconsciously perceive themselves as more important than any other person, place, or thing.

One further tip, respect your conversation partner by waiting until after he has had the pleasure of sharing his experience before you interrupt or add that you also have been there, done that, etc. Later, if your conversation partner asks why you didn't tell him earlier, you can further increase his appreciation of you with a statement such as, "I was enjoying hearing your description so much."

Use Of Subliminal Rapport Building Techniques To Develop And Maintain Relationships

Conversations typically begin with clichés and later move on to a phase that may include the introduction of facts. As rapport increases, feelings become a feature of the dialogue. Later as conversation grows deeper, conversations that are more intimate are characterized by the use of "we" and "us" as experiences are shared between conversation partners.

Good conversationalists match the mood of the people with whom they converse. This rapport establishing technique puts the conversation partner at ease. Match jovial, tranquil, or enthusiastic moods to make your conversation partner feel you are in tune with him.

The prettiest sound in the whole world is the sound of one's own name. Say the name of the person with whom you are speaking but avoid overusing it so you do not sound patronizing. Look the person in the eyes when there is a break in the conversation. Lean slightly forward. Enthusiastically ask a question that requires thought to answer with more than a simple yes or no.

A technique called captioning is the excerpting of a phrase or story from a previous conversation and relating it in some way back to the current conversation. Only the two people who shared the experience understand the meaning of the caption. This makes captioning function somewhat like a private language between communicators. It establishes a bond between communicators that is unique and gives the feeling of history to a relationship even though the relationship is new. Many business people will make a new acquaintance feel like an old friend by finding something in a previous conversation that the conversation partner liked which they highlight in a subsequent conversation. Captioning may even take the form of a private joke between two people. Caption something positive that you and your conversation partner shared.

The use of nicknames is another technique that is sometimes effective in establishing a strong subliminal bond and transitioning acquaintances into friends. For example, two acquaintances paired in a golf game at a company retreat may give each other complimentary nicknames based on a round of golf. "The Eagle" or "Ms. Par" may arise. Make sure the nickname you give someone is one the person likes.

If it seems appropriate, you may ask your conversation partner if he or she had a nickname growing up. If the answer is yes, you might ask if he'd like to be called by that name.

For instance, Robert may be asked if anybody ever called him "Bobby." Perhaps it is the name friends still call him and Robert responds that he would like new friends to call him by that name. Robert may tell new friends to call him "Bobby" instead of Robert before they ask. The sharing and encouragement of the use of a nickname often accelerates the feeling of friendship.

Two of my favorite nicknames belonged to my father and his first cousin whose names were Henry and James. I could always tell who their closest friends were because those people called them "Pat" and "Chunka." School friends gave my father's nickname to him when he was a young boy and recited Patrick Henry's address for a school assembly. James was an excellent baseball player who could really "chunk" the ball and was dubbed "Chunka" by his teammates when he was a young baseball player.

Divulging information is a technique that requires the sharing of privileged information. It may be in the form of a secret or confession that illustrates vulnerability and indicates need of help or protection. The divulged information may be confidential information given in hopes of making the new acquaintance feel special. Although the technique of divulging information sometimes may be useful, it usually backfires because the person receiving the confidential information may wonder why it is shared early in a relationship and make him suspicious of what other information is being harbored. And sadly, some people use secret information as "social currency" in hopes of advancing their own agenda.

Some business people seek to establish rapport by mirroring nonverbal and verbal language. They may mimic their conversation partner's body language including posture, stance, walk, etc. This produces subliminal rapport. In addition, they match the perceived mood of the speaker that may seem happy, enthusiastic, pensive, or sad. On succeeding encounters, the person seeking to further establish rapport may dress in clothes similar to the person's clothing with whom he is trying to develop a friendship.

Mirroring may extend to echoing the use of verbal language, including the copying of voice and diction. It is important to understand that every communicator uses speech in a way that can signal much about his education as well as socioeconomic status. Every communicator subliminally perceives his conversation partner as similar or different from himself based on speech. When the businessperson actively listens to his conversation partner's speech, he can discern the grammatical patterns, word choices, and/or accents that he may wish to adopt in order to match the new conversation partner's style. Flexing communication style is helpful to establishing rapport and minimizing differences. Sales presentations often seem to be more successful when conversation partners "speak the same language." People feel a sense of connection when they hear their own words echoed back to them. Using terms common to your conversation partner will make you sound in tune with him and increase the likelihood of mutual understanding.

You can further promote subliminal rapport by using a subtle technique that involves reflecting conversation that indicates sensory understanding. Effective business communicators can do what neuro-linguists do to identify the primary sense datum used by a speaker.

People rely on a blend of the five senses (sight, hearing, touch, smell, and taste) to interpret information as they sift through the many elements that contribute to a message although most people primarily rely on sight, hearing and touch. Start paying attention and you will notice that people talk about the world in terms of the senses they use to interpret it. They usually employ one dominant sense followed by a secondary and third style to perceive the world.

Ask sensory-based questions and listen for the use of phrases that contain words that pertain to the senses to determine a person's processing style. Use your conversation partner's sensory processing style to facilitate rapport. Below are samples of questions to help you get started.

- "Tell me about ____ (a particular experience, such as a ballgame, vacation, meeting, client experience)."
- "What did you like about it? Was is something you heard, saw, touched?"

Listed below are the five senses accompanied by samples of phrases used by speakers who interpret the world using a particular sense. Emphasis is on the three dominant senses.

Visual Orientation: Research shows that sixty percent of people in the world use sight to interpret their world. People who are visually oriented tend to have little patience, are not overly sensitive, and tend to let go of emotions more quickly than people who predominantly interpret their world through other senses. You'll hear these people most frequently use words like the following: see, look, bright, colorful, clear, foggy, picture, illuminate, dawn, flash, focus, etc. For example,

- "I see what you mean."
- "That looks great to me."
- "The way I see it ..."
- "I see the light."
- "It's clear to me."
- "Picture that."

Auditory Orientation: Auditory processors predominantly interpret the world without pictures or feelings. They like to listen to other people's stories and often ask for information to be repeated. Auditory oriented individuals have conversations in their own minds and narrate life to themselves. They are sensitive to sounds and might cover their ears when they hear harsh sounds like sirens. They tend to be sensitive to animals and kneel to talk to pets. Words auditory processors often use to talk about the world include: hear, listen, loud, sound, melodious, crescendo, discuss, harsh, crackling, tune-in, rings true. For example,

- "Can you hear what I mean?"
- "That's clear as a bell."
- "How does that sound to you?"
- "What I hear you saying …"
- "The news was music to my ears."

Kinesthetic (Touch) Orientation: People who predominantly rely on the sense of touch are called kinesthetics. They interpret sounds into feelings. Kinesthetics often speak slowly with low-pitched voices. They like tactile stimulation and are drawn to activities that involve physical contact — sports, woodworking, etc. You'll hear them use words such as: pressing, feeling, exciting, aware, clumsy, secure, hands, touch, firm, cozy, warm, snug. For example,

- "I have butterflies in my stomach."
- "I sense that you are right."
- "Let's get a handle on that."
- "Let's touch base later."
- "Is that something you feel like doing?"
- "I feel uneasy about that."
- "I've got a gut feeling about that."
- "I was touched by his remarks."
- "The project manager's appeal moved me."

Smell Orientation:

- "That deal smells fishy."
- "Smell the roses."
- "I smell a rat."
- "He can smell a buck from a hundred miles away."

Taste Orientation:
- "Transacting that deal was sweet."
- "I don't have a taste for doing business with that company."
- "Their method of advertising leaves a bad taste in my mouth."
- "The sugar coated version of the deal was just too much for me."
- "I noted his acid remarks."
- "He seasoned the deal by ..."
- "The president's salty remarks ..."

Another excellent way to increase subliminal rapport with a conversation partner is to use words relevant to the conversation partner's business and personal life. Know the trade terms used in the person's profession as well as the terms the person knows through activities away from work. This technique is powerful and requires knowledge about your conversation partner's lifestyle and interests. It subliminally makes your communication partner aware that you think like him and share his interests. For example, consider the rapport a pharmaceutical representative can more quickly establish with a doctor who is also a sports fan if he not only knows the correct medical lingo for the doctor's specialty but also uses the words the doctor is fond of using and hearing away from his life in medicine. The pharmaceutical rep's small talk with the doctor at a medical meeting could easily burgeon into a discussion of a recently televised baseball game. On a subsequent visit to the doctor's office, he could establish subliminal rapport by using sporting terms in a sales pitch. For instance, the pharmaceutical rep might say that the new medication will "cover all the bases" when used to treat "otitis media" (earaches). He has used the baseball lingo "covering all the bases" and the correct medical lingo "otitis media." Translation: the medicine will effectively treat fever, swelling, etc. (all the bases) in patients who have earaches. This technique is powerful and will make your business associate feel a stronger connection with you. After all, you speak the same language.

The last rapport establishing device involves the use of the pronoun "you" that makes it easy for the receiver to understand his role in the message. As stated earlier, people like to hear their own names spoken. They also like to easily understand what they need to understand when interpreting a message. The receiver understands the message in terms of "how does that affect me?" The sender can facilitate the person's understanding of how it affects him by phrasing the message in terms of the second person. Perhaps you can most easily grasp this concept by using the example of the pharmaceutical representative conversing with the doctor. The pharmaceutical rep could choose to tell the doctor about the method of prescribing a new drug in one of two ways. First, using language that requires the doctor to make his own translation of how to prescribe the medicine, "The drug is administered three times per day with food." Alternatively, using language in which the translation has been made for him, "You tell the patient to take the medicine with meals every day." People respond more readily to that which they easily understand and the pronoun "you" facilitates their understanding. This technique is one of the easiest and most effective of the subliminal rapport building techniques.

Gaining Control Of Conversations

Powerful conversationalists are aware of the risks and communication breakdowns that can occur at any point in any conversation. They are willing to take risks and do not hesitate to be the first to say "hello," to introduce themselves, and to initiate topics of conversation. To gain control of a conversation you must be open, friendly, and genuinely interested in every conversation partner. Be open to new ideas, topics, and people. Accept people as they are.

The Biggest Missed Opportunity

The biggest missed opportunity is not using the golden opportunity to tell a story that will turn your small talk into smart talk when someone asks, "What do you do?" or "What's new?" Be prepared to answer with more than a feeble, "Not much." "Nothing." "Same old thing." "Just working." Use this opportunity to create an actual positive short story in one or two sentences that reveals a talent, a recent accomplishment, a success story, a problem you solved, or something you've done that will help you reach your goal.

For example, a realtor might respond, "I had so much fun helping a young couple find and finance their new dream home. They were unsure how to go about financing it and I had the pleasure of working with them to make it happen."

A kitchen and bath supply salesman might say, "I helped a couple update their home. We turned an ugly kitchen into a gorgeous living space and their bathroom into a soothing retreat. It was fun to be a part of improved lifestyle changes that will also increase the value of their home for future sale."

Elicit Conversation

Asking open-ended questions will lead you to success. Open-ended questions are questions that require more than a yes or no response. For example, "Tell me about …" "What is the biggest challenge you face in your business?"

Easy Conversations With People You Don't Know

The easiest people to meet at any gathering are the

wallflowers. They will welcome your attention. Initiate your meeting by opening with a neutral compliment to the person (nothing to do with physique or personal details), introducing yourself and asking how the person knows the host, or by asking a question such as, "Excuse me, what are you eating? It looks delicious."

Showing interest in the individuals you meet by learning about their jobs, companies, interests — anything but the weather — will help you develop personal relationships that can lead to a business relationship. Demonstrate your interest by giving feedback, nodding, paraphrasing, and smiling.

Have a networking goal when you enter events for business purposes. Your goal perhaps might be to secure three to five follow-up appointments. Clarify what you hope to learn and prepare two questions to get the information you need. At large gatherings focus on real prospects like a systematic business call. Ask questions to determine valid prospects. Don't aimlessly walk around! Make others feel good and get people you meet to talk about themselves. It's okay to ask people how they happen to be attending the event. Put yourself in host mode. Act as if you belong and are thrilled to be included.

Start conversations with people you don't know by first introducing yourself, offering minimal conversation bait, and asking a question. For example, "Hello, I'm Jane Hight, one of the speakers at this convention. What are your roles at this convention?" People will generally respond by telling you their names and about their business roles. Do not talk about yourself and your business at the beginning of a conversation with a new person. You will appear to come on too strong. Do ask questions that are relevant to the occasion or the reason for the other person's participation in the event. Show interest in the individual, his job, and his company. Foster conversation in that direction instead of bringing up topics like sports, the weather, or entertainment that will not lead to sharing information that will lead to business. Conversation starters include:

- "What's been your best day at work this year?"
- "What's your favorite aspect of your job? Why did you decide to work in xyz?"
- "What was the best session you attended today? Why did you like it?"
- "What stories do people tell about the great leaders/milestones in this organization?"
- "Who's been your role model or mentor here?"
- "Which skill do you use the most in your work?"
- "What are you looking forward to?"
- "How will you spend the holidays? Does your family have any special traditions?"
- "What is your biggest priority?"
- "How are things going?"
- "What sessions are you planning to attend?"
- "What do you enjoy most about living in your city?"

People will likely begin to ask you about your business and then you can feel comfortable sharing information about yourself and your company that might lead to future business. Keep conversation brief about yourself and your business. You might offer that you'd like to send information about your business and that perhaps you could exchange business cards for this purpose. This will give you a reason to follow up your conversation in writing. Remember, you want to move on to other conversation partners about every seven to eight minutes at networking events.

Good conversation is like a good game of tennis. Verbal exchange goes back and forth between partners. Return the conversation like a serve — back to the other person. The game of conversation, like the game of tennis, is no fun if it is one-sided.

Be first to show interest in others, but when asked about yourself, remember *The Rule of Three.*

The Rule Of Three

Rule One. Reveal in the first three seconds what you do in one or two sentences. For example, when people ask me what I do, I say, "I am a writer and professional speaker. I work with people and businesses who want to reach peak performance."

Rule Two. Tell in thirty seconds who your customers are, what makes you unique, and how you help when your conversation partner asks, "Tell me more," or How do you do that?" Don't go too deep — you're networking for later! Here's what I say:

"I researched and interviewed many of the greatest winners of all time in business, sports, and entertainment to learn what made the winning difference for them. I tell their stories and explain step-by-step what they did to win top results so my readers and audiences will know exactly what they can do to win. I customize for different groups. My presentations include video and music." (Notice bait)

Rule Three. If the listener is still interested, use three minutes more to ask your conversation partner about his business. I say, "Tell me about your business." Depending on what I learn about the person's business, I respond with information about specific programs I offer that would be valuable to his business. (Selling, networking, working/ harmonizing with different personalities, leadership, teamwork, time management, customer service, or information customized for women). For example, if my conversation partner is a woman who belongs to a women's group, I say, "I present a popular program based on a book I wrote that is customized for women called *Navigating the Lipstick Jungle: Go from Plain Jane to Getting What You Want, Need, and Deserve.* This program teaches women to politely and powerfully get what they want, need, and deserve in their personal and professional lives. I present at women's conferences and charity fundraisers to raise money for women and children."

Use thirty minutes or three hours more at a follow-up meeting. When I attend an event and the person wants more information, I say, "Thank you for your interest. I'd love to learn more about you and your business. I would be happy to tell you more about how my programs help people increase business but I don't want to monopolize your time at this event. We're both here to enjoy connecting with lots of people and I don't want you to lose the chance to meet and visit with people you want to see. Let's continue our conversation when we can focus on each other. Would you like to meet for coffee later this week?"

Schedule a follow-up meeting so you won't jeopardize the present opportunity to continue networking. Exchange contact information.

It's generally best to suggest a neutral location to meet like a coffee shop so you won't seem pushy or like you are expecting a commitment. If you don't schedule a meeting, at least send a quick email or card saying how nice it was to meet.

A clever way to meet people you don't know is to use a team-up trick with a friend attending the same event. The team-up trick works this way. You and your friend separate after you have greeted the hosts and any honored guests. Circulate as previously discussed. Later walk over to the group your friend has become a part of and stand beside him or slightly back and to his side so he can see you. At a break in the conversation your friend should introduce you and offer information about you that will interest your new contacts. The most helpful part of this introduction is that you can each wow the group with accolades about each other that you would be uncomfortable saying about yourselves.

Disengage from the person or group you are speaking to by summarizing your conversation, expressing interest in future conversation, thanking the person, shaking hands or evolving gesture, and moving on. To do this, use body language to show the end of the conversation — extend your hand to shake or use an evolving alternative gesture and say something like, "Joe, I've enjoyed meeting you and hearing about your trip to London. Thank you for sharing your news and adventures. I hope we can get together soon." Smile and move on. If the person is a clinger, you might need to add, "Let's mingle a little now. I hope we see each other again before the event is over." The person you are leaving feels satisfied (you have demonstrated that you have listened by summarizing the conversation), he feels positive (you have thanked him and shaken his hand or concluded with an appropriate concluding gesture such as a slight nod or bow), and you have indicated a desire to interact later. Further, he is now free to continue his networking unrestricted contrary to a conversation that ends with "Excuse me, I am thirsty and need a drink," which may be misinterpreted incorrectly in at least three ways. First, the person may expect your return; second, he may feel welcome to accompany you to the bar; or third, he may feel that you are bored with his company.

The technique of summarizing a conversation, expressing interest in future conversation, thanking the person, shaking hands or extending an alternative gesture, and moving on is golden. Here is an example that you can modify. "I enjoyed hearing about xyz. Thank you for taking the time to share your stories/information/etc. It's been great meeting/chatting with you. I know there are other people here we would both like to chat with so I won't monopolize your time any longer as I want you to have the opportunity to connect with other attendees/guests/friends. I look forward to getting together with you in the future."

Exit Variations To Modify Or Disengage From Coversation

- "It's been so nice to meet you. I hope we see each other again soon." "Will you excuse me? I see someone I need to speak to …"
- "I've enjoyed chatting with you. I've been monopolizing you and I'm sure you want to talk with other people at this event."
- "Let's mingle. I hope we see each other again before the party is over."
- "I'll call you next week. Enjoy the party."
- "I need to speak to my friend from out of town before he leaves — please excuse me."
- "Oh wow! I see a friend I haven't seen in years! Please excuse me. It's been wonderful talking to you."
- "It's been a pleasure talking to you. I hope to see you again soon."
- "I want to ask the speaker a question about his talk before he leaves and don't want to miss the opportunity. Please excuse me."
- "Please excuse me. I need to check on something." (Shaking hands or alternative gesture) "It's been wonderful meeting you!"
- "Give my best regards to your family."
- "Forgive me. I haven't said hello to our hosts yet. It's been lovely talking to you."
- "Before we circulate, I'd like to introduce you to my colleague."
- "I can't wait to hear how xyz goes! Let's catch up at the next get together, conference, meeting etc."
- "It's been great talking to you. Thanks for telling me about xyz. Do you have a card?"

- "The next session is starting soon so I'm going to find my room. It was terrific meeting you!"

When it comes to disengaging from conversations, remember that just as you do not enjoy everyone's company, not everyone enjoys yours. Give the gift of absence to those who do not appreciate your presence.

> *Stand not upon the manner of your going,*
> *but go at once.*
> – William Shakespeare

You may find yourself conversing with someone who looks around the room instead of at you and appears uninterested in what you are saying. This conversation partner may make feeble attempts at conversation but you sense that he or she is not listening to you. In such instances, you have a couple of options. First, you can try fully focusing on your conversation partner and consider the vast potential range of his needs. It may be that he is looking at the people gathered because he is worried that he may miss something or perhaps he is searching the room for a special person. On the other hand, it could be that he becomes nervous when speaking with anyone at any length. You may finally consider that he is simply not interested in talking with you and has not learned to gracefully disengage from a conversation. In this case it's up to you to terminate the conversation as tactfully as possible and move on. Do this by taking advantage of a pause in conversation (the sooner the better) and disengaging as discussed earlier by smiling, summing up your conversation, thanking the person, shaking hands, and moving on.

Speaking of pauses, one of the most effective elements of strong communication is actually nothing at all — a pause! Powerful communicators use pauses that last three to four seconds to let the import of their messages sink in, to create drama, and to command attention. Instead of using non-words, say nothing at all. A silent pause has a powerful effect.

Business Cards

Meeting people is important but following-up with them makes a difference. You validate people when you demonstrate interest in following-up with them so always get contact information from your new contacts even though it may seem awkward. If your new contact doesn't have a business card, suggest having the person directly share contact info to your smart phone. Get an email address as well as a telephone number. After the person has left, make notes about the him or her so you won't forget information that will make it easier for you to follow-up with conversation. People appreciate when you remember what is important to them — their alma mater, children's names, etc.

Carry an ample supply of fresh business or social cards when you plan to attend a gathering. Business cards offer the name of your business, business address, telephone numbers, e-mail address, and/or anything else important to locating you in regards to business life. Social cards contain only your name and social contact information — usually a personal telephone number and address. Your cards reflect your quality. A neat professional appearance with current information is important. Do not write on your cards to correct information that has changed. Immediately print new cards with correct information when it changes.

Don't go for cardboard connections by liberally passing out your cards like candy. It will make your business card seem like it is not important. Look for a reason to hand out your card. As you listen, think about the resources you have, or the contacts you have that would be of interest or help to the other person. Listening will provide you with the reason to ask the person you are with for his card and to offer him your card. For example, "I just read a wonderful article about that. I'll send it to you." Or, "My friend Hart White works with international importers. I'll be glad to put you in touch with him."

When someone offers you information, you have the perfect opportunity to say, "Thank you so much for sending me the information. Here's my card." However, if you are with a significantly higher-ranking businessperson, it is appropriate to wait for him or her to ask to exchange cards.

Correct Use Of Business Cards

Present your business card with the print facing the person. Exchanging business cards is often expected in some cultures. Accept a business card as you would a gift. Nod with thanks and understanding as you accept another person's card and take a moment to study it. Ask questions to show your interest about information you learn from the card. Do not fold or write on the other person's card in his presence. If you want to make notes about the person, wait until you are in a private place. Place the new card in your case or other appropriate place to show respect of the card that represents the person who gave it to you. For example, do not place the card in your hip pocket where you will sit on it.

Carry cards in a case that conveys the image you want. Some cases have separated pockets for incoming and outgoing cards. Make sure you have some system for making sure you do not mistakenly hand out another person's card.

Never exchange business cards publicly if the event you are attending is a predominantly social occasion such as a wedding or small dinner in a private home. Use discretion if you want to exchange business cards at social events.

Know the business card protocol of your international

business partner's culture. Business cards are an important device for establishing and maintaining international contact. In China and Japan, it is expected that business cards will be presented during business introductions and received with both hands, thumbs on the upper corners of the card so the card will be easily readable by the recipient. However, in the Middle East and some parts of Asia, the business card is presented with only the right hand because the left hand is used for bodily hygiene and considered unclean.

Do print your information in the language of the people you are likely to meet. If you do business in the USA and in another country, consider having double-sided business cards printed with your contact information in English on one side and your contact information in the language of your international partner on the reverse side. Include your title as in some cultures the title is interpreted as an extension of the person. Print your card on high quality white or beige paper (other colors may work depending on your profession) with black ink. Your card is the tangible representation of you that others will use to remember you.

The Winners Attitude

A happy attitude will increase your ability to achieve the results you desire. If you display a negative attitude, if you are angry, frustrated, anxious, overwhelmed, etc., you will send out vibes that negatively infect those around you. If those who support you in your quest for success do not have a positive attitude, your progress and power will be impeded. People who are not supportive of your goals, who do not believe in you, who belittle your dreams and goals and give reasons why you will not succeed will hold you down. Like Pharrell Williams, stay away from "stinking thinking" if you want to optimize your success. Let YOUR thoughts and YOUR actions control YOUR destiny.

> *It's your road, and yours alone.*
> *Others may walk it with you,*
> *but no one can walk it for you.*
>
> – Rumi

Surround yourself with positive people. Stay away from toxic people whose favorite party is a pity party. Negative people who talk against almost everything use chatter full of "couldda shoudda woulddas and I'm so sorrys." Energy-sucking vampires drain power to enjoy life and reach goals.

People interested in buying products, services, or ideas want to know what you can do. Tell them what you can do and what you're good at.

Ineffective people who don't reach their goals often self-deprecate and easily buckle under business and social pressure. Don't put yourself down! You do not have to tell people your flaws. Everyone has flaws. George Brett, Major League Baseball Hall of Fame, Kansas City Royals, thirteen-time All-Star, World Series champion, AL MVP, Gold Glove Award, three-time Silver Slugger Award, and three-time AL batting champion says what made the difference to him was, "Knowing what I'm capable of doing and doing only what I'm capable of. Always play to strengths because you will get the most out of your ability."[16] Sometimes people will make fun of what you know is the best way for you to achieve your goal. You'll need to have the courage to do what you know is the best way to achieve your goals regardless of others.

Spectators including the media made fun of basketball player Rick Barry for his underhanded granny style free throws even though his shot was virtually flawless. They said he looked like a sissy and shot like a girl. Barry became the only player to lead the NBA, ABA and NCAA in scoring and was a twelve-time All-Star and nine-time all-league first teamer who scored more that 25,000 points in his career. At the time of his retirement, Barry held the record for the highest free-throw percentage in history. What made the difference for Rick Barry? Doing what he knew he could do to win and having a high social threshold to do it to win. Barry explained why other players would not use the granny shot and chose the overhand shot that yielded a low free throw average that adversely impacted final scores. "It's all about the ego. They don't think it's macho enough for them."[17]

The way you respond to life and the people in your life will make a difference in your success. You will meet people in every corner of the world who are not helpful and are unfair. Identify people and businesses that are positive, fair, supportive and provide opportunities for you to be an authentic positive person who will excel and be productive. Knock on every door until the right doors open.

Who can you trust? People leave clues that reveal who they are. For example, if someone tells you they will return your call, attend a meeting, send you a check, etc. and they fail to follow through doing what they said they would do when they said they would do it, observe the clue. If they do the same thing or something similar a second time, observe a pattern. You cannot change a person's patterns of behavior. People show who they are with their actions. To win, look for clues, observe patterns, and choose wisely the people with whom you associate. Run as fast as you can from people who play the role of victim blaming others for their situations, justifying their situations, and complaining about their situations. Negative mindsets are like contagious diseases. Choose people in your circle of influence who take responsibility for their lives. People with positive mindsets move forward. Your association with positive people will move you forward.

*People don't change.
They are merely revealed.*

– Anne Enright
First Laureate for Irish Fiction and Winner of the Man Booker Prize

A writer named Peter Voogd explains what it takes to win six figures. His plan includes an essential shift of circle of influence. According to Voogd, the people who surround us and from whom we take advice impacts our success because who we associate with determines who we become.[18]

*If you hang around five intelligent people,
you will be the sixth.
If you hang around five millionaires,
you will be the sixth.
If you hang around five idiots,
you will be the sixth.
If you hang around five broke people,
you will be the sixth.
It's inevitable.*[19]

In other words, you are the average of the five people with whom you spend the most time. Who you associate with, what you read, listen to or watch influences your success. Your total environment influences what you think and will either drive you towards or away from the achievement of your goals. Surround yourself with people, books, and media that drive the success you want.

Eighteen months after walking into Abbey Road Studios, an impoverished provincial band without a record contract, found themselves in the center of mass hysteria and global fame. They were original, authentic in every way, and refused to record music except the songs they wrote themselves. They remained humble, ever mindful of their roots. In an interview about fame and how long The Beatles would last, John Lennon said, "People can say, 'How long are you going to last?' You can be bigheaded and say, 'Yeah, we're going to last ten years,' but you can't say that. As soon as you say that you're lucky if you last three months."[20] The Beatles remained humble as they became one of the most successful money-making bands of all time and inspired the most significant social change in Great Britain since World War II and beyond.

> *It's all right to be Goliath, but always act like David.*
> – Phil Knight
> American Billionaire, Co-founder and Chairman Emeritus of Nike

Knowing this background about The Beatles, it may not surprise you that when Steve Jobs, co-founder, chairman, and CEO of Apple, Inc. was asked about his business model on *60 Minutes*, he replied:

> My model for business is The Beatles. They were four guys that kept each other's negative tendencies in check; they balanced each other. And the total was greater than the sum of the parts. Great things in business are never done by one person, they are done by a team of people.[21]

Your success, like that of The Beatles, depends on people. You can't sell anything if you don't have people to sell to so treat others as you treat your finest possessions. They are.

People like people who have humility and demonstrate interest in learning from others. Be open to the possibilities of what people share. Listen to the ideas, suggestions, and needs of others to take you from an ego-driven state to an enlightened state focused on others. It will free your mind to be fully present.

Take time to get to know people. Life is so rushed that people often feel ignored and unappreciated. One of the greatest needs of all people is to be valued. You can show that you value others by taking sincere interest in them and what is important to them. They will notice and they will be grateful. Don't expect people to be interested in spending time with you to learn about your products, services, or ideas if you haven't first shown interest in them and what is important to them.

Respect the time of others just as you respect your own time. Show up fully and on time. Do what you say you will do when you say you will do it. If you don't, you will likely never get what you want, need, and deserve. People know you by the actions that back up your words. If your actions do not back up your words, people will not want to invest their time with you because they will feel you do not deserve their time and effort required to conduct business.

Give people your time but give it wisely. Take a good look at your customer base. Twenty percent of the people probably give you eighty percent of your business. Take good care of them. Do not place them on your back burner.

> *There is very little difference in people,*
> *but that little difference makes a big difference.*
> *The little difference is attitude.*
> *The big difference is whether it is positive or negative.*
>
> – W. Clement Stone
> Insurance Billionaire and Philanthropist

Alfonso Ribeiro, current host of *America's Funniest Home Videos* who played Will Smith's spoiled, wealthy cousin Carlton Banks on *The Fresh Prince of Bel-Air*, had a willingness to try new things from a young age. Ribeiro landed the leading role in the Broadway musical *The Tap Dance Kid* when he was only eight years old. He went on to dance many parts in life that brought lots of joy — and lots of money. His Carlton character was so famous for dancing to Tom Jones' "It's Not Unusual" that his dance move became known as "The Carlton Dance." Loveable Ribeiro unabashedly continues to dance "The

Carlton Dance" without limiting himself to the mansions of Bel-Air. While I held his infant son, he danced "The Carlton" on the third floor balcony of the most iconic house in surfing — Pipeline legend Gerry Lopez's Volcom House overlooking Oahu, Hawaii's North Shore. In the presence of Pipe royalty, with the best surfing taking place only a stone's throw from this legendary kingdom's deck, no one on the balcony or the ground below, jammed with up-and-coming surfers, could stop looking and grinning at Alfonso. All eyes will be on you too when you try new things in new ways in new places.

No matter how good something is no one wants the same thing all the time whether its food, music, or conversation. Be interesting. Learn about life around you and experience different activities in different places. Read a variety of books, sample a variety of entertainments, learn new dances, etc., and evolve. Engaging in new experiences opens the door to authentic conversations about various aspects of life.

Connect With Words

Use language not only to connect to people but also to get them to work with you so you can get what you want. People won't listen, help, or support you unless you acknowledge three basic needs all human beings have. Those needs are to be valued, needed, and respected. Choose words as well as actions to convey that you value, need, and respect others.

To choose how best to do this, especially in challenging conversations, consider Steven Covey's advice, "Seek first to understand, then to be understood." To understand, you must listen. Count to a minimum of three before you speak in any controversial situation so you can choose how you want to express yourself without sabotaging a relationship. It takes practice but it is important if you want to reach the top.

Five Positive Ways To Use Language When Working With Others

1. Make your point and stop talking. Pauses are powerful. Execute your power with the power of the pause!
2. Eliminate the word "but." People don't believe what you say before "but," only what you say after it.
3. Use positive words to describe situations. Words like "challenge" and "opportunity" are received better than words like "problem" or "issue."
4. Use the word "would." When you want people to change or do something, avoid using the word "should" which is demanding. The word "would" acknowledges the control of the listener to make a decision without being told what he "should" do.
5. Show unity with words like "we" and "ours." These words show respect in the part others play in success. For example, say, "Our team" instead of "My team."

A wise man once said nothing.

I speak two languages, Body and English.

– Mae West

Chapter Four

Open The Window And Shout: How To Package And Promote To Reach The Top Of The Charts

> *The meek might inherit the earth but it's not going to be in your lifetime.*
>
> – Joan Williams Hight
> My Mother

A minister wrote a book that was turned down by every publisher. So frustrated was the preacher that he tossed his manuscript in a trashcan. His wife pleaded with him not to throw his work away, but he was adamant that his rejected work was no good and forbade her to remove it from the trash. The next day when the preacher was away, his wife took her husband's work to one last publisher. The publisher was curious when the woman entered his office carrying a large paper bag from which she pulled a trashcan. She explained the reason for the odd presentation and her full belief that her husband's work was valuable and should be read. Her unwillingness to give up on her husband's work, the eye-catching paper bag packaging, and her ardent promotion resulted in the publication of *The Power of Positive Thinking*. Its author — the person considered one of the most positive people ever to live on this planet — Dr. Norman Vincent Peale.[1] Promoting and packaging for success takes perseverance and is a challenge for everyone — even for the most positive among us.

> *Without promotion,*
> *something terrible happens ... nothing!*
>
> – P.T. Barnum
> Co-Founder Barnum and Bailey Circus

Barbara Walters told "Her Story" in an *ABC News Special*. "I believe in promotion. I think if you are going to do something you should tell people about it. I promote every interview I do. What's the point of doing it and working that hard and not telling people about it? At least open your window and shout!"[2] It was a window that saved her career.

Excellence in promotion made the difference in Walters' remarkable career and it was a window that saved it. However, she did more than open a window and shout to make the G.O.A.T. list in news journalism. Walters knew *how* to look through the window to see what was out in the world. She used what she saw to climb out of the window and up to the rooftop in her field. She knew *how* to open the window in the right way. And she knew *how* to shout so she could be heard.

Early in Walters' career, women were not accorded respect as news journalists. The news business was considered a man's business and nobody thought it was possible for a woman to do the job. When Walters worked with Frank McGee on NBCs *TODAY* show, McGee went to the head of the network and asked that Walters not be allowed to ask any hard news questions. It was determined that for every three questions McGee asked, Walters could ask only one — unless she asked questions outside of the studio. She began to look for interview opportunities outside the studio window. She excelled. When McGee died, she became the first female co-anchor of the *TODAY* show — and also the first female co-anchor on any network. Later she became the first female co-anchor of the evening news on *ABC with Harry Reasoner* — and also the first female evening news anchor on network television. Walters was a pioneer leading the way for future women wanting to report hard news. Today there are women reporting hard news on every network.

In addition, important to Barbara Walter's success was her persistence. She realized that when life shut a window she could open it again. After all, windows are windows and that's how you work them. For Walters, there was a time when the public said she was failing and all the windows seemed to be crashing down. When she was paired with Harry Reasoner on *ABC Evening News*, Reasoner did not like her. The on-air tension between Reasoner and Walters was so obvious that high profile comedians like Johnny Carson made jokes about her. A newspaper headline read, "Barbara Walters Failure."[3]

In a 2014 interview with National Public Radio's (NPR) Steve Inskeep, Walters remembered what made the difference and kept her going during this time:

> It was lonely and it was painful. At one point I was on the air with a male partner who really didn't want me on and made things quite difficult for me, but what saved me — two things that I think: one was letters from other women saying, 'We're going through the same thing,' in whatever field they were in, in whatever job they had, and 'hang in there.' And I knew I had their support. And the other thing was a telegram, believe it or not, that said, 'Don't let the bastards get you down,' and it was signed John Wayne. And I felt the cavalry was coming! So it was a difficult time, but if it helped other women — and maybe it did — then it's a legacy I'm extremely proud of.[4]

Margaret Thatcher, the first female and longest-serving Prime Minister of the United Kingdom for over 150 years, struggled early in her career to be respected and taken seriously as a strong leader. Fellow members of Parliament thought her weak. They condescendingly referred to her as the "Lady Member." Thatcher set about changing her personal package to facilitate the perception of herself as a strong woman to reach her political goals. Her story is a terrific study of how clothing, nonverbal and verbal packaging impact career.

In her autobiography, *The Path to Power*, Thatcher wrote, "Every politician has to decide how much he or she is prepared to change manner and appearance for the sake of the media. It may sound grittily honourable to refuse to make any concessions, but such an attitude in a public figure is most likely to betray a lack of seriousness about winning power."[5]

Thatcher repackaged and transformed her frumpy dowdy housewife image without compromising her authenticity. Masterminding Thatcher's makeover was a former television producer named Gordon Reese. He advised her to exchange her fussy bows and garden party hats for bolder elegant ensembles. With regards to her appearance, Dr. Daniel Conway, a lecturer in politics at Loughborough University shares, "She was the first one who had to make an effort to change the way she looked. Thatcher's transformation was among the first to tailor a politician's image to fit the media age. She was lower-middle-class and from the provinces — and this could have been used as a symbol of her unsuitability."[6] She began wearing elegant, simple, bold, bright, and structured suits.

Thatcher meticulously considered every detail, including her handbag. She opted for a solid, rigid, structured leather handbag instead of a traditional black briefcase. According to her political secretary, John Whittingdale, "It was a prop. She would produce it very visibly at big meetings to show she meant business."[7] The word "handbagging" became a reference to Thatcher's businesslike demeanor that became so widely referenced when referring to Thatcher that it entered the Oxford English Dictionary. It defines the verb *to handbag* as: *(of a woman politician), treat (a person, idea, etc.) ruthlessly or insensitively*. Lady Thatcher herself once told an interviewer: "Of course, I am obstinate in defending our liberties and our law. That is why I carry a big handbag."⁸

Thatcher realized her high-pitched voice was stalling her success. Laurence Olivier, the famous actor, recommended a tutor from the Royal National Theatre to teach Thatcher to lower her shrill pitch and to develop a calm, more resonant and authoritative tone. Thatcher took Olivier's advice and trained her voice to project power. She replaced warm, fuzzy words and stories with direct speech and cold facts to quickly get to her point. Repackaging worked. Not only Parliament but the world took notice, recognizing her as a strong woman — a Soviet Red Army newspaper nicknamed her "The Iron Lady." Thatcher's repackaging is easy to see and hear on YouTube, where you can compare videos of her early career to later videos of her as a powerful Prime Minister.

The most famous princess in the world, Diana Princess of Wales, watched a recorded television interview of herself after her separation from Prince Charles. In the interview she famously said, "There were three of us in this marriage so it was a bit crowded."⁹ According to voice and presentation coach Stewart Pearce whose clients included Margaret Thatcher, Diana secretly hired Pearce after the interview because while she felt proud of what she said, she did not like the way she sounded and looked. "Shy Di" decided to take charge of her destiny. She mustered the courage to decide what her future dreams would be, then took the actions she needed to achieve results to match her vision.¹⁰

Pearce writes in his book, *Diana: The Voice of Change*, that Diana's brave candid interview was "an emancipatory act ... She was doing something that no other member of the royal family had done for 900 years, I mean, which woman has said such things about the heir apparent and not lost her head?" When Diana was no longer Her Royal Highness, Pearce asked Diana to share her vision and personal goals. She wanted to project herself as a victor not a victim who controlled her own destiny not the destiny the royal family directed. She believed in herself despite her challenges, made her own goals, and believed she could accomplish her goals with effort, determination, and kindness. Once Pearce understood, he set to work to equip her with the information, techniques, and skills she needed to achieve her goals and to publicly project the vision she had of herself.[11]

Pearce says first he taught Diana breathing techniques just as he had for Thatcher starting with the elimination of the "startle reflex" or gasping for air in speech. As for body language, "What I did was to actually lift her head so that the whole of her spine was elongated. If we have an aligned spine, we always communicate confidence."[12] Diana, no longer Her Royal Highness, became known and beloved as The People's Princess and The Queen of Everyone's Hearts.

You risk not getting what you want if you sugar coat or beat around the bush to get what you want. For example, if you are cold and you would like someone to turn up the thermostat, you will more likely get the desired result if you say, "I'm cold. Would you please turn up the thermostat?" than if you say, "It's cold in here."

Volume and tone are important to getting what you want. You must be loud enough to be heard and to receive the attention you need to get what you want.

Avoid making statements that sound like questions. Speak with conviction. Record a conversation you have with another person. You may be surprised to hear an upward lilt at the end of your statements. Many people do this — especially women. Awareness of your voice will help you to correct many vocal issues. Hire a speech coach if you have trouble making progress.

Speak up when you have something to say to get credit for your ideas. Not only will speaking first prevent others from saying what you are thinking first, it also will demonstrate your leadership, credibility and willingness to take risks.

Muhammad Ali mastered packaging and promotion to become the first global icon. He is undoubtedly one of the most memorable self-promoters. At a time when others on the star track relied on managers to promote them, Ali created news about himself with his actions and stories. He labeled himself, "The Greatest of All Time," he used rhyme, in the ring he danced the "Ali Shuffle," he wore out opponents with the "rope-a-dope," and to draw attention to injustice he told a story about throwing his Olympic Gold medal into the Ohio River after being refused service at a Louisville, Kentucky restaurant.

You are ready to build on your foundation when you have a strong knowledge base and clear direction. This chapter will teach you what you need to know to capture the attention of the people you interact with to facilitate personal and professional achievement. Self-promotion when done right is not dirty or annoying. Relevant packaging and promoting is useful not only to the achievement of your goals but also to others who can benefit from what you offer. You can't be shy. While communication is 50/50 with a sender and a receiver, it is 100% up to you to communicate your 50 percent of the message.

Communication begins before you arrive and it continues after you leave. Think about the book you are holding. What made you decide to read it? Probably you heard me speak, heard someone else talk about this book or about me, or read about the book or about me. Most people go into a bookstore to buy a specific book — they seldom go into a bookstore to buy a book they haven't heard of by an author whose name they don't recognize. When they do buy a book they haven't heard of, it's likely because of its cover.

People often initially choose those they interact with the same way they pick the books they read. First, they rely on advance information — a book review or a personal recommendation. A resume, a letter of recommendation, and a phone call are all like a book review. When there is no review, people rely on the cover.

When a first-time meeting occurs it is like looking at a book for the first time. The front cover is important. Buyers of books spend only three to five seconds looking at the front cover. The cover is what initially catches the eye. If buyers like what they see, they flip the book over to read the back cover for ten to fifteen seconds. If and only if they like the initial presentation, they thumb through the pages to assess chapter titles, glimpse content, check clarity and readability including font and size. If upon cursory inspection the potential buyer determines the writer has something valuable to offer and can maintain the reader's interest, he will buy the book. Like it or not, that is also how people decide who they will hire, who they will date, and from whom they will buy. Presentation matters.

People make purchasing decisions within sixty seconds. It's scary, but that's what happens. What are you doing to improve your ability to convince others at the outset that you are the person with the best product, service, or idea? And if you are initially successful, do you know how to ensure others return to you in the future?

According to Dale Carnegie, "There are four ways, and only four ways, in which we have contact with the world. We are evaluated and classified by these four contacts: what we do, how we look, what we say, and how we say it."

The first way people evaluate you is by the most basic form of communication — your manners. Good manners are universal — respectful treatment of fellow humans no matter what their origin. People around the world have the exact same human needs — to be valued, needed and respected. If you want people to help you win the game, the gig, or the job you first need to satisfy their human needs. Communication quickly deteriorates with people who are not shown that they are valued, needed, and respected. People have a human need to belong, to be in control, and to reach their potential. Let them know how they are an important part of your plan. Make others feel special whether they are young, old, rich or poor by taking them seriously and listening to them to show that you understand them. You have great power through your words and actions to change how others see themselves. Satisfy the primary need of others to be needed, valued, and respected and you will find yourself on the fast track to success as a respected leader who wins excellent results.

A girl sitting next to me in French class hurt my self-confidence when I was a teenager with seven words, "Can't you do anything with your hair?"

Despite no one else ever saying anything to me about my hair, for many years I felt that my hair was ugly, making me unattractive. My self-esteem lagged. Four words from someone else changed that.

Helen Hayes, "First Lady of American Theatre," won an Emmy, a Grammy, an Oscar, a Tony, the Presidential Medal of Freedom (America's highest civilian award), and the National Medal of Arts. She visited my hometown when she was 85 years old to collect one more award for her eighty-year contribution to American films, theatre and broadcasting — The Albert Schweitzer Medal. Hayes at the time was a spokeswoman for the rights of the elderly and hosted a syndicated radio program, *The Best of Time*, dedicated to improving the image of the elderly. She took time out during her visit to Wilmington, NC, to meet with residents at a local retirement home. Celia Rivenbark, then a writer for the local newspaper quoted Hayes in an article:

> I stumbled into working with older people after I did a documentary on nursing homes for the Public Broadcasting System. Although there were some nice places, most weren't. We covered some of the

most depressing homes. For so many years, older people were apologetic for their very presence on the earth. But they are very important and we all have something to contribute, at any age, even if it's just a punk hairdo.[13]

I met Helen Hayes at a reception after the Schweitzer Award ceremony. Four words soothed the old wound. Hayes warmly shook my hand with her right hand, placed her left hand on top of mine, looked directly into my eyes as if I were the only person in the ballroom and said, "I love your hair." Maybe my hair looked awful and she was just being nice, but she looked and sounded sincere. It was a little thing for her to say, a trite comment, but her thoughtful comment made a difference. The tiniest gestures often do.

There is truth in the Japanese proverb, "One kind word can warm three winter months." Hayes' words made a difference to the elderly that day at the retirement home, to her on-air listeners, to readers who read the article, and to me as her words thawed old hurt and continue to warm me not only for three months but years into the present. Your words affect your clients, colleagues, family, and friends either dragging them down or lifting them up as they journey through inevitable obstacles in an unfair world.

> *One of the greatest victories you can gain over someone is to beat him at politeness.*
>
> – Josh Billings
> American Humorist and Author

A knee-jerk reaction when someone says something that is not respectful or honorable is to respond with something equally disrespectful. Remember, most people are doing the best they can with the limited skills they have. They don't know any better. My Southern mama used to say about these unfortunate people, "Bless his/her heart, he/she just can't help it." This was her way of forgiving ill breeding and/or stupidity. She advised me to be smarter and kinder. When desired, you can politely learn what the person really means in order to address the issue in a way that would validate the person's need to express the issue with you or someone who is with you. Be polite, but don't let anyone push you around. Smile and say one of the following phrases to get the best results possible when dealing with people who "just can't help it" due to their limited skill set:

- "That's interesting, why would you *say* that?"
- "That's interesting, why would you *do* that?"
- "That's interesting, why would you *ask* that?"
- "That's interesting, why do you *want* to know?"

> *Be kind to unkind people.*
> *Sometimes they need it the most.*
> – Ashleigh Brilliant
> History's Only Full-Time Epigrammatist
> and Author of *The Haight-Ashbury Songbook*

It's not just your words that make a difference in the way you package yourself — it's also your actions. Bigger and stronger George Foreman, a two-time world heavyweight champion was favored to beat Muhammad Ali at the "Rumble in the Jungle" fight in Africa. Foreman had the following to say about Ali's victory despite Ali not being the biggest or the strongest:

> He [Ali] didn't have the best power or the best anything but his presence. You got into the ring with him and you knew this is something different ... he [Ali] said, 'I came in here pretty, I'm going to leave out pretty'. His greatest power was his presence. He made me feel so important. If you sit around

him you felt important. You really felt like you were something special. And he'd just sit there and made you think, wow, and he's paying some attention to me and he wouldn't yawn much, he'd just listen to you.[14]

Anna Paquin, New Zealand born star of several major motion pictures who at eleven years old won an Academy Award for her role in *The Piano,* demonstrated and explained to me what she knows makes the difference in getting the results you wish for on your birthday and any day.

Anna was in my hometown the summer of her 13th birthday to film Carson McCuller's *The Member of the Wedding.* To celebrate, a filmmaker friend working on the movie with Anna rented a stretch limousine to drive Anna and the new friends she'd made while on location to a party at a surprise location. My daughter, Win, was among them. Anna's mother, Mary Brophy, kept a close eye on Anna. She didn't want to cramp her new teenager's day by riding in the limo with the girls but she did want to be a part of the celebration. I was happy to drive her. We followed behind the limo in my old Chevy Suburban.

We drove ninety miles south to Myrtle Beach's Grand Strand. Soon after we entered the city limits, Mary spied an out of place pyramid standing an imposing 70 feet high guarded by two massive sphinxes. Her laughter erupted with disbelief when she saw and realized that the pyramid was the party destination — The Hard Rock Café. She laughed saying that she'd never seen anything like this in her native New Zealand or in Canada where she also had lived.

Rock and Roll music blasted as we entered the pyramid and continuously played as we checked out authentic memorabilia on display including guitars from rock legends like Carlos Santana, Eric Clapton, B.B. King and Brian Wilson, a cape that belonged to Elvis, Paul McCartney's wool suit, and black leather boots worn by the man in black himself, Johnny Cash! Even though we were in a pyramid, our food was all-American hamburgers. Anna's mom and I watched the girls from a nearby table. Anna seemed to be enjoying every minute including her anonymity. And then it happened.

Just as we took the last bites of our burgers, out of nowhere, led by the restaurant manager carrying a cake, what seemed to be the entire staff came marching towards Anna singing happy birthday at the top of their lungs so loud that they drowned out the Rock and Roll music playing overhead. Anna quickly said something to the girls and they all scrambled under the table. Everyone in the restaurant turned to look in the direction of the singing procession but when they did they could not see anyone sitting at the long empty table the staff was approaching. The perplexed staff looked foolish singing to a vacant table.

The disappointed manager deposited the cake with thirteen flaming candles on the empty table. The waiters shrugged their shoulders, mumbled something, and left. When the coast was clear, the girls came out from under the table and the party resumed with the girls laughing and encouraging Anna to make a wish on the short but still burning thirteen candles.

I wanted to know what Anna had said to the girls before ducking under the table and how she'd thought of dodging being the center of a spectacle. My chance to ask came that evening when she spent the night at my house and the girls found me to say goodnight. I told Anna how much I had enjoyed celebrating her birthday. I ventured, "You handled dodging mass attention really well today, but I'm curious. What made you think of ducking under the table and getting all the girls to go down with you?"

Anna smiled, "Did you see the movie I was in last year called *Fly Away Home*, the one about the Canada geese that fly from Ontario to North Carolina?"

"Yes, I did and you played your part very well, but what does that movie have to do with ducking under the table today?"

Anna explained that before the movie she knew nothing about Canada geese and had learned about them to prepare for the film. Among the things she told us is that geese fly together in formation because it creates lift for the flock — just like being with friends on your birthday adds lift to the occasion. When a goose falls out of formation or gets sick, other geese fall out of formation to help. She explained that having friends with you when you're down and need help reduces drag. Anna wished to blend in and to have a normal birthday so when it looked like her wish would be ruined, she'd thought to ask the girls to fall out of formation with her and to duck under the table to reduce the drag. Canada geese honk to help each other keep up and fly their best. The girls had honked to help cheer Anna on as she celebrated a relatively normal thirteenth birthday.

I read about Canada geese after the girls went off to bed to verify what Anna had shared and to explore how understanding the natural actions of geese makes a difference. What Anna said is true. Combined action makes the difference to Canada geese survival, to their lift, and to their success. Anna is smart. She correctly figured that what was good for the goose would be good for the girl. It's also good for the rest of us.

Working together as a team improves flock performance by seventy-one percent. Synergy creates uplift and reduces drag when you work together. If someone on your team falls, help him or her back into your team's formation. Honk/encourage others to do their best. It makes a difference.

> *I've never scored a goal in my life without getting a pass from someone else.*
>
> – Abby Wambach
> Two-Time Gold Medalist, FIFA Women's World Cup Champion, and Six-Time Winner of the U.S. Soccer Athlete of the Year Award

The second way people evaluate you is by your use or lack of use of the traditional written rules followed by a group of people in a particular area. These rules are referred to as etiquette. Basic knowledge of etiquette in the area in which you live and work will increase your confidence and impact your success. Understanding the etiquette subscribed to by a group reduces anxiety you might otherwise experience about the expectations people have of you. Etiquette is different from place to place. The etiquette of one group is no better than another. The important thing is to understand the etiquette so you can flex your behavior just as you would adjust your language to the language of the people in another country in order to be understood. The elimination of anxiety about yourself when you know the etiquette of a group will free you to focus on giving and sharing with others. When you give and share with others without thinking about yourself you will experience happiness. This book does not provide basic etiquette information but my books *The Etiquette Advantage*® and *The Dance Steps of Life* are available for readers who want an easy guide covering all the basics without the burden of a boring tome.

> *Your manners are always under examination,*
> *and by committees little suspected, awarding you*
> *or denying you high prizes when you least think it.*
>
> — Ralph Waldo Emerson

Body Language

Reading the body language of others is an inexact science made even more difficult when we consider that nonverbal signals vary from city to city, state to state, and country to country. However, because people do read each other's silent communication signals, it will serve you well to be aware of some of the most common nonverbal signals you may encounter in the business world. In addition, knowing how body language is perceived will help you to send the signals you intend.

It's a bit daunting to consider that 99% of you is invisible and that the way people perceive you is based, at least initially, on the 1% others see. Everything about you sends a message to the people who might want to hire you, promote you, fall in love with you, or do business with you. According to clinical psychologist Linda Blair, author of the book *Straight Talking*, "It takes only seven seconds for us to judge another person when we first meet."[15] A poor first impression can take a lifetime to undo. Be sure that everything about you is sending the signal you want. Your signals include more than your words and the sound of your voice. Your signals include what people see.

> *60% of all human communication is nonverbal body language; 30% is your tone, so that means 90% of what you're saying ain't coming out of your mouth.*
>
> – Alex "Hitch" Hitchens/Will Smith
> 2005 Movie *Hitch*

Words account for only a fraction of your message. Your posture, the way you sit and stand, the gestures you use, distractions you carry (cell phones, PDAs, newspapers, books or magazines), the non-words (e.g. uhs, ands, etc.) you utter, give clues as to your competence. Be careful what you carry! Understanding the signals and knowing how to respond to signals you receive will help you get what you want, need, and deserve.

In the 1870s, Morse Code was the most sophisticated mode of long distance communication. Morse Code jobs were highly sought as they paid well and were prestigious. A company advertised for a new hire Morse Code operator. A young woman went to apply for the job. When she entered the office, she walked over to the reception desk where a sign read, "Thank you for coming to apply. Please sign in, take a seat, and wait to be called into the inner office for an interview."

The young woman signed the sheet of paper and took her seat in the waiting room filled with applicants. After about a minute and a half, the young woman rose from her seat and walked into the inner office.

The other applicants in the waiting room were angry that the young woman had jumped in front of them and began making comments like, "Who does she think she is?" "Can you believe the arrogance of that woman?" Another said, "Well, she'll never get the job. People like that are always found out."

In a few minutes, the president of the company emerged from the inner office with the young woman. The president said, "I appreciate your interest in the job. The job has been filled. Thank you for coming." An uproar began with people yelling, "That's not fair!" "We were here first and waited for our turn." "She jumped ahead of us for an interview!"

The president raised his hands motioning for the angry would-be applicants to calm down and said, "While you were waiting, a Morse Code message was transmitted in the waiting room for you to hear. Its translation, 'If you can understand this message, come inside. The job is yours.'"

The applicants lost their chance for a well-paying job because they failed to know the signals. Know the signals sent to you so you won't lose opportunities to get what you want.

In addition to understanding signals sent to you, you need to be aware of the signals you send. People subconsciously consider your nonverbal signals to make judgments about your socio-economic and educational background. They make decisions about you based on the clarity and effectiveness of your actions, as well as your choice of words. You will appear more authoritative and confident the less you rely on gestures.

In fact, studies show that the higher individuals are on the socioeconomic scale, the fewer gestures they use because they rely more on vocabulary to send messages. Extraneous gestures often compensate for a limited vocabulary. Increase your vocabulary through reading, listening carefully to others, and incorporating new words into your speech. Sprinkling your presence with non-words and distractions can overshadow your message.

> *What you do speaks so loud*
> *that I cannot hear what you say.*
>
> – Ralph Waldo Emerson

What are you physically doing when you try to sell your products, services, or ideas — in business, at home, or in a social setting? What can you physically do to optimize your message that will make a difference in your success? Sometimes we see and send signals without realizing their meanings. Consider a few of the most common examples of what people notice about your appearance.

Posture is the first thing people notice about your appearance. To show you are confident, stand up straight. You can easily check your posture with a simple technique. Stand up. Stand straight with your legs six to eight inches apart. Position your chin so that it is parallel to the floor. Your posture should now be in alignment. Keep your chin parallel to the floor. Now lace your fingers behind your back. This pulls your shoulders back and down. Release your hands and place them by your sides. Voila! Your posture is perfect. Do this until you get the feel of it and keep doing it throughout the day. Erect posture will do more for your appearance than anything else. Watch royalty walk. Notice that they often place their hands behind their backs to adjust posture. Royal posture is erect.

Walk at an even pace. You'll look frantic, lacking poise, and out of control if your pace is too fast. You'll look lazy if you move too slowly.

Keep your body posture open and ready to move forward to show that you are ready to take on responsibility. Folding your arms in front of your body makes you look like you are protecting yourself or are cold. This body position physically appears to block the conversation partner from you and therefore sends the subliminal message that you are not interested in conversation.

Placing hands on the hips indicates dominance and perhaps communicates that there are "issues." According to Amy Cuddy, Harvard Business School professor and author of the book, *Presence: Bringing Your Boldest Self to Your Biggest Challenges*, this posture can also increase confidence. "It's critical to know that changing the way you carry your body will change the way you feel about yourself. So sit up straight, not to respect others, but yourself." Cuddy's research shows that body language constantly communicates information to your mind so you can trick it into sending a signal to relax when you are stressed so you will perform well:

> In our studies we find that if people stand like Wonder Woman for two minutes their testosterone increases significantly, their cortisol drops significantly, they are more risk taking ... we find that their pain threshold is higher, they think more abstractly, and they are more likely to do well in very stressful situations like interviewing for a job.[16]

Leaning against a wall, table, or chair indicates a sloppy and casual attitude.

Shoving hands into a shirt, blouse, jacket or pocket sends the message that the person is non-professional, secretive, and unwilling to openly communicate. After all, hands deeply thrust into the pockets are not available for shaking or for any other form of tactile communication. Preoccupation with money (either too much or not enough) is another interpretation when the hand in the pocket jingles loose change.

Stand Up! Standing up shows self-respect and respect for others. Gone are the days women remained seated and waited until properly introduced to speak to others. Modern women and men STAND UP! Always stand up.

How to sit. Choose a rigid chair when you sit because it is difficult to look perky and powerful when you are swallowed by an oversized piece of furniture. Have a powerful sitting posture by approaching your chair and finding the chair with the back of your legs. Sit on the chair's edge and slide your hips back. Sit up straight.

Spreading out when sitting sends off unfavorable messages for both men and women. However, the unfavorable message is different for each sex. The man who spreads out is signaling that he is taking over, while men interpret a woman who is spreading out as overstepping her bounds. However, if the woman places only one arm on a nearby chair the nonverbal message is that she wants to be perceived as having equal authority. Women who want to be taken seriously generally find it useful to slightly lean forward while resting their elbows on the table and lightly clasping their hands. In addition, women who sit next to the most powerful person in the room are perceived to have power.

Manspreading or man-sitting is the offensive practice of some men who sit with their legs wide apart in order to prevent others from sitting next to them. It is so offensive that it is banned in Madrid. The Metropolitan Transit Authority in New York has even released an official anti-manspreading campaign. The most formal and correct way for men to sit is with feet parallel on the floor.

The Duchess Slant for women when sitting is to have legs firmly together slanted at an angle with ankles touching. Variations include placing feet with either both feet flat on the floor, crossed at the ankles, or crossed at the knees. Be aware that you run two risks when you cross your legs at the knees — varicose veins and appearing nervous if you swing your legs.

How to place your feet. Showing the soles of your feet is an insult in some cultures. An embarrassing international incident occurred during a meeting between Russian President Nikita Khrushchev and American President Richard Nixon when Khrushchev crossed his legs and turned up his foot revealing a large hole in the sole of his shoe. The faux pas was reported all over the world by the international press and the editors of the *New York Times* chastised Khrushchev for his bad manners. Be careful of the message you send — even with your feet. Look at signals sent by royalty in their portraits and remember to keep both feet parallel with your toes pointed in the same direction when you sit.

Tucking one foot underneath your body when sitting will make you appear ungrounded and girlish. Appear grounded by placing both feet on the ground.

Crossing the leg over the thigh is called the "know-it-all" position. It is a seated position more common with men than women, but both sexes can be guilty of it. People who sit like this rarely change their minds, especially if they place their hands behind their heads. Don't bother trying to bring a person sitting like this around to your way of thinking when you are in the dealing phase of business communication.

Crossed arms and/or legs tend to indicate a defensive frame of mind and placing a hand over the mouth or chin are signs of a person deep in thought. These body positions do not invite contact. Attract contact by keeping your arms loose by your sides and keeping your hands away from your mouth.

Lean forward when you speak to others. This demonstrates interest and shows that you are listening.

Smile. Smiles bring the same joyful feeling and good will to every person in every culture on every continent. According to Dale Carnegie:

> There is a simple reason for this phenomenon: when we smile, we are letting people know we are happy to be with them, happy to meet them, happy to be interacting with them. They in turn feel happier to be dealing with us. Of course we don't always feel like smiling, but if we make the effort, we not only make those around us happier but also become happier ourselves.[17]

*When you feel happy, notify your face.
Notify your body to smile
when you are not happy to cheer up yourself.*

The Beatles played to a sold-out frenzied audience in Milwaukee in 1964. Christine Cutler, a 14-year-old fan, had planned to see the show but she got sick and was hospitalized. A doctor's wife called the *Milwaukee Journal* newspaper which then got a message to McCartney. Before the Beatles left town the following afternoon, McCartney telephoned Cutler at St. Francis Hospital. At the conclusion of the conversation McCartney told the young girl, "Well now, I've got to hang up, you see, but you will smile though. That's the main thing, you know." The nurses cried, and Christine said she wanted to take the telephone home with her.[18]

Your smile costs nothing and is a gift you can easily share. Smiling requires the use of fewer facial muscles than frowning. A smile is the greatest indication of a friendly and positive attitude and a willingness to communicate. Your smile will make the other person feel more receptive towards you. A smile can make or break a conversation. A smile can make or break a relationship.

Groom in private. This includes picking teeth, brushing hair, applying lipstick and powder.

Remove sunglasses when you first meet people so you can make eye contact.

Look people in their eyes. It is the custom in North America to look a communication partner (CP) in his eyes 40–60% of the time and to let the eyes travel around his face the rest of the time. In our culture, we usually look directly in our CP's eyes for 5–7 seconds and then let our eyes travel around our CP's face, perhaps gazing at the forehead, cheek, and chin. Look at the other person's face at approximately five-second intervals to avoid seeming to stare him down which will make him uncomfortable and make you appear critical. Do not look the person up and down to check clothing as it will seem that you are judging the person.

Pay constant attention and do not look over the person's shoulder and around the room. Do not gaze away while your CP is speaking. When you talk, continue to look your CP in his eyes but also look away from time to time when you are thinking of your words. Never look away to check out who is in the room to determine who might be more interesting or more attractive than your CP. You might notice someone, but you will lose credibility the instant your expression reveals that you are not focused on your communication partner. Show that you understand your CP by nodding from time to time.

Sam Walton realized the importance of positive body language and eye contact so much that he instituted a "Ten-Foot Attitude" that is one of the secrets to Walmart's customer service. He asked his associates (his name for employees) to take the following pledge. *I solemnly promise and declare that every customer that comes within ten feet of me, I will smile, look him in the eyes, greet him, and ask if I can help him.* Walton said:

> I learned early on that one of the secrets to campus leadership was the simplest thing of all: speak to people coming down the sidewalk before they speak to you ... I would always look ahead and speak to the person coming toward me. If I knew them, I would call them by name, but even if I didn't I would speak to them. Before long I probably knew more students than anybody in the university, and they recognized me and considered me their friend. I ran for every office that came along.[19]

At the University of Missouri, Walton was president of the senior men's honor society, an officer in his fraternity, president of the senior class, and captain and president of the ROTC's elite military organization Scabbard and Blade.

Psychologist Jane Templeton shared her observations regarding the value of knowing eye language communication signals to business in her article, *"How Salesmen Can Find Out What's Really on a Customer's Mind."*

> If a prospect's eyes are downcast and face turned away, you're being shut out. However, if the mouth is relaxed, without the mechanical smile, chin is forward, he is probably considering your presentation. If his eyes engage you for several seconds at a time with a slight, one-sided smile extending at least to nose level, he is weighing your proposal. Then if his head is shifted to the same level as yours, smile is relaxed and appears enthusiastic, the sale is virtually made.[20]

It's important to note that in some cultures it is poor manners to look a person in the eyes because it is considered too personal to look into another's "window to the soul." Do your homework to learn about a person from another culture before your meeting.

Constant touching of a wedding band (especially when the communicator is discussing a spouse) is observed as a sign that the marital relationship is experiencing difficulty.

Holding hands or objects such as a briefcase or magazine in front of the body indicates an anxious person desiring a communication barrier. Pulling objects from a briefcase or purse when entering a room gives the message that the person is not prepared or may be stalling for time.

Quick-paced walk accompanied by freely swinging arms suggests a person who is goal-oriented.

Walking with hands in the pockets as a habit suggests that the person is secretive and negative.

Walking with hands on the hips suggests a person who is in charge and wants to cover the most territory.

Touch appropriately. Touching others is generally inappropriate in a business environment and can send misinterpreted messages in social settings. Do not reach out to touch people you have just met, people with whom you are not completely comfortable, or people who are senior to you in business. Before the Coronavirus pandemic, the only acceptable form of professional touch in North American business culture was the professional handshake. Due to the virus, the ancient custom of beginning and ending conversations with a handshake was suspended and threatened with extinction.

In the United States, a handshake traditionally has been used between people making a deal so much so that despite the pandemic a *Washington Post* article professes, "The handshake will return. It's too much of who we are."[21] The pledging of words between people who trust each other is valued more than many written contracts between people who distrust each other.

The handshake is the accepted greeting for men and women in almost every country around the world. Even the Japanese will bow *and* shake hands when beginning and ending a meeting in the Western world. Physical meetings, conferences, networking events and occasions to "seal the deal" traditionally include the ancient custom of shaking hands. This book includes what you need to know regarding the traditional handshake to prepare you for business. In addition, we'll discuss a variety of new replacements that began during the Coronavirus pandemic so you will know how to handle awkward situations as customs evolve.

When it is safe to shake hands, don't hold back — immediately extend your hand. You are judged by your handshake. Women take their place equally beside men. The woman's handshake, like a man's, should convey warmth and sincerity while making a positive, tactile connection with another person. Stand when you shake hands — it shows respect for others and respect for yourself. Powerful women stand when they greet people hello and they stand when they say goodbye. If a person is a visitor in your office or home, stand and walk them all the way to the door. This is important enough to repeat: Walk your visitors all the way to the door. If there is an elevator, you may want to walk your visitors all the way to the elevator.

The professional handshake is firm and web-to-web with three to four pumps from the elbow. Accompany your shake with a smile, direct eye contact, and open body posture.

Keep your right hand free — ready to give and to receive handshakes. A good professional handshake is dry and pleasant to the touch. Keep your shaking hand (the right hand) dry by holding iced drinks with your left hand and perhaps momentarily sticking your hand in your jacket pocket to warm it before shaking hands.

The weak limp-fish handshake sends the subliminal message that the person is weak and looks to others to make decisions. The person who offers a weak handshake is viewed as not truly interested in shaking hands and interacting.

The fingertip-extender handshake sends a subliminal message similar to that of the weak limp-fish. Rendered more frequently by women than men, it almost appears to be extended for the purpose of receiving a kiss on the hand.

The bone-crusher handshake. This handshake's subliminal message is that the person is aggressive and seeking to intimidate. Further, the person may be viewed as angry. Sometimes the person giving this handshake will turn the hand so that it is on top of the other person's hand. This power play is read, "I'm on top." Remove rings from your right hand before entering into multiple handshaking situations to reduce risk of overly firm bone-crusher handshakes.

The gloved handshake (sometimes referred to as the preacher handshake) is given by placing the left hand on top of the shaking hands. It is effective for consoling but not for doing business.

Some people are not comfortable shaking hands because they have hyperhidrosis, commonly known as sweaty palms. A secret tip is to keep a small powder puff or handkerchief in your pocket or purse so you can periodically touch it to absorb excess moisture. If your problem is severe, tell your physician who can prescribe a product called Drysol that eliminates the problem of sweaty hands. A simple surgical procedure performed by thoracic surgeons can eliminate hyperhidrosis.

If for some reason you cannot shake hands, explain it to the person who has extended his hand to you. For example, "I would like to shake your hand, but I sprained my wrist when I moved furniture, repaired the computer, fell off a horse, etc." Comments such as these not only break the ice but also serve as conversation bait.

Body language with physically-challenged individuals. A person with a disability does not have a contagious disease and should never be pre-judged or defined by his disability or treated differently. People with physical challenges use the same body language as everyone else in so far as they are physically able. Shake hands with the person's left hand if you meet someone who has limited use of his right hand or an artificial limb. If the person is blind, say, "I'd like to shake your hand."

Alternatives to Shaking Hands

- *Hand or Fist Across Heart:* Place your right hand over your heart for a few seconds while maintaining eye contact.
- *Bow Your Head:* The deeper the bow the greater show of respect in Asian countries.
- *Wai Bow:* This Thai custom is one of my favorites. Press your palms together near your chest, lower your head and raise your hands until your thumb touches your nose and your index finger touches your head between your eyebrows. Bring your hands to your head while you bow.
- *Namaste Gesture:* Place the palms of your hands together in front of your chest and accompany with a slight nod of your head.
- *Mime a Fist Bump*
- *Tip Your Hat* (males if you wear one)
- *Salute*
- *Air-Five:* A spin-off of a high five done without touching hands in the air. This is the greeting given in the TV series *The Office* when Pam and Jim air-fived from across the room. Often accompanied with the high-fiving sound "Whoopish."
- *Air Kiss, Blown Kiss, or Thrown Kiss:* The lips are pursed as if kissing but without touching the other person.
- *Wave*
- *Foot Shake:* Tap sides of feet
- *Elbow Bump*

The hands can be effective in communicating ideas. It is important to be careful when using body language transculturally. Learn the body language customs of your transcultural communication partners before you meet.

Pointing the finger at any one in any culture is likely to generate ill will. However, the fingers can be used effectively to reinforce communication that contains numerous items.

Using the fingers facilitates conversation that includes several points. Try to keep oral lists to three items as more than three increases the difficulty of oral comprehension. North Americans begin the count with the index finger, followed by the middle finger, and then the ring finger. Europeans typically begin enumerations with the thumb followed by the index finger and then the middle finger.

Heavy fragrances should be avoided so you won't come on too strong when meeting people.

Removing clean eyeglasses to clean is viewed as a procrastination technique.

Placing eyeglasses in the mouth is thought to indicate that the person is either hungry or searching for additional information while extending time to make a decision.

Ear pulling, eye rubbing, nose rubbing, chin rubbing, and covering the mouth are interpreted by people who read body language to indicate concealment of information, uncertainty, or an untruth being spoken by the communicator.

An analysis by neurologist Alan Hirsch and psychiatrist Charles Wolf of President Bill Clinton's body language during his testimony to the Grand Jury regarding his extramarital affair revealed that Clinton did not touch his nose when he told the truth. However, when he lied, the analysis found that Clinton gave a split-second frown and touched his nose once every four minutes for a grand total of twenty-six nose touches.[22]

Read body language in gesture clusters and consider the setting and the individual. For example, the person rubbing his eyes and nose may be demonstrating an allergic reaction to the cat in the room, not that he is hiding information from someone and cannot look at him. The person covering the mouth may be tired and not unintentionally conveying, "I shouldn't say that." The social yawn on the other hand can indicate more than fatigue. Often this person is trying to buy extra time when facing a mildly stressful situation.

Touching the hair or tossing it back implies that a person thinks positively about his or her personal appearance.

Twirling strands of hair indicates confusion, uncertainty and nervousness.

Running a hand through the hair generally conveys a sense of being unsure of what to say or do next. The professional woman who wears her hair up is conveying that she is in control or at least wants to be in control. Women who wear their hair down are generally perceived in a more sexual than professional way.

Stroking the chin is a promising sign that means the listener is interested.

Showing the hands palms up indicates an open and receptive communicator.

Steepling is the gesture of pressing the fingers together and resting the chin or mouth on the fingertips. This gesture indicates deep thought as though the communicator is praying for an answer. Additional interpretations, especially when read as part of a cluster of gestures which involve posture and eye contact, suggests that the person is confident, proud, and perhaps pontifical. It is thought that the higher the position of steepling the more confident the person.

Tugging at the collar is an indicator that the communicator's body temperature has increased. Yes, it might be hot in the room which does need to be considered, but the person who knows how to read nonverbal communication is also aware that body temperature increases when people lie. A hand automatically reaching up to let air in by loosening the collar may mean that a person is hot under the collar because he is nervous or anxious.

Stroking a scarf (or stroking a necktie for men) is a nonverbal signal that the communicator is trying hard to please and is desirous of making a good impression.

Jiggling the foot back and forth when the legs are crossed exudes nervousness.

Tapping the foot on the floor exudes impatience and anxiety.

Biting nails, twisting hair, cracking knuckles, and chewing gum show lack of poise and sophistication and can subtly sabotage your career.

Giggling excessively and without reason is conversational filler which denotes nervousness and anxiety. It is often a weak ploy to gain acceptance.

Slightly tilting the head can indicate that the listener is interested in what he hears. Charles Darwin first noted this in animals as well as humans. Frequently tilting the head to the side to listen is most often interpreted as indicating submission. It is power-depleting. Leave the head tilt to flirts.

Nodding the head periodically is an active listening technique in North America that shows approval, understanding, and that you wish the person to continue speaking. Nodding too frequently is like wearing too much rouge — you'll look overdone and insincere as if you are not actually listening. The way a nod is given does not mean the same thing in every culture.

My daughter, Allison, traveled to India. When she arrived in Mumbai, she went to the airport's ATM machine to get money. A burly guard holding an Uzi submachine gun stood in front of the money machine. She asked the guard if she could get money from the ATM. He bobbled his head right to left and said, "yes." The guard said "yes" but his head to her American understanding indicated "no."

Allison respected his gun and did not want to misinterpret so she repeated her question. Again, the Indian guard bobbled his head right to left while saying, "yes." Allison was perplexed and afraid to go past him. But she needed money. Therefore one final time she asked, "Are you sure it is okay for me to get money?" This time the guard barked, "Yes!" Allison got her money. It was a quick awakening for her that body language varies in different places in the world.

People like to do business with those they perceive to be like themselves, or at the very least, indicate an understanding of them. Take the time to learn about the customs of your communication partners when you do business with global partners and show them that you understand their customs. The message you send when you do not know their communication customs is that perhaps you are stupid, ignorant, or simply don't care enough to learn the most basic things about them or their business culture. Equipping yourself with the tools you need in the business jungle can mean the difference in getting a job in the USA or being barked away in India!

A handsome young man born and raised in Spain shared his story with me one day after a training class I conducted for a global business based in Fairfax, Virginia:

> I moved to this country to attend the University of Virginia where I played on the golf team. When I lived in Spain, I did well in school. My teachers liked me. I had many friends. I never had difficulty getting a date.
>
> I struggled to fit in for a long time at UVA, never understanding that the way I successfully conducted myself in Spain was causing me relationship problems in the United States. In America, no one seemed to want to be near me or have anything to do with me. I became depressed. One day during golf practice, my golf coach came over to me and said, 'You are standing too close to people.' I had thought that Americans were cold and standoffish while they were thinking that I was aggressive and invading their personal space. I now understand. The skills you are teaching are vital not only to professional success in this country but also to personal success. Thank you.

> This information will make my life easier. I wish I had learned it sooner.

The young man was referring to the interpersonal zone or spatial distance between communicators. He was previously unaware that the average North American is most comfortable interacting with communication partners at a distance of 18 to 24 inches. Not knowing this caused relationship problems for him and made him unhappy. It made a difference in his ability to be successful once he understood. The interpersonal zone varies within this distance according to each individual's personality, self-concept, and attitude towards conversation partner, cultural background, and perceived or real rank. In addition, the study of proxemics shows that extroverts and people with high self-esteem tend to stand closer to a conversation partner within the acceptable range, while introverts and people with low self-esteem stand on the outer limits of the acceptable peripheral range. Not knowing a regional spatial zone that is closer or greater than your culture's acceptable zone can cause miscommunication as it did for the UVA student from Spain. Other examples are conversation partners in the Middle East, Southern Europe, and Latin America who typically converse while standing closer together than people from Northern Europe and North America.

Etiquette and social customs change with time. The Coronavirus is changing many personal and professional customs with new distance guidelines from healthcare experts advising us *to stay at least six feet away from people outside of our households*. Be aware of evolving regional customs and flex your style as appropriate while remaining safe.

The business world is global. Take time to learn about your communication partner's customs that may be different from your own. Know the culture of your conversation partner in advance when possible. Learn cultural values, local phrases, and what makes people laugh who live in regions different from your own. What is humorous in one culture may be offensive in another. Learn the signals. Read the signals of the people in your business culture. Be aware of the signals you send.

Dress That Makes The Difference

Madeleine K. Albright was born in Czechoslovakia before World War II and fled to the United States as a refugee. She was determined to earn an education and completed her doctorate while raising three children. At age 39, Albright accepted her first professional job. During her career, she worked as a university professor, a businesswoman, and as an adviser on world affairs, ultimately becoming the first female United States Secretary of State in history. Albright understood that clothing and accessories are tools — and when carefully selected can be powerful tools for transmitting nonverbal diplomatic messages.

As U.S. Ambassador to the United Nations, Madeleine Albright established a tradition of wearing pins to send nonverbal diplomatic statements after Saddam Hussein referred to her as an "unparalleled serpent." At her next meeting with Iraqi officials, she wore a golden snake brooch. Albright said, "I found that jewelry had become part of my personal diplomatic arsenal. While President George H.W. Bush had been known for saying, 'Read my lips,' I began urging colleagues and reporters to 'Read my pins.'"

Albright selected pins to visually express hopes, determination, impatience, or warm feelings. She was named the first female Secretary of State in 1997 and at the time became the highest-ranking woman in the history of the United States government. A fascinating collection of over two hundred of her pins is part of a traveling exhibit, *Read My Pins: The*

Madeleine Albright Collection, organized by The Museum of Arts and Design. The exhibit is a strong testament to the effectiveness of strategic packaging to promote a winning perception.

Uniqueness is critical to becoming memorable. "The Greatest," and "The Fab Four" shared admiration for an A-Lister who became known as "The King of Rock and Roll." The following are the reasons Muhammad Ali, The Beatles, and other notable winners believe Elvis Presley lives on as the "The King."

1) "Before Elvis, there was nothing." "Nothing really affected me until I heard Elvis. If there hadn't been an Elvis, there wouldn't have been The Beatles."[23] (John Lennon)

2) "A lot of people have accused Elvis of stealing the black man's music, when in fact, almost every black solo entertainer copied his stage mannerisms from Elvis."[24] (Jackie Wilson)

3) "Elvis is the greatest cultural force in the twentieth century. He introduced the beat to everything, music, language, clothes, it's a whole new social revolution — the 60s comes from it."[25] (Leonard Bernstein)

4) "When I first heard Elvis' voice, I just knew that I wasn't going to work for anybody; and nobody was going to be my boss ... Hearing him for the first time was like busting out of jail."[26] (Bob Dylan)

5) "There have been a lotta tough guys. There have been pretenders. And there have been contenders. But there is only one king."[27] (Bruce Springsteen, "The Boss")

6) "I don't think there is a musician today that hasn't been affected by Elvis' music. His definitive years — 1954–57 — can only be described as Rock's cornerstone. He was the original cool."[28] (Brian Setzer)

7) "He's just the greatest entertainer that ever lived. And I think it's because he had such presence. When Elvis walked

into a room, Elvis Presley was in the f**king room. I don't give a f**k who was in the room with him, Bogart, Marilyn Monroe."[29] (Eddie Murphy)

8) "I don't admire nobody but Elvis Presley was the sweetest, most humble and nicest man you'd want to know .... People don't realize what they had till it's gone. Like President Kennedy, there was no one like him, The Beatles, and my man, Elvis Presley."[30] (Muhammad Ali)

Louisville Magazine calls Butch Polston "The King Maker."[31] The documentary "Fit for a King" is about Polston's business that makes Elvis costumes. Polston tells the following story about the robe Elvis had made for Muhammad Ali:

> Elvis and Ali had developed a friendship. Ali saw some of Elvis' clothes and said, 'Man thems some fancy duds.' Elvis decided he wanted to give the champ something really unique that the champ would really be blown away by all the artistic work on it. Elvis had Gene Doucette who designed many of his most famous and recognizable stage outfits make a robe "Fit for a King" for Ali.[32]

The robe adorned with rhinestones and jewels with "The People's Choice" inscribed in large letters on the back is known as "The Robe" and is on display in the Muhammad Ali Center in downtown Louisville, Kentucky.

The Beatles lacked a unique sellable package (including jeweled robes) until Brian Epstein met them and became their manager. They originally wore torn jeans and leather jackets. They swore, smoked, drank, and ate on stage. Epstein, like Elvis and Ali, understood the importance of packaging. His formal education included study at the Royal Academy of Dramatic Art where he was interested in costumes as a way to convey onstage character. He realized the value of dress and body language in conveying not only character but also message. Epstein convinced The Beatles to repackage themselves in order to attract dance hall promoters who did not like them but could pay them the money they wanted.

At first The Beatles balked at the idea of cutting their hair and exchanging jeans and leather jackets for suits, but they were fully committed to achieving their goal to make a lot of money. Lennon explained in an interview:

> So it got to be like Epstein said, 'Look, if you wear a suit you'll get more money.' I said ... all right I'll wear a suit. I'll wear a f**king balloon if someone's going to pay me. I'm not in love with leather THAT much.[33]

Repackaging themselves did not compromise their music or their message and it worked. While The Beatles' packaging for the photo-op mentioned at the beginning of this book didn't work to get a photo of them with Sonny Liston, the photos taken with Muhammad Ali became some of most iconic of the century. By the time The Beatles ceased to be a group they had replaced tattered jeans for hundreds of brand-promoting clothes to help them sell their music — and their ideas. Epstein taught The Beatles how to package themselves in many ways including having them end performances with a synchronized bow to show appreciation to their audiences.

The Beatles were luckier than most people because typically no one will tell you how to dress to facilitate the accomplishment of your goal. Correct clothing generally follows unwritten rules that you are expected to decode for yourself. Failure to decode correctly can sabotage your progress and leave you wondering why you didn't rise to the top when everything else you did was excellent. How you package your message is important if you want to create your own version of Beatlemania.

Equipping yourself with the right skills as well as packaging and promoting yourself to accurately reflect the person you are makes a difference. I use different types of music and video to illustrate when I speak to groups. The description below is of a video of one of my favorites — *The Washington Post's* "Pearls Before Breakfast"[34] experiment that illustrates how perception, taste, and priorities are influenced by packaging and promotion.

On January 12, 2007 in the Washington, D.C. Metro Station at L'Enfant Plaza, a violinist casually dressed and wearing a baseball cap played six pieces of Bach music for 43 minutes during which time over a thousand people passed through the station. After three minutes, a single middle-aged man slowed his pace and paused. After four minutes, a woman placed one dollar in the violinist's hat and continued on her way. After six minutes, a young man leaned against a wall and briefly listened before continuing to walk. After ten minutes, a three-year-old boy stopped but his mother pulled him along. This happened with several other children whose parents wouldn't let them stop. Only six other people briefly paused to listen. The violinist played for an hour without recognition and when he finished no one noticed or applauded. Twenty people had given a total of $32.17.

The violinist was Joshua Bell, one of the finest violin virtuosos of the era, who was playing some of the most beautiful and intricate pieces of music ever composed. His instrument was one of the finest ever made — a Stradivarius made in 1713 for which Bell paid 3.5 million dollars. Only three nights before Joshua Bell filled Boston's Symphony Hall where audience members had paid an average of $100 a ticket.

Consider the very different response to the free D.C. Metro event if it had been effectively packaged and promoted. Packaging and advance promotion can make or break your career. You can be as talented in your field as Joshua Bell is in his, but if you don't take care to market yourself for success, you will likely earn a pittance of what you are worth. It's critical that you present yourself with a sellable package if you want to maximize results. Remember Joshua Bell and *The Washington Post* experiment if you want more than a few dollars for your products, services, or ideas.

Carol Meyrowitz, one of the highest paid female CEOs ever and current Executive Chairman of the Board of a Fortune 500 Company, obviously understands clothing is important to clients and customers. She leads the largest international apparel and home fashions off-price department store chain in the United States — more than 3000 discount retail stores in six countries, including T.J. Maxx, HomeGoods, and Marshalls. Meyrowitz discusses what is key to driving business in a *Harvard Business Review* article. She says, "Buyers must thoroughly understand consumers and fashion ... They have to develop relationships with vendors ... how to communicate with vendors."[35]

Business people consciously and unconsciously identify others by their clothing and make judgments accordingly — even before they speak. How people perceive you directly impacts how people will relate to you, including how they will reward or deny you job opportunities, promotions — or friendship. The good news is that you can control and train the perception others have of you with management of your nonverbal and verbal messages.

Carla Harris, Vice Chairman, Global Wealth Management, Managing Director and Senior Client Advisor at Morgan Stanley, says the adjectives people use to describe you when you are not in the room are important because all the important decisions about your career are made when you are not in the room. Compensation decisions are made when you are not in the room. New assignments are given out when you are not in the room.[36]

Harris advises people to choose three adjectives that you

want people to use when they describe you when you aren't in the room. For Harris, "tough" was one of the words she wanted people in her business to use to describe her. An "aha" moment for her was when a colleague told her, "You're smart, you work hard, but you're not tough enough for this business." Harris knew she was tough and strategically set about changing the workplace perception of herself. She says, "For 90 days I would walk tough, talk tough, eat tough, drink tough." A phrase she used in conversations about herself was, "You know I'm tough."[37] Later when her name came up in conversations when she was not in the room and considered for a job that required a tough candidate, she was described exactly as she had programmed those around her to see her by walking tough, talking tough, eating tough, drinking tough. Consistency in your behavior, speech, dress, and actions determines the perception others have of you.

Harris believes, "Perception is the co-pilot to reality."[38] Your verbal and nonverbal communication determines whether people believe you are able to do what you can do or want to do. If you do not demonstrate your abilities with your body language and dress to match what you say to reflect who you are and what you can do, you will not be awarded the opportunities you want.

> *When I get asked, "What's the secret to success?"*
> *I just say, 'Early to bed, early to rise,*
> *work like hell and advertise.'*
> — Ted Turner at Montana State University, 2011

The clothing you select sends a message about you, so be careful to choose clothing that sends the message you intend. Archibald Leach was a poor uneducated working-class man from Bristol, England who realized that he not only had to change his name but dress the part to make the difference in his career. He used clothing to totally reinvent himself. Leach became a famous actor in the United States known as Cary Grant. He said that he never bought anything when he first saw it but only the next day if he still thought about it.[39]

What was important to the Netflix series *Schitt's Creek* becoming the first-time winner of all seven major comedy and drama Primetime Emmy Awards? According to series creator Daniel Levy:

> Wardrobe is probably the most important element in story telling outside of actually writing because we as people say so much about who we are and what we believe in and about what we want and what we think of ourselves by the way that we dress. So to me, wardrobe was a huge focus, making sure that we really thought through each of our characters making sure that the details were there.[40]

Virginia Smith, Fashion Director, *Vogue Magazine*:

> I think that is what was different about *Schitt's Creek*. It's as though the clothing was thought of at the same time as the character development and everything else so it became inherent to the show.[41]

Rachel Giese, editorial director, *XTRA:*

> I think the investment put into wardrobe was a smart investment because it said so much about who the characters were. You had a whole visual story and a whole way of understanding the characters through the clothing.[42]

Carol Burnett:

> The outfits become the person when you look in the mirror you see, 'Oh that's who she is.'[43]

Catherine O'Hara (Moira):

> When you get these kinds of clothes on you stand differently, you move differently, people look at you differently ... and I feed off of all of them.[44]

It's easy to sabotage your success with your clothing unless you research and consider the message your clothing choice will send about your professional ability and your values. Clothes are an important part of nonverbal communication and contribute to establishing in the minds of others who you are, where you are from, and what you can do.

> *Clothes make the man.*
> *Naked people have little or no influence in society.*
> – Mark Twain

Choose quality over quantity when you invest in your wardrobe. Shop early in the season when you have more options. Classic colors such as black, gray, navy, beige, and taupe tend to have a longer wearing time than bright trendy colors. Find a good tailor and have your clothes properly altered. Trousers start at the natural waistline and break at the in-step. A good investment is a quality clothes brush. Dry clean and wash your clothes as little as possible to prevent them from looking limp — clothes quickly lose their sizing after cleaning.

Business clothing is not about personal style or comfort. Business clothing is about showing respect for others and their positions. Clothes are tools. If you're smart you'll put a lot of thought into the clothes you wear because it can be a factor to your success in business. Choose the business attire that is appropriate for your industry and the industry functions you attend. The business dress for your industry may require that you dress up or down in order to fit in with the people with whom you wish to do business. It is appropriate to ask what to wear if you are unsure. Asking shows your interest in fitting in and being a team player.

Business people are often confused about what to wear because dress codes vary in different business cultures in the United States and abroad. To further complicate what to wear, every business has a unique set of behaviors, protocols, and styles that define its culture. In the United States, we recognize three broad types of corporate culture, each with its own dress code. The three types are conservative, modern, and unstructured. Women have more clothing options in each of these environments than men, and because of the options they often sabotage themselves when they fall victim to fashion whims.

> *Count to three. Get up, dress up, and show up because you never know who you might meet.*
>
> – Joan Williams Hight

Leadership studies prove that people follow those who are well dressed in the style to which they aspire. Dressing in a manner that closely matches the person is a powerful subliminal rapport building technique. Consider your business culture.

> *You may dress unconventionally, but the more strangely you dress, the better you have to be.*

Conservative Business Culture is characterized by an autocratic style of leadership. The environment exudes conservatism and its established patterns are slow to change. The atmosphere is quiet. Offices tend to be well designed and traditional. The mood is serious. Examples are old established law firms, banks, and blue chip companies that are highly structured.

Conservative business culture employees are businesslike. Conservative culture dress code tends to be formal. Men wear traditional dark-colored suits, silk ties or bowties. Hair and sideburns are short. Facial hair, if any, is groomed. Tattoos, if any, are not visible. Piercing of any sort is extremely rare.

Successful women in conservative business culture most often wear suits in navy, black, or beige. Jackets are paired with skirts more than dresses or trousers. Skirt length is generally slightly below the knee or at the knee but rarely above the knee. Other colors are worn, especially red. Red and black are considered the ultimate power colors. The higher the quality of the fabric, the greater the range the suit color can be. If you are in this environment, choose simple, well-cut suits or dresses instead of faddish items. Make sure undergarments are not showing and that clothes do not cling to your figure. Women's brightest clothing color in conservative business culture is typically splashed on with a scarf or blouse that does not reveal cleavage. Blouses are cotton or silk, most often white or pastel. Shoes are usually closed-toed with 1" to 2" low heels. Hosiery should be flawless (no runs) and conservative in color and in harmony with the shoes *(no light hosiery with dark shoes)*. Makeup is minimal — some mascara, no color shadow, soft rouge, powder, and lipstick. Hair tends to be short, but if it is long, hair is pulled back and away from the face. A light briefcase or portfolio case made of leather is often carried in place of or in addition to an unostentatious handbag that is usually small and in a dark color that matches the shoes. Jewelry is high quality, not flashy. You'll often see women wearing pearls, gold necklaces, earrings that do not dangle, and bracelets that do not make noise. Except for a single pair of earrings, body piercings (nose rings, eyebrow rings, etc.) are not visible. Perfume is so faint you need to be in an intimate interpersonal space to smell it.

Modern Business Culture. Modern business culture is characterized by a team approach to management. The environment appears open to new ideas and exudes confidence. The furniture tends to be sleek and modern. Displayed artwork is colorful. Office doors generally are open. Examples are consulting, architectural, and advertising companies. The employees appear friendly, approachable and helpful and often socialize together after hours.

Professional dress for men in modern business culture is relaxed. Men wear suits that may be light in color as well as casual trousers and sport jackets. Dress shoes may or may not be laced. No sandals. Hair is typically short but when longer it is groomed. NASA's "Mohawk Guy," Bob Ferdowski, is a good example of how modern business culture is more receptive to a serious dose of cool than conservative culture.

Women in modern business culture wear suits that may be light or colorful as well as tailored trousers. Shoes may be heeled, wedged or peep-toed, but not sandals. Shoe colors are generally limited to dark or neutrals. Legs may be bare especially if the shoe has a peep-toe. Hosiery is in tone with the shoes. Opaque hosiery has little or no design. Briefcases may be microfiber or leather. Handbags are stylish but for the most part unadorned. Makeup is polished and may have a slight shimmer that is missing in a conservative culture. Perfume is faint and minimal. Hair is groomed, close to the scalp, and in place whether short or long. Jewelry tends to be sleek.

Unstructured Business Culture. The third and most chaotic of the business cultures is the unstructured. Unstructured business culture is characterized by democratic leadership and because it is less structured it is difficult to read. One person may wear different hats. This may be a new organization that has not defined its structure or management approach. The rules are less defined and the noise level may be loud with audible music. There may be no set work hours. Office décor is not a priority and furniture may be mismatched due to changing styles and growth and may very well come from an attic. Examples are startup companies based in a garage or a business conducted from a spare bedroom.

Men in an unstructured business culture may wear just about anything including jeans, shorts, and sandals. Hair may be long or short. Facial hair and male piercings may be found. Female employees in unstructured business cultures may appear casual and familiar. They do not wear suits or jackets but prefer slacks, jeans, or fun dresses. Shoes run the gamut from sandals, stilettos, to boots in all colors. Legs are often bare. Hosiery may be colored and textured. Briefcases are seldom carried but totes, hobo bags, textured leather, and cloth bags with decorations can appear. Makeup may be totally lacking or heavily applied. Body piercings may be multiple. Perfume or cologne may be obvious. Accessories are trendy, large, and often dangle.

The most important thing to remember when choosing clothing for your particular business culture is that in business, clothes serve the same purpose as a book's cover. Clothes are tools for sending messages. Use psychology. Let your clothes reflect who you are and the business you are capable of conducting. When in doubt, ask, and err on the side of formality when there is no one to ask. The very best advice for dressing in your particular business culture is this: Dress not for the job you have, but for the job you want. You absolutely need to look the part. The adage is true, "Only birds with the right feathers are admitted to the nest."

Global wearing of masks in the post-pandemic workplace likely will be commonplace. Choose masks with care as masks send subliminal messages about you and your ability to do the job. In general, wearing a dark or single color mask in business settings is a safe choice. Logos, graphics, and patterns project business brand because everything about you projects your personal, professional and company's brand.

Business Casual evolves and is different for conservative, modern, and unstructured business cultures. The advent of Covid-19 hastened its evolution as athleisure and sweatpants became common attire for people working remotely. Consider the subliminal message these and other clothing suggests when you do business in person or via a virtual meeting. Extremely comfortable casual clothing may sabotage your professional credibility and the perception of your ability to fit in with your business culture.

Business casual is different from culture to culture, but every business casual look should include:

- Clean mask
- Good grooming, including clean hair and fingernails
- Clothing in good repair
- Well-maintained shoes appropriate for the job
- Appropriate hosiery or socks

The pendulum swings with clothing trends, as in all things, to both extremes and then back to the middle. Many companies are re-thinking, revamping, or completely abandoning dress-down policies initiated in the 1990s after discovering the downside of dress-down. A survey conducted by the employment law firm Jackson Lewis showed that 44% of the 1000 companies surveyed noticed an increase in tardiness, absenteeism and "flirtatious behavior" after implementing dress-down policies.[45] An Incomm Center for Research and Sales Training poll revealed that less than half of trade show customers responded favorably to sales people in casual attire, whereas 86% responded favorably to those dressed in business attire.[46] Those statistics underscore the economic sense of the current return in many businesses to require formal business attire be worn by employees who interact with clients on a daily basis.

Try as we might, we cannot change the perception others have of us — but we can influence it. Perception is reality.

Dress-down attire sends the subliminal message that the person is thinking about personal comfort and convenience. Professional attire signals a person in control with focus on business, the customer, and service to the customer. Dress professionally if you want to be perceived as a professional. Even in places where the rules have changed, the one thing that remains constant is the need to look professional, confident and competent.

Women, remember that men are hardwired. Your stylish professional outfit with a low neckline or tight hip fit may not look sexy to you or to other women. However, two-legged males in the corporate jungle will see you the same way four-legged males in the natural jungle see females. Males are visual. Don't lose power by losing sight of the perception created by your clothing choice.

Shaunti Feldhahn, author of *The Male Factor: The Unwritten Rules, Misperceptions, and Secret Beliefs of Men in the Workplace*, conducted a study to test the difference in men's and women's perceptions of dress. He asked white-collared men and women what they think when they see a woman dressed in a way that emphasizes her figure. Seventy-six percent of the men surveyed believe a woman wants the men around her to look at her body, while only twenty-three percent of the women surveyed agreed. One man chuckled, referring to the men who said they were not affected and said, "That is the 'liar, liar, pants on fire' cohort."[47] For most jobs, provocative clothing is career and goal sabotaging.

Consider the venue, the situation, the age and sophistication of the business people with whom you interact as you choose the most effective clothing to help you send the message you intend. When you do choose to wear business casual clothing, remember it is always "business" first and "casual" second. Err on the side of formality. Casual Friday is not power friendly. It magnifies the differences in the way men and women are perceived. Men have the advantage of wearing khakis and a short-sleeved shirt and still looking somewhat powerful. Casual wear options for women often send a powerless message. Women run the risk of sending the message that they are more interested in and better suited for a party than for a leadership role when they wear heels that are too high and makeup that's heavy or bright.

What to wear in an environment in which you want to reach optimum success depends on the nature of the business culture. Not all businesses are the same throughout the world. Business cultures in Asia are different from the business cultures in the Middle East. The courtroom is different from the boardroom. Take time to learn about business cultures in different regions of the world when you want to optimize your international success. If you want to fit into a corporate setting, blend with the environment, but know when to be flexible.

Carl Sandburg told a story about a chameleon who got along very well, adjusting moment by moment to his environment, until one day he had to cross a scotch plaid. He died at the crossroads heroically trying to blend with all the colors at once. Maintain personal integrity in every business culture you're in but be flexible enough to change when change is needed.

You need different tools and skills for different business and social cultures. Consider the five high-power Ps: Prior Planning Prevents Poor Performance. To be successful you must not only know yourself but also know the people with whom you wish to interact.

Think carefully about every detail. Before you go anywhere, consider who, what, when, where, why and how.

- Who are the participants?
- What is the purpose?
- When will you be there?
- Where will you be?

- Why are you going?
- How can you be the most effective in accomplishing your goals?

Detective work will pay off if you are unsure about the typical business attire for a particular industry. A large international consulting company I worked for required consultants going into a new business to drive their cars to the place of business, sit outside, and observe the clothing people wore as they entered and exited the building. After observing, management told consultants to dress accordingly to begin a business relationship. The company knew that people like to do business with people they perceive as like themselves and that similar clothing is a subliminal way to minimize differences. Similarly styled clothing is an easy way to establish that you fit in a particular business culture.

If you are going to an event and are unsure of the attire, call the host and ask. Don't be shy. Your call demonstrates initiative that shows you care — and that you belong.

How To Best Present Yourself For A Virtual Meeting

Look professional at all times including your participation in virtual meetings. Paying attention to what the virtual viewer sees on the webcam affects the perception others have of you. A little attention to the following details will help you shine.

Dress. While business casual dress is expected for virtual meetings, you still need to look professional and well-groomed. Avoid distracting patterns. Choose solid colors that do not match the background. For example, you'll be lost if you wear gray clothing against a gray wall. Bright colors are not generally professional in a business setting but bright colors will help you stand out on video or webcam. Bright white and dark black look like "blobs" on camera.

Background. Viewers will see a limited amount of your environment. You want the focus on your face, not on what's behind you. Make sure your environment looks professional, for example no beds, no dirty dishes, no clutter. Consider sitting in front of a bookcase without trinkets or in front of a piece of good art.

Lighting. Use as much natural light as possible. Sit facing the light or opposite the light so light will shine on your face. Sitting with lamplight or sunlight directly behind you or sitting by sidelights will make you into a silhouette. A small investment in circular lights to place in front of your face will make a huge difference. They are portable and easy to set up.

Eye Level. Eye to eye contact is the best connection, so look straight ahead at the camera. Stack books under your device if its webcam is physically below your eye level so the webcam is not looking up at your nostrils.

Perspective. The cameras on smartphones and webcams are wide-angle. Step back from the camera to avoid a distorted "wide-angle face."

Sound. Remember to remain close enough to the camera so the microphone can hear your voice. Close doors to rooms where children and pets are. Mute the microphone when you are listening so it won't pick up sounds of your typing or rustling papers. An accessory microphone plugged into the USB port of your laptop will improve the way you sound. In Zoom, select the accessory microphone instead of the microphone from the webcam.

Act as if what you do makes a difference. It does.

– William James
American Philosopher, Psychologist and
First Educator to Offer a Psychology Course in the USA

*I remind myself every morning:
nothing I say this day will teach me anything.
So if I'm going to learn, I must do it by listening.*

– Larry King
American Television and Radio Host,
Winner of Two Peabodys, an Emmy, and Ten Cable ACE awards

*Most of the successful people I've known
are the ones who do more listening than talking.*

– Bernard M. Baruch
American Financier and Presidential Advisor

Chapter Five

You Don't Ask, You Don't Get: How To Talk Your Way To The Top

You're short on ears and long on mouth.
— John Wayne

Winners are not shy. You must ask for what you want in life. People cannot read your mind. According to research conducted by Lewis Schiff, executive director of Inc. Business Owners Council, only one in four people ever asks for more money when hired for their first job despite the willingness of nine out of ten employers to pay more if, but only if, the employee asks.[1]

Healthcare data king Greg Beier, known for retooling data collection while President of Novant Health, grew up in a family of ten children, attended school in Kansas, graduated with distinction as valedictorian and at the top of his class in college. He needed financial aid to attend an elite graduate school. His hard-working father was too proud to ask for money and would not fill out financial aid applications. Greg needed an academic scholarship. He applied to Northwestern University and to the University of Chicago. Each awarded him a full scholarship. Both schools were roughly the same cost but the financial package at Chicago was greater. Greg told the dean at Northwestern the financial package Chicago offered and that it would affect his decision. The dean refigured the financial package and beat the Chicago academic award. Greg chose Northwestern.

Greg remembers his first day of class, "I wore jeans to class just as I had back in Kansas. My classmates wore neckties and I wondered how I would fit in."

When it was time for grad school elections, some students who had gotten to know the relaxed and friendly Midwesterner asked Greg to run for president. Greg remembers:

> Two students running against me circulated fliers listing their impressive credentials. I knew I had to do something different to win so I thought about what I could offer that was different and would enhance the rigorous Northwestern MBA experience where students are competitive and highly focused on success. I wanted to add levity to the program because I believe that there is more to education than academics. I omitted my credentials and devised a different strategy without focusing on myself but on what I would do as president to benefit my classmates. I proposed Friday afternoon beer blasts on the lakefront, two semester dances, and free donuts in the lounge every day to foster fellowship.[2]

Greg won, but the reality of winning meant following up on his campaign promises — a challenge as the current Northwestern grad school activities budget fell short of the money Greg needed. He appealed to the dean using a mock business plan explaining the benefits of an increased activities budget to the dean who was in the business of creating generous alumni. Greg posed that as a result of an enriched student experience, future alumni would more generously participate with financial gifts and recruitment help.

"I was so surprised when the dean doubled the student activities budget that I wondered if I should have asked for more money! I asked the dean why he doubled the budget. The dean said, 'The budget is the same it has always been. It has never increased because no one has ever asked. I increased the budget because you asked.'"[3]

Asking for what Greg wanted made the difference. Asking specifically for what you want will make the difference for you. Ask for what you want. BE SPECIFIC.

*When negotiating,
if you don't get it in writing you probably won't get it.*

Morgan Freeman narrates a music video for American country music artist Steve Azar's song "Waitin' on Joe" because according to Freeman, "This song matters."

> I don't know about anywhere else but I "reckon right here in the Delta a man waits about seventy percent of his time just waitin'. Waitin' on somebody. Waitin' on something ... Chasin' that elusive dream ... most of us will keep waitin' here until our time here is over ... sometimes I wonder if what we're really waitin' on is ourselves. Maybe there is a lot of Joe deep down inside of each and every one of us. We focus so much on what we're waitin' for that we miss or forget to appreciate what we got ... or we could wonder if we are just wastin' our lives 'Waitin on Joe.'[4]

Many of us make the mistake of waiting until everything is perfect so we won't make a mistake. That time is not coming. When I met songwriter Azar in a Myrtle Beach bar and asked him about what made the difference in his success he said, "The mistakes I've made. How I overcame them, what I learned from them. How I wrote about them and got better from all the lessons in my life. Mistakes are important as long as they are not too big, you can overcome any of them."[5]

Azar says the following about asking actor Morgan Freeman to narrate "Waitin' on Joe:"

> It was one of those things where if you ask, the worst thing they can say is 'no.' You never know. He had moved back to Mississippi. My mom grew up on Highway 61 in a grocery store, on top of it. And my cousin's got this famous barbeque place called Abe's Bar-B-Q that Paul Simon and Elvis Costello and Robert Plant, you name 'em, they've been there. My cousin's barbeque place sits right down the street from where my mom grew up on Highway 61 and the 49 split. When people talk about the crossroads and all that, well, it's crossroads in there. It's crossroads in a lot of places in a lot of people's minds, in the history and the lure of the Delta. But with that said, he (Morgan) had moved back to a town that was back in Charleston, Mississippi, that was just down the street. And we just called. Morgan heard the song and he goes, 'You know what? This song matters. I'll not only do the narrative, I'll be in the video.' And it was just a wonderful gift. I was on the same label that Shania was, and they had spent gobs of money on her video at the time, and we had spent pennies on the dollar compared to that, and we had Morgan in it. He didn't even charge me anything.[6]

Don't wait on Joe. Ask. Persevere. Many of Azar's songs reflect his perseverance trying to make it in the music industry. If you're looking for a song to inspire you, listen to his song, "The Underdog."

I saw Michael Jordan teach this critical lesson to a young boy who was part of the gallery watching Jordan play golf at Shadow Creek Golf Course in Las Vegas. The boy wanted

Jordan's autograph and extended a piece of paper and a pen to Jordan when he walked past him on the way to his Carolina Tar Heel blue golf cart with his jersey No. 23 monogrammed on the seats. Jordan stopped, smiled, and looked the boy in his eyes and asked, "What do you want?" The boy stared up at Jordan not saying a word as he continued to extend pen and paper to Jordan. Jordan repeated, "What do you want?" The boy continued to stare and to hold the pen and paper towards Jordan. Jordan spoke to the boy as he walked away, "You don't ask. You don't get. You won't get anything in life if you don't ask."[7]

When you need assistance, ask this way:
"I've got a problem.
I wonder if you would be kind enough to help me?"

Clearly identify the person you want to help you and let the person know he is the one you need. This is important for every request and in a large setting where there are many people, it can literally save your life. Fascinating research discussed in Robert Cialdini's book, *Influence: The Psychology of Persuasion,* reveals why people often do not respond to the needs of others in their presence even when the need for help seems obvious. Not only do they not know what or when help is needed, they also do not know if they should be the person to help. Cialdini's advice if you have an emergency and are in a large crowd "... isolate one individual from the crowd: Stare, speak, and point directly at that person and no one else: "You, sir, in the blue jacket, I need help. Call an ambulance."[8]

Many people, especially women and minorities, are socially conditioned not to ask for anything. They are taught behaviors that will hold them back while giving an advantage to others. They are encouraged to be accommodating, compliant, shy, demure, not to "rock the boat," or hurt anyone's feelings, and to avoid leading conversations and asking questions, as well as to avoid saying or asking anyone for anything that might put another person in an awkward position. In addition to undermining your self-confidence, this behavior will guarantee you submissive roles both personally and professionally. It primarily benefits those seeking to dominate or take advantage of you by minimizing competition. Taking your place on the A-List requires confidence and courage to ask for what you want, need, and deserve. It also requires the willingness to take some heat from those who want you to "know your place." You have to speak and ask for what you want.

In addition, personality types that have a need to connect with others also tend not to ask for what they want. Make a deliberate effort to reprogram your attitude to begin asking for what you want, need, and deserve if you're reluctant.

More often than not you'll have to ask for what you want more than once. Don't be shy. On average, people have to hear a message seven times before they remember.[9]

And finally, not everyone is like the young boy who knew what he wanted but didn't ask. Many people don't know what they want or need. You can learn what people need if you ask them, listen to them, and then if your product, service, or idea will help them you are on your way to a win-win outcome. Listening is as important as asking.

I heard a story at a medical conference about a man named Buford who went to a doctor's office. The receptionist asked what he had and Buford replied, "shingles." The receptionist wrote down his name, address, health insurance number, and told him to have a seat.

Fifteen minutes later a nurse's aid came out and asked Buford what he had. Buford said, "shingles." So she wrote down his height, weight, and complete medical history and told Buford to wait in the examining room.

A half hour later a nurse came in and asked Buford what

he had. Buford said, "shingles." So she gave Buford a blood test, a blood pressure test, and an electrocardiogram and then she told Buford to take off all of his clothes and wait for the doctor. An hour later the doctor came in and asked Buford what he had. Buford said, "shingles." The doctor looked at him and asked, "Where?" Buford said, "Outside on the truck. Where do you want them?"

This medical joke is a good reminder to listen to your customers, your neighbors, or the people you'd like to date. They will tell you what they want. Many people are passive listeners. Passive listeners hear the words but they do not do anything to interpret the message using verbal and nonverbal clues like the ones discussed earlier in this book.

It's important to clarify what you hear by asking good questions. Effective questions are open-ended, meaning they cannot be answered with only yes or no. The answer to an open-ended question requires an explanation.

Probing questions will also help you clarify what you have heard and are used for follow-up and for eliciting details. The following useful phrases will help you when you need to probe for additional information.

- "Tell me more ..."
- "Explain why ..."
- "Say more about ..."

Actively listening to others is a skill that involves mental engagement. It requires interpreting the message, evaluating the message and responding to the message. Active listeners attend to the message by focusing on the speaker and controlling distractions. Do the following to facilitate active listening:

- Face the person.
- Adopt open posture.
- Lean towards the person.
- Give full attention.

- Listen using your senses.
- Listen to words and tone.
- Observe body language.
- Use encouraging words and gestures.
- Avoid interrupting.
- Do not immediately form judgments and responses.
- Strive for two-way communication.

Everyone has something to sell (an idea, a product, a service, a talent) and everyone has something he wants to buy. Listen so you will know and understand what it is people need so if your product, service, or idea is a fit, you can match the needs of others to what you have to sell. If you ask good questions and listen to your communication partners, you will learn what it is that you may have that can meet their needs. Once you know what others want, you must tell them how what you offer meets their needs.

Clarify what your communication partner tells you to ensure mutual understanding. Ask for feedback if you are not clear about what the person tells you. In addition, make sure your communication partner understands the value of the product, service or idea that you offer. Do this by asking for feedback to ensure understanding. The following phrases will help you:

- "Do you have any questions/thoughts/suggestions?"
- "If I understand you correctly ..."
- "What I think you are referring to ..."
- "This is what I understand you are telling me ..."
- "So you are saying that ..."
- "This is what I understand you are telling me ..."

People know what they want. Don't waste your time or theirs trying to sell them what they do not want. I show to sales groups a fun video clip from a BBC TV program, *Rutland*

Weekend Television, to illustrate how people will tell you what they want and will do what they want regardless of what you say. In the sketch, host Eric Idle introduces The Beatles' George Harrison and announces to the audience that Harrison is on the show to sing "My Sweet Lord."

Harrison walks onto the set dressed as a peg-legged pirate. Using the voice of a pirate, Harrison tells Idle that he has not come to the show to sing but to act in a pirate sketch. Idle does not listen to Harrison and repeats his announcement to the audience that Harrison will sing "My Sweet Lord." The music intro begins, but when it is time for the lyrics to be sung, Harrison acts like a pirate and sings the "Pirate Song" — doing exactly what he told Idle he would do.[10]

People will tell you what they want. Listen to them. They will get what they want and it might as well be from you!

Most of us believe that when we engage in opportunities to interact with others that we are listening, when often we are doing something that is causing interference with the listening process. Listening is a skill that can be learned and like any skill it must be practiced. Active listening is important if you want to get what you want.

Active listening requires mental involvement with the person who is talking. Make a mental outline of the important points and think of questions or challenges to the points. Active listening involves participation on the part of the listener. Active listening is not the same in every situation.

In any given day we are faced with many different listening situations when we seek what we want. It is often challenging to listen because so much is going on around us. Knowing and being aware of four basic types of listening will help you in various situations: listening for information, listening critically, listening reflectively, and listening for enjoyment.

Listening for information requires identifying the main idea, identifying supporting material, forming a mental outline, predicting what will come next, relating points to your experience, looking for similarities, questioning, and paraphrasing. We not only listen to information in large formal settings, but also in interpersonal and small group settings. In both settings, the forms of active listening that apply are relating points to your experiences, looking for similarities, questioning and paraphrasing.

Critical listening includes determining the speaker's motives, challenging and questioning ideas, distinguishing fact from fiction, recognizing our own biases, and assessing the message. Critical listening also requires all of the steps of listening for information. In critical listening, we listen for the motives of the speaker and mentally challenge the speaker's ideas and information. In reality all communication should be listened to critically.

Critically listening for "opportunity words" will help you win when a speaker using them believes he is definitively telling you "no" without realizing that his word choice provides you with an opportunity to gain information you can use to get to yes. The opportunity words to listen for are "decided" and ones ending in "ly." Let's look first at the hidden opportunities offered by these two words; then how using a third word, "because," will help you leverage information you can realize from the "opportunity words" so you can win.

The first opportunity word is "decided." When a person tells you he or his company has "decided" something that is not in your favor, seize the opportunity the word "decided" offers to change the decision. "Decided" means the decision has not been implemented so there remains opportunity to change the decision. Further, "decided" means that an option was considered before making the as yet unexecuted decision.

The flexibility of "decided" is that the speaker or his company could have "decided" something else — perhaps what would make possible the decision you need to win. The word "decided" invites you to ask a follow-up question so you can learn the alternative option. Perhaps you have information you can share that the person or his company did not know to consider. Knowledge of what you can share beyond what was originally used to make a decision can make the difference in changing a decision before it is executed. Remember, if you really want to win, never settle for a current decision that is not in your favor without learning the other options the decision-maker considered, because what the person or company initially "decided" has not been acted upon, thus providing you with a chance to offer unconsidered information to affect the change you need to win. Use the opportunity "decided" provides to learn the option; then leverage the more favorable option to win by giving the reason(s) beneficial to the person or the company that decision-makers may not have considered.

The second "opportunity word" speakers may inadvertently use to tell you "no" will also help you change what does not work in your favor to what will — a word ending in "ly." Examples of the "ly" word are *typically, basically, normally, usually, generally, etc.* The opportunity these words offer is the signal that there are exceptions to what is *typically, basically, normally, usually, generally, etc.* done. For example, the speaker may say to you, "Usually we don't do/give/have/offer/provide xyz." "Ly" words clearly indicate that there are and have been exceptions in the past. You may merit the exception, so be sure to ask about the exceptions/options; then leverage your reasons for the exception as it pertains to you so you can win what you want. Here's how.

Use one of the most the powerful persuasive words in the English language — "because." "Because" is powerful because the words that follow reveal the benefits of the desired change. To do this say, "Because xyz" and follow with the reasons choosing the alternative option will benefit the person and/or his company.

To win, you must critically listen, ask questions, and take action to win even when your actions seem pushy. You might not win every time, but one thing is sure just like my mama said, "The meek might inherit the earth, but it is not going to be in your lifetime." And like Michael Jordan said, "You don't ask. You don't get."

Reflective listening is for the purpose of hearing the speaker's message and his feelings so you can communicate back to him that you have heard him and realize his emotional feelings. In this type of listening it is not listening for main points or criticizing ideas that are important, it is listening for feelings or what is called empathic listening. It usually occurs in interpersonal communication when counseling others. To demonstrate reflective listening use phrases such as:

- "You sound really ..."
- "You feel ... is that so?"
- "What I think you ...?"

Listening for enjoyment is a type of listening that uses many techniques taken from the other areas of listening. With this genre of listening one will most likely find it useful to enjoy more complicated information. However, listening for enjoyment can require skills as complex as those needed in other listening situations — the only difference is that it is fun!

Do The Following To Master The Art Of Listening.

- Make predictions about the given message.

- Assess what you've heard. Pay attention to the message and tune out the unwanted message.
- Give meaning to the message by selecting and organizing the material that you have heard.
- Select what you need to remember.
- Apply "The Rule of the Second." Pause a full second before you respond to a person. This signals that you have listened. If you speak immediately after your communication partner speaks, you signal that you have been waiting for the person to stop so you could speak what you think is more important — your words, thoughts, opinions, and ideas.
- Look at the person while he is talking. Do not fidget or laugh.
- Think about the meaning of what the person is telling you and try to understand what he is feeling from his point of view.
- Let the person finish what he has to tell you before you talk. Some people mistakenly finish a sentence for another person thinking that doing so demonstrates understanding. What this really does is annoyingly snatch the thought and control of the conversation from the speaker.
- Repeat back to your communication partner what he has told you in your own words to let the person know that his feelings have been heard. It is appropriate to ask questions related to what he has told you if you do not understand.
- Listen for what's important to the speaker (children, vacation, interests, etc.) and reflect back later in conversation.
- Avoid judging or criticizing or telling your communication partner what to do.

Even the technology that promises to unite us, divides us. Each of us is now electronically connected to the globe, and yet we feel utterly alone.

– Dan Brown
Author of *Angels and Demons*

Chapter Six

Understand One Word: How To Use Technology For Peak Performance

*Technology is a queer thing.
It brings you great gifts with one hand,
and stabs you in the back with the other.*

— C.P. Snow
English Novelist, Physical Chemist, and Government Administrator

The lead medical director for a global pharmaceutical research company with offices in 42 countries contacted me about a big problem. Production was lagging. A scientist in Brazil did not want to collaborate with a team member in Germany. A team member in England did not want to work with a colleague in India. Everyone on the eighteen-member team was hostile to a scientist in Texas. Team members had never met face-to-face. Language was not the problem. Everyone spoke English. Technology made collaboration possible. All members knew how to use it. However, the way technology was used caused resentment among team members that impeded timely success. The problem was fixed with actions you'll learn in this chapter that make the difference.

Technology and long distance communication tools play a vital role in 21st century success. These tools are used at every level of business from research, development, production, and sales to delivery. Businesses are so dependent on technology that if it were taken away business operations would grind to a halt. However, no matter how sophisticated the technology used to facilitate a decision or sale, buyers are social creatures who rely on relationships with people they know to help them find solutions to problems and to help them with a variety of decisions.

Long distance communication tools and technology support virtually every business and career in the modern world by providing a vast repertoire of opportunities to help us know people. The beauty of these long distance tools is that when used effectively we can meaningfully connect with large numbers of prospects and customers to help them solve their problems. Those people in turn help us reach our goals. Knowing how to effectively use tools from the most basic to the most complex is vital if you are to win. People buy from people — and when all things are equal, they buy from people they feel a connection with, often dismissing other factors like costs and quality.

Technology is like a piano.
You won't get any music from it unless you play it.

– Jane Hight
Author of *Navigating the Lipstick Jungle*

Sam Walton had one word for the tool that made the difference for his booming business, "damncomputer." He didn't like it, but he understood its power. He knew enough about the "damncomputer" to know it could help keep costs down and profits up by keeping a tight control on inventory, making it possible to order just the right items at just the right time. A Walmart store is located within 10 miles of 90 percent of the people living in the United States but according to Walton that is not the reason for its juggernaut success. "People think we got big by putting big stores in small towns. Really, we got big by replacing inventory with information."[1]

Walmart was the first business to use electronic scanners at cash registers linked to a central inventory-control computer. Walmart's computer database is one of the largest in the world, just slightly behind the Pentagon's in capacity. Like Walton, you don't have to be an expert at every type of technology but you do have to understand and know enough technology to make the difference in success.

Your messages will fall flat if you simply bang them out on a keypad or bark facts into a transmitter without being sensitive to the humans receiving your messages. Communication technology is meant to enhance, not replace relationships. To be sure you use it to facilitate your goals, the most important consideration is context. The United States, Canada, and northern European nations are considered low-context cultures, meaning that the verbal content of a message is more important than the way it is delivered. Video conferencing and emailing, previously accepted as efficient ways to connect in predominantly low-context cultures as a substitute for face-to-face interaction, is now accepted throughout the world in high-context cultures due to the global Coronavirus pandemic.

High-context cultures, including Asia and the Middle East, traditionally have relied more heavily on the setting, including nonverbal cues, to convey meaning beyond the literal words of a message. These cultures have highly ritualized business transactions that include physical exchange (handshake or bow) and nonverbal cues (facial expressions, gestures), immediate feedback, and tone of voice. The manner of communication matters more than the words in high-context cultures where value is placed on in-person interaction. To be successful you must understand your communication partner and flex to his style. If you are not sure how your communication partner prefers to exchange information, ask for a face-to face meeting or at least a videoconference to agree on a way to use technology to communicate.

Telephones

The telephone continues to be the most dominant global communication tool for selling, buying, and making lasting impressions. It is also the dominant source of frustration. Callers who feel disrespected tell on average seven to nine people when they have a poor telephone experience.[2]

Making connections over the telephone is a lot like making connections with people face-to-face. Do the same homework and know as much about your telephone conversation partner before you talk on the phone as you would if you were going to meet in person at a networking event. Your verbal impression on the telephone conveys 87% of your education, background, ability, and personality in as little as sixty seconds.[3] Be enthusiastic, confident, and attentive. Small talk is huge talk over the phone. It sets the tone for communication at a distance.

Use the same body language you do speaking over the telephone as you do in person. People can "hear" your smile when you begin with a pleasant greeting. People can also hear when you are eating food, drinking a drink, chewing gum, and multi-tasking on the computer. Be polite and professional as you stay focused on the person at the other end of a call.

Say hello and immediately give your first and last names to the person you call. Never say, "Guess who this is?" Ask the person you call if it is a good time to talk if your call will last longer than a few minutes. This shows your respect of his time. Tell the person how much of his time you need so he can schedule a time to talk to you if you are going to need more than three to five minutes during your impromptu call. If you tell the person that your call will take five minutes, then do not talk longer than five minutes or you will jeopardize trust. If the person you call says that he only has a specified amount of time, respect his time and limit the length of your call. Time is more precious than money because we can always get more money, but we cannot get more time. Do not rob people of their time or force them to give you more time than you said you would take from them or they have to give you.

Prepare an agenda and speak from notes. That way you won't waste time — yours or theirs — and you'll appear smart and efficient. Identify your purpose early in the conversation. Anticipate questions and possible objections to avoid additional calls.

Asking for feedback is important because you cannot see the face of your communication partner to make sure that what you are saying is understood. Elicit feedback by asking, "Do you have any questions/thoughts/suggestions?" Clarify what you hear by saying, "If I understand you correctly ..." "So you are saying that ..." "This is what I understand you are telling me ..."

Take care not to sound abrupt by using phrases like "Hang on." "Hold on." "Who's calling?" "Speak up!"

Schedule a follow-up conversation and include a time and deadlines. You can do this by saying, "I'll get back to you on ..." Then follow through and do what you said you would do when you said you would do it.

If you need something from the other person, be sure to say "please" as in "Would you please ...?"

Demonstrate what you have the power to do when someone asks you to do something. Avoid saying that it is not your job and that you cannot help. Better choices are saying, "While I'm not able to ..." "I will speak to someone about your concern." "I'll find out ..."

The way you close a call creates a lasting impression. State the action you will take on the business discussed. For example, "Here is how I can help . . ." "Here is what needs to be done ..."

When you end the call say, "Thank you" and speak in the past tense. For example say, "Thank you, I'm glad we chatted." End with a professional, "Good-bye," not "Bye-bye," "See ya," or "So long."

Answer incoming phone calls by the third ring. Greet the caller in a friendly manner. Protect your time by politely saying at the beginning of the call, "I only have five minutes." Schedule return calls for longer conversations.

Show respect for others who are giving you their time face-to-face by not answering incoming calls when they are in your presence. If you must answer an incoming call, excuse yourself to answer the call and make your conversation brief. Not doing this sends the message that the caller's time is more important to you than the time of the person with whom you are standing face-to-face.

Your answering machine should have a professional greeting on it that is brief and polite. Be current if your message includes a holiday or an auto responder.

When you leave a voice mail message, say your first and last names. Say your name slowly at the beginning of your message. Spell your name if it is somewhat complicated. Providing your telephone number early in your message saves the listener from having to listen repeatedly to your entire message if he needs to listen for your number a second time. Your message should be brief, not exceeding two minutes. Say please and thank you as you clearly state what you need from the person. Let the listener know the best time to return your call to avoid telephone tag. Don't leave a teaser message like, "Call me. I have something important to tell you."

Cell Phones

Your phone should have a professional ring. Turn the ringer off or change to vibrate mode when you carry your phone in public. Using cell phones in public is rude. Excuse yourself from a group if you must talk on a cell phone. The ringing of cell phones and subsequent conversations in restaurants, theatres, etc., is annoying and unprofessional. You send the message that the person on the phone is more important than the people spending time in your presence. The people standing in front of you may tell you they do not mind that you ignore them while you talk on the phone or text, but make no mistake, you are being rude and insulting by devaluing their presence and their time. Exceptions are for extraordinary situations such as when a person is on a kidney transplant list or leaves children with a baby sitter. Even then, monitor calls with caller ID and let voicemail record messages. Return non-emergency calls later and in private.

Instant Messaging/Texting

Instant messaging/texting is wonderful because ... well, it's instant. Be brief. It's not for serious, emotional, or confrontational issues. Be courteous when you use it. Be aware that you will likely offend those in your presence if you text on your phone in public places and in meetings. Be careful not to appear to place technology ahead of those you are with face-to-face.

When you do text or instant message, check the availability of those you contact. Use "busy" and "away" message features to avoid misunderstandings and to let people know that you are not ignoring them. Use spell and grammar check regardless of the mode used. Emoticons appear unprofessional and rushed so be careful using them.

As a courtesy to your instant messaging/texting partner, summarize attachments and send large quantities of information as attachments instead of copying/pasting into the message. Courtesy remains important when you text. Use PLS/THX. Be professional at all times.

IM/Texting shorthand will help keep your messages brief. The following are a few of the most common:

- BFN (bye for now)
- CID (consider it done)
- CU (see you)
- FYI (for your information)
- IMO (in my opinion)
- IOW (in other words)
- L8R (later)
- NRB (need reply by date)
- NRN (no response necessary)
- PLS (please)
- THX (thanks)
- TIA (thanks in advance)
- TY (thank you)
- TBA (to be announced)
- YW (you're welcome)

X Formerly Twitter

The biggest name in skateboarding, legendary Tony Hawk known as "The Birdman" for his high-flying maneuvers, gives an example of how you can mobilize the masses by touching only a few keyboard characters on your phone or computer. Hawk unleashed an amazing display of social media savvy with a #hawkhunt in my hometown, Wilmington, NC. He did so with a tweet, now referred to as an 'X,' containing 140 characters.

My cell phone rang one hot summer day. It was my daughter, Win, calling me from Winter Park, Florida.

"Mom, what are you doing?"

"I'm in my car driving home from the beach."

"Go to the airport right now!"

"Why?

"Tony Hawk is in Wilmington and tweeted that he has hidden a signed skateboard somewhere in town. He is having a "Hawkhunt," like a scavenger hunt. He is tweeting clues and I am figuring them out. I want you to go find it."

"Huh? A tomahawk? Why do I want a tomahawk?"

"Aggghhh ... Mom, really? Tony Hawk is the most famous skateboarder of all time. Just go! Probably not that many people in Wilmington who follow him on twitter are reading his tweets this instant. I will figure out the clues and you can find his skateboard for me."

"Oh. Hmmm. Really? I'm wearing my swimsuit and cover up. I'm not exactly dressed to be out in public."

"Please Mom. Do it."

"Okay. Because I love you. I'll do it."

I drove to the airport parking lot. The parking lot at my quiet, small-town airport that is never crowded was for the first time ever jammed with cars circling the parking lot. I telephoned Win.

"The parking lot is full. It's so crowded that it's crazy for me to even try to drive into the lot."

"I've figured out his clue. Mom, get out of you car! Run to the Hertz lot! Look in the bushes behind space #37."

"The things mothers do." I laughed, pulled the car over, and semi-jogged in my flip-flops to the Hertz lot. I don't mind telling you that I felt silly going into the bushes wearing my swimsuit and cover up, bending down and spreading apart the bushes. I felt like an oversized child at an Easter egg hunt.

"I found it!" I shouted to the circling cars as I held up the board to many disappointed faces. It was like I'd found the golden egg!

Hawk's creative use of only 140 characters created excitement not only with folks in my small hometown, where we mistakenly thought few were following Hawk, but with his

3.66 million followers from all over the world. Effective use of X can make the winning difference.

X is for the purpose of answering, "What are you doing or thinking?" X is free and much faster than logging into a website content management system to transmit information to a large audience. Use it to instantly inform millions of people about news happening in real time including public safety and business developments and to solicit feedback.

X messages, formerly called tweets, are currently expanded to 280 characters. DM (Direct Message) character limit is 10,000 characters to enhance use that allows users to message each other more freely. It's a quick way to connect with people and the results for you can be amazing as Tony Hawk demonstrated.

Think of X as a micro-blog to update your network. The great thing about Xing is that it humanizes you to a very large group. If you're not Xing, you should! According to a recent NM Incite statistic, 71 percent of people who experience a quick and effective response on social media are likely to recommend that company to others.[4]

You can use X to network, brand, and market to win the game, the gig, or the job. However, use X to moderately promote or you will lose followers. The exception is when you set up an X account named after a product or service for the sole purpose of promoting. In that case, your followers have a different set of expectations.

X Power Points

- Answer direct questions.
- Share knowledge/Give value.
- Avoid excessive linking.
- Re-X good tips and give credit to others.
- Be up-to-date on things.

- Respect others' privacy.
- Don't ask for re-Xs unless broadcasting a question.
- Avoid aggressive following to prevent X suspension.
- Add a small number of interesting people to build your network.
- Avoid ghost Xing.

Email

Email often causes problems in the workplace because people sloppily dash off words that poorly convey their meaning and thus cause problems. To avoid this, think of email communication like face-to-face communication.

Effective use of email requires that you attend to six elements:

1. *The "To" field.* Check and double check the address you select just like you would take care to call a person by the correct name when you are face-to-face.
2. *The "From" field.* Use your full name in proper caps to clearly identify you as the sender.
3. *The "Subject" line.* Avoid using the word "hi" and spam words in your subject line. Change the subject line for your replies. Subject lines that clearly indicate the content of your message between 1–20 characters in length have the highest average open rate (18.5%).[5] Think of your subject line as a news line in the newspaper that attracts you to read an article.

An example of a weak subject line is a one word subject such as *Meeting*. A stronger subject line for an email about a meeting might be:

| Urgent meeting May 20 @ 2 pm in Computer Center! |

A technique for ease and speed is to simply use the subject line for the entire message. Do so by placing either your initials or the letters EOM (end of message) at the end of your message. Here's a sample of this technique:

| Mon doesn't work. How's Wed? — JHM |
| Wed is NG. How's Th? — EOM |
| Th is fine. — JHM |
| See you Th @ 3:15 — EOM |

4. *The "Greeting"* is like a personal handshake. Don't omit it. Begin with "Hello" or "Dear."
5. *The "Body"* of your email should have correct grammar. Just because it is instant communication does not mean that it can be sloppy. Using positive phrases in your messages such as "Hope all is well," "Please," "May I," "Great job," "Good thinking," "Congratulations," create good feelings.
   - Respect space. Use plenty of white space.
   - When you ask for something in an email don't forget to say, "I appreciate your help," or "Thank you in advance."
   - Be clear and be sure to give a concrete request/task/time deadline when you ask someone to do something via email.
   - Send requests to only one person to avoid diluting responsibility.
   - If you really want somebody to do something, copy (CC) someone powerful.
   - Seek feedback by directly asking for it, as in "Let me know what you're thinking." Verify the recipient's understanding of your message and confirm important time lines.

Nagging with a repeat email request is okay because if someone has not responded to your email request within 48 hours they probably aren't going to respond. This also applies to telephone message requests.

Email often causes problems because we cannot hear vocal inflection, see facial expressions, or read body language. You can however set the tone with punctuation.

The dash (—) can heighten what's enclosed as if you're raising your voice. For example, The Global Business Company — winner of the service award — just introduced its new product line.

Parentheses ( ) can play down what's enclosed as if you're lowering your voice. For example, The Global Business Company (winner of the service award) just introduced its new product line.

Commas (,) can neutralize what's enclosed. For example, The Global Company, winner of the service award, just introduced its new product line.

Just as you use gestures in face-to-face communication, you can use **bold**, <u>underscore,</u> and *italic* features to gesture in your email.

Keep your correspondence reader focused. Avoid limp language and jargon. Say what you mean. If you forward an email, tell the recipient why you are forwarding and what is expected. People get annoyed with mail that clogs their inbox and seems forwarded for no apparent reason.

6. *The "Closing"* of your email is like a handshake that you extend at the end of a face-to-face communication. Conclude with "Best regards," "Warm regards," "Sincerely." And finally, write your first and last names.

You can use your signature as powerful passive promotion of your business but keep the basic info to 70 characters — 4 to 6 lines max. You don't need to include everything. Use caps correctly and avoid colors and graphics.

Ten E-Mail Commandments

1. Avoid hasty, error-filled messages.
2. Reply promptly or use a current autoresponder. It makes people feel important.
3. Be concise. Avoid lengthy messages. Do not include earlier messages that require people to scroll past to get to your new message. Summarize!
4. Avoid personal messages not relevant to business, i.e. jokes, inappropriate material.
5. Don't use email to transmit sensitive material or relay bad news.
6. Save email that is business related or personally significant. A record of communication can be valuable.
7. Avoid spamming/mass-emailing commercial material and chain letters.
8. Be careful forwarding e-mails and pressing "reply to all."
9. Avoid flaming and shouting (all caps).
10. Avoid sending attached files to people who may not have the necessary software to decode or whose inbox may have a small size limit.

Facebook

"Facebook. Ruining marriages, friendships, and families since 2004." Be careful what you post on Facebook. Employers frequently look at employees' public profiles to determine the suitability of job candidates as well as to learn information about current employees. Post public photos that reflect you as a professional. Be careful not to offer too much information on your Facebook page. Carefully friend and de-friend people. Use the appropriate privacy setting. Create a limited profile. Keep a friendly tone by avoiding ALL CAPS and sarcasm.

LinkedIn

LinkedIn is a business-oriented social networking site predominantly used for professional networking. It is the largest professional network with more than 822 million registered global users in more than 200 countries and territories. Use it to maintain a list of contact details of people with whom you have a professional connection.

LinkedIn can help you in a number of ways. First, it can help you connect with people you know and to people your connections know. You can gain an introduction to others through a mutual contact. LinkedIn is a terrific tool demonstrating the power of weak connections. Very few people who get jobs actually know the person who hires them. People most likely get jobs because somebody recommended them. The person recommending is not necessarily the best friend with the person who hires, but there is a connection. LinkedIn helps you identify connections who can link you to others.

You can use LinkedIn to find jobs, people, and business opportunities. You can review the profile of potential employers and determine which of your contacts can introduce you to a potential employer or connection you want to meet. Posted photos on LinkedIn help to identify you and help you identify others.

Use LinkedIn to increase your visibility. People do business with people they know. Adding connections on LinkedIn increases the chance that people searching for a person with your skill set will find and choose you. According to LinkedIn research, people with more than twenty connections on LinkedIn are thirty-four times more likely to be approached with a job opportunity than people with less than five.[6]

Include a link to your LinkedIn profile as part of your email signature. This is a tasteful and appropriate way to let people see your credentials.

Use LinkedIn to prepare for conversation. Read about those you'll meet at an event, interview with for a job, or approach to sell a product, service, or idea.

Written Correspondence

When products and services are equal, people choose to do business with people who treat them with courtesy and respect. In business, it's not just who you know, but who you thank. An important way to strengthen your business relationships is by showing appreciation to everyone who is valuable to you. Everyone likes to feel appreciated. Thank people you do business with and everyone who is helpful to you.

There are no "little people." Thanking support personnel is important. They make you look good so don't neglect them. Most employees do not mention their pay or other perks when asked what motivates them to perform at their highest level. What they do mention is that they are more willing to work hard when they know they are appreciated. Showing appreciation to your staff for their efforts improves their performance which in turn is good for your business. Don't forget to show appreciation to the maintenance crew either — they make your business look good. No one can read your mind. You must take action to let people know the value of their efforts to you. Silent gratitude is useless.

A powerful way you can be polite is to write a handwritten thank you note to the people who help you. The sooner you write it the stronger its impact — aim for within two business days after a courtesy is extended to you.

Silent gratitude isn't very much to anyone.
– Gertrude Stein
American Novelist, Poet, Playwright, and Art Collector

Black ink is most professional, followed by dark blue ink. Use your own personal paper — not company letterhead. Company stationery is for correspondence that reflects company policy. Never use it for personal correspondence. Men traditionally use correspondence cards or letter sheets to write personal notes. Traditional paper choices for women include correspondence cards, letter sheets, and fold-over notes often referred to as informal notes. (Traditional etiquette cautions men not to use informal fold-over note paper because it is a traditional paper used by women). Avoid cute floral paper when thanking someone for anything connected to business. Choose quality to reflect the quality image you intend.

I once had a twenty-eight-year-old client who lost his job as a banker in New York City. His mother asked me if I would do a one-on-one coaching session with him to prepare him for upcoming job interviews. During our coaching session, I discussed the importance of a handwritten note to thank people who would be interviewing him. He scoffed at my advice and adamantly refuted the idea saying, "No one in New York writes handwritten thank you notes. They email." I listened and then offered that perhaps because no one else seemed to be writing handwritten notes in New York that he might want to consider writing a note to differentiate himself from his competition.

About three weeks later, a colleague from Boston conducted a business dining tutorial in New York for the wealth management division of a global financial services firm. When she arrived at the training site, the person who hired her led her into the room where the training would occur. He pointed to personalized boxes of William Arthur stationery positioned at the place setting of each banker who would attend the seminar. He said, "I know we didn't discuss thank you notes in the training you agreed to provide, but would you please explain to our bankers the importance of handwritten notes to our customers?"

The handwritten thank you note may be rare, but it is very much alive in New York among people who wield power and win. Say thank you and write notes. You won't be totally alone, but you will stand out.

A simple "thank you" doesn't require much effort but the payoff of your tiny investment is that you will favorably stand apart from the rest of the pack. People choose to do business with people they favor when services and products are equal.

Saying thank you is expected for invitations that cross over from business to social occasions such as family entertainments, cocktail and dinner parties including a spouse or significant other, office parties, or events at which you are a guest. A verbal thank you to the host is sufficient when you leave events such as an office party at a restaurant where you share a meal in the ordinary course of business. Some business people opt to reiterate their thanks for these routine business invitations in their next business correspondence instead of writing a separate thank you note.

Unexpected thank you notes mean a lot. Consider thanking people for their business and/or for what they have done for you throughout the year at nontraditional times like Thanksgiving instead of Christmas. Personally sign all correspondence including printed greeting cards with an appropriate closing that will not be misinterpreted. "Sincerely," "Yours truly," "Best regards," or "Warm regards" are safe choices. Omit any honorific due you, but do sign both your first and last names. For greater impact, add a short handwritten note of thanks.

The Beatles sent thank you notes to people who made a big difference in their careers like DJs who played their music. The Beatles also sent thank you notes to people who were simply kind to them. A fun example of one of the notes they sent was to the owner of a shop called Magee's House of Nuts in the Los Angeles' Farmers Market who gave them peanut butter. "Thank you for the Peanut Butter. It was fab!" The personally signed note by all four of The Beatles became a Magee's treasure and testament to their goodwill.[7]

Thank people when they offer kind words about you or your business. Let them know you appreciate the positive feedback. They will also appreciate it when you take the time to recognize their accomplishments or good work.

Thank people for their support and advice. Take this opportunity to let the person know about your areas of expertise and willingness to be available should they need you.

The well-written thank you note will mark you as a polished professional and will set you apart as one with savoir-faire. The best notes are personal, specific, brief, and prompt. Differentiate your note from most notes that begin with the same two words "thank you" and end with "thank you again." Make the note about the person, not about yourself. For example, an average business note that gets average results might be written in the following way.

Dear Greg,

Thank you for everything you did to make my experience working on your project positive. I enjoyed working with you and hope to work with you in the future.

Thank you again.
Sincerely,
Jack Smith

The following note is different. It is not about the writer and what the writer enjoyed. It is about the receiver of the note and uses the person's name within the note.

Dear Greg,

Your creative idea for the project was typical of your ingenuity. You brilliantly executed the plan and kept everyone on schedule. The result of your effort will make the difference in the lives of many people.

Greg, I sincerely hope to work with you again in the future because I know your efforts produce excellent results.

All the best,

Jack Smith

Personal notes are no exception. Remember, it's not about you and what you enjoyed but about the person receiving your note. Focus your thought on the person instead of yourself. For example, instead of writing, "I had a nice time at your party. Thank you for inviting me," write "You are an exceptional hostess. Lynne, you thought of every detail to make Friday evening unforgettable." This type of thank you note facilitates the excellent results you want — being invited back for business or for future entertainment.

Personally thank the people to whom you owe gratitude, including the person who entertained you, or if you entertained, the support staff or others who helped make the affair run smoothly. Tell exactly what you appreciate and don't exaggerate or continue at length. A few well-written sentences are plenty. Be prompt, but if you can't be, remember it is never too late to say thank you or to send a note of appreciation.

A follow-up telephone thank you the next day is nice, the e-mail or faxed thank you is better than nothing, but the handwritten note is by far the most appreciated and effective means of saying thank you. The handwritten note demonstrates the personal touch — something that is often lacking in business and therefore highly prized. The old Crane Stationary advertisement said it best, "To the best of our knowledge, no one ever cherished a fax."

The advantage an emailed thank you has over a handwritten note is its ability to be sent as a copy and forwarded to others for public recognition of a job well done. A sample of an email note of thanks appropriate for distribution to everyone in a department might read as follows:

Dear Frank,

Your idea for the Freemont project was exceptional. As you know, this was a really important project for our company and it is thanks to you that the project was successful.

Your team is one of the best in the industry. They brilliantly executed the plan and on time. Hats off to every member!

Best regards,
Brandt Jacobs

Special Gestures Of Appreciation

Show appreciation whenever and wherever you can. A campaign to thank military service people was started by Scott Truitt. It is a simple and easy way to thank military men and women you do not know without having to approach them. Here are the steps to the Gratitude Campaign thank you sign:

- Place your hand over your heart like you do when you say the Pledge of Allegiance.
- Pull your hand down and out.
- Bend at the elbow and do not bend your wrist.
- Stop around your belly button with your hand flat, palm up and angled towards the military service person you are thanking.

One machine can do the work of fifty ordinary men.
No machine can do the work of one extraordinary man.

– Elbert Hubbard
Little Journeys to the Homes of the Great

Sandra's seen a leprechaun,
Eddie touched a troll,
Laurie danced with witches once,
Charlie found some goblins' gold.
Donald heard a mermaid sing,
Susy spied an elf,
But all the magic I have known
I've had to make myself.

– Shel Silverstein
"Magic"/*Where the Sidewalk Ends*

Chapter Seven

Wave A Wand: How To Conjure Hollywood Magic

One of the deep secrets of life is that all that is really worth doing is what we do for others.

– Lewis Carroll

What do Mark Zuckerberg, Dr. Phil, Denzel Washington, Dolly Parton, Ellen DeGeneres, Bill Gates, Oprah, Warren Buffett, Barbara Streisand, and Andre Agassi have in common? They are givers. They know that giving is magic. Here's how it works.

Oprah is a shining example that doing what you love and helping others pays off. Her creed, "What you put out comes back all the time, no matter what."[1] Her list of "20 Things I Know for Sure" includes, "The happiness you feel is in direct proportion to the love you give." The Beatles last lyric on the last album they recorded imparts the same philosophy, "And in the end, the love you take is equal to the love you make." Elevated happiness is a common denominator shared by winners who consistently give. No matter where you are on your path that is riddled with your unique obstacles, and no matter what your goals, no matter where you live, no matter how much money you have or do not have, you should give value to others. It is not only good for others — it is good for you. Help others. Help solve problems that you can make better when you notice opportunities.

Sincere unselfish help given to others without expecting anything in return results in something that seems almost magical. Karma. Karma seems magical because what you give without expecting anything in return has a strange way of coming back to you. Oprah reportedly has given away over $40 million dollars. She is a billionaire. It is no small wonder that Oprah's "Favorite Things" television episodes were the most watched episodes each year of *The Oprah Winfrey Show*. The audience members present during the taping of these episodes received Oprah's favorite things for free. Other popular TV personalities do the same. Ellen DeGeneres' "Twelve Days of Giveaways" became so popular that giving away prizes became a standard feature of *The Ellen DeGeneres Show*.

Involve people and invite them to join you in giving whenever you can. Welcome everyone. The Beatles organized a "Magical Mystery Tour," an unscripted film in which ordinary people travelled on a bus to share magical adventures and the enjoyment of six new Beatles' songs. The album that resulted as part of the film was number one on *Billboard's* Top LPs listings for eight weeks. Three years after the tour, George Harrison and an Indian musician friend, Ravi Shankar, became aware of the dire situation of refugees from a little known place in East Pakistan called Bangladesh. They wanted to help and came up with an idea to raise international awareness and fund relief efforts for refugees who were suffering and starving after a cyclone and civil war in 1970. Harrison and Shankar got in touch with people in their network and asked them to join them in a concert. Ringo Starr, Bob Dylan, Eric Clapton, Billy Preston, Leon Russell, and the band Badfinger agreed. The concert was the first-ever of its kind and magnitude. Decades later, Shankar would say of the overwhelming success of the event, "In one day, the whole world knew the name of Bangladesh."[2] It was a fantastic occasion and the rewards reaped by the selfless coming together of Harrison, Shankar, and the musicians they invited to join them for one day resulted in on-going aid to Bangladesh.

A best selling live album, a boxed three-record set, and a documentary film followed The Bangladesh Concert. Sales of the live album and DVD release of the film continue to benefit the George Harrison Fund for UNICEF which raised $1.2 million for children in the Horn of Africa in a 2011 campaign marking the album's 40th anniversary. George Harrison's estate, reportedly worth in excess of $400 million at the time of his death, gushes royalty money each month to his heirs that is greater than what most people receive in a lifetime.

Help people even when there is no profit in it for you. Karma. What you give comes back — and obviously can be worth much more than tenfold.

Many people worthy of the A-List get little attention or never get noticed even when they are talented, smart, and attractive. Ohio native Haley Bennett was one of them for nine long years. Her career took off when she showed up bearing a homemade lemon meringue pie for director Tate Taylor *(The Help)* at a lunch meeting to discuss a role in *The Girl on the Train*. She got the part. When asked where she got the idea of sweetening up Taylor with a pie, she laughed, "I wish I would've caught on to this a little bit earlier. I would have started making pies sooner ... It was a great icebreaker. It was a *smart* icebreaker."[3]

The way to have what you want
is to give what you need — emotionally and spiritually.

– Oprah

Bishop T.D. Jakes, a best-selling author, successful film and television producer, and preacher inspires millions including Oprah who is one of his biggest fans. Jakes offers five steps he believes make a difference in happiness. Read Jakes' books or watch his videos on YouTube to learn more.

1. You have to own your own happiness by taking away the responsibility for your happiness from other people.
2. You have to change your own story focusing on the script you want for your life with the good that is in it and the story that you want without blaming the past. You wrote the script. Change the story. Change the dialogue.
3. Enjoy the journey of life not the destination. Don't delay the happiness until you reach the finish line (get your degree, get married, etc.) Realize happiness at every moment you live life.
4. Put yourself on your calendar because if you don't see yourself as valuable no one else will. Start your own party first so others won't draw you into the cyclone of their own drama.
5. Balance work with play. If you play all the time you will be hungry.[4]

You don't have to be rich to give or to make the difference in the lives of others. Muhammad Ali had a trademark surprise. He added magic to interactions with people he knew as well as those he did not. Paul McCartney remembers Ali as not only being a great boxer but also a gentle man "with a great sense of humour who would often pull a pack of cards out of his pocket, no matter how posh the occasion, and do a card trick for you."[5]

My parents once took my brother and me on vacation to the Great Smoky Mountains. We arrived at our hotel after a long day of traveling. I was at the age that I was having doubts about Santa Claus, the Easter Bunny, and the tooth fairy. The first night of our trip, just before we went to dinner, a back tooth fell out. I didn't tell my parents or big brother and decided this was an opportunity for me to confirm my suspicions. I placed my tooth under my pillow with a note that said:

Dear Tooth Fairy,

I am not telling my parents that I lost my tooth. I will know if you are real when I wake up tomorrow.

Everyone was exhausted when we returned from dinner. I instantly fell asleep the minute my head touched the pillow on the bed turned down by the housekeeping service. The next morning when I awoke I remembered my tooth. I was ecstatic when I discovered a quarter under my pillow and happily explained to my parents what had happened. My parents were delighted and told EVERYONE for years about the magical service rendered by the hotel's tooth fairy. We returned to that same hotel every summer for many years and everyone my parents told wanted the name and location of the hotel so they could also stay at the magic "tooth fairy's hotel" when they traveled to the Great Smoky Mountains. That one small gesture by a thoughtful housekeeper made the difference between an ordinary and an extraordinary experience. People love to get more than they expect and the smallest things — even a quarter — can be the magic that makes the difference. I don't know the amount my parents tipped the housekeeping service, but my guess is that it was a lot more than a quarter.

Dave Yearwood is a professional surfer and one of the coolest and most authentic people I know. He glides daily across waves on anything from a classic single fin to one of his own custom made Yearwood Surfboards that he crafts into a variety of different fish shapes. Dave sees that his soul is worked into each new board and while the boards under his feet occasionally change, the smile on his face always remains. He is well-loved across the globe — at least where there are waves — and not just because he is a great surfer. Dave takes time to give and share, not only with other surfers, but also with the people he meets including those whose language he does not speak. His smile overcomes language barriers that are part of his global path. Dave says, "When I am on surf trips and not in the water,

I love spending time with people trying to make them laugh and smile. Even if you can't speak the same language you can share something like a smile or a laugh. Or buy a bunch of kids cokes."[6] One photo I found of Dave is of him sitting ocean side in Panama with kids drinking cokes he purchased for them.

Dave showed me pictures and told me stories about each one. One photo was of a boy in El Salvador who wanted to swim but had to swim naked because his family did not have enough money to buy swim trunks. Kids made fun of him. Dave gave the boy a pair of his swim trunks. Another photo was of a young boy in Nicaragua who would watch the traveling surfers when they came to catch waves. Dave asked the boy why he did not try surfing. The boy replied, "No Tabla" (surfboard). Dave took care of that. No wonder the surfer community loves him — and no wonder Yearwood Surfboards sell well. If you would like to take one of the best glides of your life on one of Dave's boards, he'll take time to meet you, learn about you and custom shape a board just for you. www.yearwoodsurfboards.com. Doing unexpected things for others without expecting anything in return makes a difference.

Make magic action happen every opportunity you have. Unexpected and inexpensive gestures will help you win without your ever having to say a single word in the language of your customer. Invest in relationships and if you want to be a champion, do for others first and do more for them than they do for you. Doing for others does not have to require an investment beyond your time. Share information, news articles, etc. that people you know will find valuable. Make introductions to your network that will be interesting and/or helpful. Invite your connections to attend events with you including simple gestures such as enjoying a cup of coffee together. Actions that show your interest in others foster trust that brings magic to every connection.

Customers expect the goods and services they buy to be good. Top-drawer goods and services are not simply good. They are excellent. Exceed expectations by doing one thing more to make the difference in your customer's experience. People love to get more than they expect and will return to buy from you in the future if they have an experience beyond what they expect. My bank offers coffee and cookies in the lobby to customers, while the drive-through teller gives candy to customers and dog treats to accompanying canines. TOMS shoes is a for-profit company that has incorporated an added action into its business plan by operating a non-profit subsidiary, Friends of TOMS. A pair of TOMS shoes is given to a child without shoes whenever a pair of TOMS shoes is sold. In addition, when TOMS sells a pair of eyewear, part of the profit is used to save or restore the eyesight of people in developing countries.

Leave others better than you find them every opportunity you have. You will discover that if you go out of your way for someone else, there will be a good chance they will do the same for you. The ability to develop relationships is key to winning, and the only way to develop relationships is to take a sincere interest in others and then add meaning and value to every interaction you have with them.

Giving is life's magic. We make the world a better place and ourselves happier when we help others by selflessly giving value to others. People with overwhelming reasons to feel unloved and worthless due to obstacles like poverty, homelessness, mental, physical, and sexual abuse who nonetheless give value to others are examples of the good that always seems to follow when they believe in themselves, love themselves, and extend love to others.

Generosity is the thing that is at the begining of prosperity.

– Tim O'Reilly
American Entrepreneur, Inventor, and Founder of O'Reilly Media

You will only be remembered for two things:
The problems you solve or the ones you create.

– Mike Murdock
Singer-Songwriter, Author, Television Host of The School of Wisdom

Chapter Eight

The L.A.S.T. Result: How To Turn Problems Into Super Star Solutions

*It's not a problem that we have a problem.
It's a problem if we don't deal with the problem.*

– Mary Kay Utech
Founder of Mary Kay Cosmetics

General Mills, Inc. sponsored a fundraiser for The First Tee at Blessings Golf Club in Fayetteville, Arkansas where I met Joan Cronan, the Women's Athletic Director at the University of Tennessee, who along with Coach Pat Summitt turned the Lady Vols into a national brand. Cronan is the winner of a slew of awards: NACWAA and NACDA Athletic Director of the Year, Sports Hall of Fame Administrator of the Year, and Women's Basketball Coaches Association Leadership Award winner. She was quick to tell me she believes, "Three Ps make the difference in success — passion, pride, and people." She explained, "*Passion* about what you're doing. *Pride* in what you're doing. And being smart enough to surround yourself with the right *people*." If you do that you will avoid lots of angst in your life because it's true, "Iron sharpens iron."[1] However, even when you mind the "Three Ps" and surround yourself with the "right people" to "avoid lots of angst," the nature of life makes the total avoidance of angst impossible. This chapter will teach you what to say and what to do when problems arise dealing with others.

Otis Redding wrote a song back in the 1960s that was a man's plea for respect and recognition from a woman. However, it was the Queen of Soul, Aretha Franklin, who made the song famous using it to sing out not about a man's need for respect but about a woman's need for respect at a time when a woman could not live with a man and receive government welfare money. The song she sang, "R-E-S-P-E-C-T," is about a woman who is willing to give a man all of her money — including her welfare money — for just a little bit of respect. More than thirty years after the song's release, *Ebony* magazine editorialized, "R-E-S-P-E-C-T" had become "a personal and collective anthem not only for Aretha Franklin but for everybody living in the shadows, for abused and undervalued Sisters as well as undervalued Brothers, for women and men of all races who wanted, needed, had to have that respect."[2] "R-E-S-P-E-C-T" is often considered the best song of the Rhythm and Blues era and is ranked number five on Rolling Stone's list of The 500 Greatest Songs of All Time.[3]

> *There are two things people want more than sex and money — recognition and praise.*
>
> – Mary Kay Ash

According to prominent psychologists including Sigmund Freud, John Dewey, and Abraham Maslow, a primary need of all people — men like Redding was writing about, and women like Franklin was singing about, is to be respected and valued. Conflict occurs when people believe they or what is important to them is not respected.

Avoid controversial topics like politics and religion. Use one of the following phrases to get your conversation back on a productive track when others bring up topics that are uncomfortable for you:

- "I'd like to suggest we change the subject."
- "This makes me uncomfortable."
- "Let's move on to other topics."
- "Let's agree to disagree."

Take the high road — be respectful of others even when people are unfair. Remaining cool, treating others with dignity even when they are not respectful sets a positive tone for conflict resolution.

Acting immediately without running from a problem you need to address regarding the serious mistakes of others is important if you want to reduce your anxiety and retain the power and authority you've achieved. Do what is right even if it is painful to people you like. Deal with problems quickly so you can move on.

Powerful people are in control of their emotions. People who raise their voices are perceived as disagreeable hotheads, so instead of raising your voice when you are angry, respond with powerful and descriptive language expressing the actual reason for your anger. The loser of an argument is often perceived as the person yelling loudest. You'll look like a loser if you lose your temper and yell.

Tears lessen power. If you become angry or tearful, remove yourself from the situation until you've regained composure saying, "Excuse me. I'll be back in a few minutes." If you need more time say, "This is not a good time for me to talk. Let's discuss this later."

Try as hard as you like, you are human and will inevitably make an unintentional conversational blunder — something that hurts or upsets your conversation partner (CP). Mistakes are part of being human. The more adept you are at acknowledging your humanity, the more quickly others will forgive you — and like you. Your unintended comments are not intended to be insensitive, but for your CP the comment is uncomfortable and/or painful. You likely will be aware that you have uttered something you wish you had not as soon as you speak. You likely will recognize this because your CP may fall silent, snap back at you, or perhaps even tell you that your comments are not appropriate or that your comments are mean.

Your words matter. "I wish it hadn't happened" is not an apology. Using the word "if" as in, "I'm sorry if you ..." places the responsibility on the person you're apologizing to rather than on you where it belongs. The best way to apologize is by immediately addressing the blunder. For example, say, "I'm sorry. I did not realize that would upset you." As an alternative you might say, "Please forgive me. I feel terrible. I did not intend to hurt your feelings."

Body language can help convey sincerity. Look the person in his eyes, relax your face, and let your hands be at rest by your sides — not defensively crossed in front of your body.

Never ruin an apology with an excuse.
– Benjamin Franklin

The offended person will likely forgive you and appreciate your contrition if your apology is warm and sincere.

Look at people and listen to them. If their words don't tell you how they are feeling about you, their body language will. Make it easy for people to give you feedback and to let you know their complaints when they have them. Complaints provide an opportunity to demonstrate respect and value of the feedback. Seize the opportunity to shine.

Deal with problems honestly and immediately. The truth always comes out — if not immediately it eventually will. The winds of gossip magnify problems the longer you wait to tell the truth and accept responsibility. Taking immediate ownership will help you retain control over a problem and diffuse the energy of detractors. After all, you will have said everything including that you are sorry, so there is nothing else detractors can add. The problem is certain to fester if you do not accept ownership early. Take responsibility for your actions when you make a mistake without making excuses. Making excuses sets you up for criticism. Avoid rationalizing aloud, offering explanations, justifying your actions and making excuses for your errors. People really do not care why you screw up — they just want you to correct the problem.

> *Three things cannot be long hidden:*
> *the sun, the moon, and the truth.*
>
> – Buddha

A great way to show R-E-S-P-E-C-T to others when there is a complaint or conflict is with a L.A.S.T. technique. L.A.S.T. is an acronym for Listen. Apologize. Solve. Thank.

Listen carefully when a person voices a complaint and allow the person time to vent. Clarify what you have heard by repeating back the complaint. Use these phrases to help you clarify what you are told:
- "If I understand you correctly ..."
- "So what you are saying is ..."
- "This is what I understand you are telling me ..."
- "What are your ideas, thoughts, etc. ..."

Apologize/**A**cknowledge. **A**pologize no matter whose fault the problem is. You do not have to agree. If possible, apologize face to face. If you can't be in person, telephone so the person can hear your voice. Write a letter or email as a last resort. This is not the time to send a text. **A**cknowledge the person's anger, feelings, frustration, and/or disappointments. Most people respond to criticism or complaints with a knee-jerk reaction that is not respectful. Instead, give yourself time to listen to the full complaint and to show your interest in having a complete understanding of the problem. Ask for feedback. Encourage the person to vent with a phrase like, "That's interesting. Tell me more." You must listen to others first if later you want them to listen to you. Find out what the person wants before you offer any options for resolution.

Use a caring tone when you convey a caring attitude to show sympathy/empathy for the situation that is the source of the problem. Recognize the effect of the situation on the person (embarrassment, inconvenience, frustration). You don't have to agree. Your apology does not have to say that you admit that you are wrong — only that you are sorry for the trouble the problem causes. Apologizing validates the other person's frustration and shows that you are sorry for that problem. Helpful phrases to convey your apology are:

- "I'm really sorry this happened."
- "I apologize for the trouble you are having."

Solve the problem by taking action as quickly as you can. Don't allow the conflict time to grow. Take action by solving, helping to solve, or by suggesting a solution to the complaint. For example you might say, "Let's figure out how we can resolve ..." If there is something you can do to make the problem better then tell the person what you will do — and do it.

After you solve a problem, do one thing more. Adding one thing more than is expected to the correction of a problem will set you apart from other people. Seize opportunities to create magic with every apology. The opportunity to solve a problem and to overdeliver with an unexpected action makes the difference by demonstrating your willingness to go the extra mile. This extra action creates a tremendous opportunity to identify yourself as someone who respects, values, and cares about what is important to your client, colleague, or customer. Examples of problem-solving actions that make the difference include unexpected gestures such as sending a hand-written note thanking the person for the opportunity to correct the problem along with a token of atonement such as a gift or gift certificate.

Thank the person for bringing his anger, disappointments, feelings, or frustrations to your attention. Thank him for the opportunity to express your apology for the feelings that are the result of something you have said or done. Use the person's name when you thank him. Ask if there is anything else you can do. Follow-up with the person later to get more feedback on the solution you provided. You can ask questions like, "How was everything? Did ___ work for you? Did the solution meet your expectations?" If his answer is, "No it did not," you have another opportunity to implement L.A.S.T. (**L**isten, **A**pologize, **S**olve, and **T**hank) to convey that you value and respect the person and what is important to that person.

> *The greater the obstacle,*
> *the more glory in overcoming it.*
>
> – Molière
> French Playwright, Actor, and Poet

At the birthplace of Walmart in Bentonville, Arkansas is the original WALTON'S 5 & 10 store. It is now a museum with artifacts documenting the store's history. A large freestanding column prominently stands like The Code of Hammurabi in ancient Mesopotamia for all to see listing Sam Walton's "10 Rules for Building a Business." Number 8 reads:

> Exceed your customers' expectations. If you do they'll come back over and over. Give them what they want — and a little more. Let them know you appreciate them. Make good on all your mistakes, and don't make excuses — apologize. Stand behind everything you do. The two most important words I ever wrote were on that first Walmart sign: 'Satisfaction Guaranteed.' They're still up there, and they have made all the difference.[4]

Among the memorabilia hanging on a nearby wall are returns made to Walmart along with Sam Walton's hand written apologies to customers. My favorite was a defective merchandise slip for a fishing pole listing the reason for the return, "Fishing pole didn't work — no fish."

Our personal histories and individual life experiences make us unique. These differences cause conflict with others because we do not naturally respect differences. Factors that influence conflict are personality, behavioral characteristics, regional differences (North vs. South, urban vs. rural), cultural background (ethnicity or country of origin), family background (family approach to conflict), religion, mental or physical abilities, gender, sexual orientation, generational differences, and business experience including how conflict was handled in previous places we have lived and worked. Lack of understanding and failing to value diversity will yield complaints that impact your ability to make it to the top of whatever career you choose.

Comments that attack and show that what is said is not valued include:

- "That's not true."
- "You're wrong."
- "You're confused."
- "You don't know what you are talking about."
- "Stop interrupting me."
- "Hold on a minute."
- "Leave it alone."

Phrases that express that you are listening without attacking another person include:

- "My facts don't agree with those."
- "I disagree."
- "There's some confusion here."

- "There are some issues you may not be aware of."
- "Please let me finish what I started to say."
- "Let's wait a moment."
- "I'd rather handle this myself."

Respectful phrases to use when you ask for something without appearing to demand or take advantage:
- "I'm sorry to trouble you."
- "Would you be so kind as to ___?"
- "Won't you please?"
- "Would you mind?"

Follow requests by saying, "Thank you."

Keep a positive attitude when you deal with a negative situation. If you are angry, frustrated, anxious, overwhelmed etc. you will send out that message and further increase the negativity of the situation.

A situation that occurred during the height of Beatlemania is an example of what can go wrong, how not to handle complaints, and how to handle complaints when there is misunderstanding.

During the height of The Beatles' success, John Lennon made a comment to a British journalist that was part of a harmless lifestyle story. Lennon took the reporter on a tour of his home and as they walked through his home he told her about different items in the house — costumes, bric-a-brac, books, etc. His collection of books included volumes about different religions. He commented, "Christianity will go. It will vanish and shrink. We're more popular than Jesus now; I don't know which will go first — Rock and Roll or Christianity. Jesus was all right but his disciples were thick and ordinary. It's them twisting it that ruins it for me."[5]

The remark in its original context went unnoticed and provoked no ire in Great Britain but five months later an American journalist used the quote in a different context in a different article. American readers found it so offensive that anti-Beatles demonstrations were organized. Many fans turned against The Beatles picketing their concerts and organizing bonfires to publicly burn their music and photographs. Radio stations stopped playing their music. The comment seriously affected sales of The Beatles' music. Concert plans were jeopardized. The furor in the United States spread to other countries including Mexico, South Africa, and Spain — even the Vatican issued a public denouncement of Lennon's comments.

In an effort to undo the damage, Brian Epstein, The Beatles' manager, flew to the United States and held a press conference. He chastised the American journalist who wrote the article and publicly criticized the publication in which the out of context comment appeared. This tactic did little to assuage the public's anger.

What finally did help was John Lennon's public acknowledgement of the problem, an apology, and a thank you. At a press conference held in the United States, Lennon began by acknowledging and verbalizing what had occurred. He apologized although he accepted no blame. He also found an opportunity to say thank you. The *Apologize Album* was a result of this event. He said, "I wasn't saying whatever they're saying I was saying. I'm sorry I said it really. I never meant it to be a lousy anti-religious thing. I apologize if that will make you happy. I still don't know quite what I've done. I've tried to tell you what I did do but if you want me to apologize, if that will make you happy, then OK, I'm sorry."[6]

Lennon later said, "I always remember to thank Jesus for the end of my touring days; if I hadn't said that The Beatles were 'bigger than Jesus' and upset the very Christian Ku Klux Klan, well, Lord, I might still be up there with all the other performing fleas! God bless America. Thank you, Jesus."[7]

Lennon's handling of the situation by acknowledging, apologizing, and thanking remedied the harm done. The

Vatican responded forgiving The Beatles saying, "The remark by John Lennon, which triggered deep indignation, mainly in the United States, after many years sounds only like a 'boast' by a young working-class Englishman faced with unexpected success, after growing up in the legend of Elvis and Rock and Roll."[8]

The time is always right to do the right thing.
– Martin Luther King, Jr.

Smile and say, "My pleasure" when people thank you for listening and solving their problems but demonstrate respect even when people ask you for something you cannot provide. Maintain your integrity at all times and be polite when you must say "no." Explain why you must say "no" and apologize for not being able to say "yes."

Once the situation is resolved in the best way possible you might find that you need to do what four-time NBA MVP NBA star LeBron James did that made the difference in his career. Bury the hatchet.

James got his start playing seven seasons for the Cleveland Cavaliers. When he left to play for the Miami Heat his fans in Ohio including the owner of the Cavaliers, Dan Gilbert, were angry. Gilbert wrote a scathing letter to James in which he called James "disloyal, a coward, a quitter, and a narcissist"[9] but James did what he believed was best for his career.

James told *Sports Illustrated* writer Lee Jenkins about his actions that upset people, how his actions propelled his career, and about burying the hatchet:

> Remember when I was sitting up there at the Boys & Girls Club in 2010? I was thinking this is really tough. I could feel it. I was leaving something I had spent a long time creating. If I had to do it all over again, I'd obviously do things differently, but I'd still

> have left. Miami, for me, has been almost like college for other kids. These past four years helped raise me into who I am. I became a better player and a better man. I learned from a franchise that had been where I wanted to go. I will always think of Miami as my second home. Without the experiences I had there, I wouldn't be able to do what I'm doing today.... When I left Cleveland, I was on a mission. I was seeking championships, and we won two.[10]

James grew with the Miami Heat. He and his team went to the NBA Finals four times. After four seasons, James wanted to return to his home state. Reflecting on the booing of the Cavalier fans, the burning of jerseys, and Gilbert's letter, James says:

> It was easy to say, 'OK, I don't want to deal with these people ever again.' But then you think about the other side. What if I were a kid who looked up to an athlete, and that athlete made me want to do better in my own life, and then he left? How would I react? I've met with Dan (Gilbert), face-to-face, man-to-man. We've talked it out. Everybody makes mistakes. I've made mistakes as well. Who am I to hold a grudge?[11]

Gilbert shared on twitter, "Welcome Home @KingJames. I am excited for the fans and people of Cleveland and Ohio. No fans and people deserve a winner more than them."[12]

> *Evolve so hard they have to get to know you again.*
> – Mike Mills
> Legend of the Barbecue World, Four-Time World Champion, Three-Time Grand World Champion at Memphis in May Otherwise Known as the Super Bowl of Swine, 1992 Grand Champion of the Jack Daniel's World Invitational Barbecue Cooking Contest, and Winner of the Jack Daniel's Sauce Contest

Success is earned. You'll often find that to do what is in your best interest won't be popular with a lot of people who want you to do what they think you should do even though it is not in your best interest and also perhaps not in their best interest. It must be you who determines what you need to do that is best for your career and it must be you to determine when to do it.

LeBron James says about his own success that began in Akron, "In Northeast Ohio, nothing is given. Everything is earned. You work for what you have."[13] It was uncomfortable for James when he set about doing what was best for his career. He ticked off a lot of people. In your lifetime you also will likely inadvertently tick off people you didn't mean to upset. You'll need to do what LeBron did if you are to grow. Bury the hatchet. LeBron's decision to bury the hatchet made possible continued growth for LeBron James and for Gilbert's team. If you don't want to be average or mediocre, you have to do what you've got to do, say what you have to say, and bury the hatchet.

> *To keep your marriage brimming,*
> *With love in the loving cup,*
> *Whenever you're wrong, admit it;*
> *Whenever you're right, shut up.*
>
> – Ogden Nash
> American Writer of Humorous Poetry

*I hated every minute of training, but I said,
'Don't quit. Suffer now and
live the rest of your life as a champion.'*

– Muhammad Ali

Chapter Nine

Pay To Play:
How To Take Championship Actions

> *You don't open on Broadway.*
> *You open in New Haven.*
> — Political Consultant Stuart Spencer to Ronald Reagan

Medinah Country Club, the setting for the 39th Ryder Cup, provided me with a chance to verify a story that circulates around the medical center in Chapel Hill about Michael Jordan. We were on the porch of the NBC Hospitality Tent in between walks on the golf course near Chicago to cheer for the USA team against the European team. Jordan is from my hometown and we are both UNC Tar Heels so as we waited for golfers to arrive at the tee box near the tent we made small talk about North Carolina.

As a college freshman at UNC-Chapel Hill, Jordan hit a 16-footer with 17 seconds left in the NCAA collegiate basketball championship to win against the Georgetown Hoyas 63–62. Jordan didn't feel well the day after the victory and was taken to North Carolina Memorial Hospital where Newton Fischer, Chair of the top ranked Otolaryngology (Ear, Nose, Throat) Department, examined him. According to department legend, medical interns and residents lined the examination room and silently watched with interest as Fischer examined the Tar Heel hero. Fischer focused on Jordan's medical complaint, made his diagnosis, prescribed treatment, and dismissed Jordan without mentioning the previous night's winning shot that was front page and broadcast headline news on every major and minor media outlet. Nor did the interns and residents mention to Jordan "The Shot" as it is customary for student doctors to only observe without speaking to a patient when an attending/teaching physician examines a patient. According to those who were present, Jordan couldn't stand it any longer so as Fischer was leaving the room Jordan said, "Hey, Dr. Fischer, did you see the game last night?"

Fischer turned back to Jordan and momentarily stopped before walking out of the door to see his next patient. "Why yes Michael, I did, and I think you should go out for the team again next year."

I asked Jordan if the story were true. He studied me with astonishment wondering how I knew about his postgame doctor's visit. Then he turned his head to the course for a long gaze.

"I'd forgotten that. But yeah, I remember that vividly. I had an abscess and it really hurt. It was a terrible pain," he said staring at the course. Jordan stopped talking, reflected, then turned his head back to me nodding and chuckling, "Yeah, I remember Dr. Fischer. He was a good doctor. He fixed me up." Jordan looked out again at the golf course and then smiled back at me not saying a word.

"Well," I said, "Is the story true or not?"

He got a serious look on his face and paused before replying, "It was good for the motivation."[1]

Staying motivated makes the difference if you want to maintain excellence in anything whether it's practicing medicine, basketball, or banking because the minute you stop doing what made you a winner is the minute you stop winning. Read trade journals, business books, listen to motivational recordings, attend professional meetings where you can meet people with new ideas and hear speakers in your field, etc. to keep inspired. Reveling in the limelight, coasting, and taking it easy is tempting when you're at the top. After all — you're at the top of your game! You cannot take it for granted that you will "make the team" or remain the top winner in any profession if you do not stay motivated to do what it takes to maintain excellence. Continue to "go out for the team" when you make it to the top. To achieve and to maintain personal excellence you have to consistently and persistently practice so you can "make the team" every day. Hidden habits determine shine.

> *You can map out a fight plan or a life plan, but when the action starts, it may not go the way you planned, and you're down to your reflexes which means your preparation. That's where your roadwork shows. If you cheated on that in the dark of morning, well, you're getting found out now, under the bright lights.*
>
> – Smokin' Joe Frazier
> Heavyweight Boxing Champ 1970-73

> *Work never bothered me like it bothers some people. You can outwork the best player in the world.*
>
> – Ben Hogan
> One of the Greatest Golfers in History

One of Jordan's friends and one of the greatest to ever play football, Hall of Famer and Super Bowl champion Jerome Bettis aka "The Bus," put it this way, "The way you become great is a daily process. You say to yourself, 'Every day I'm going to do whatever it takes in order for me to get better.' The process is one day at a time. What you have to understand is the other guy is getting better."[2] Winners like Jordan and "The Bus" continue in retirement to practice personal excellence "going out for the team" initiating new projects including raising money for various charities.

> *The minute you step off that podium is the minute you start preparing for the next world championship. That's kind of how I work.*
> *You celebrate for a brief moment, then you move on.*
>
> – Abby Wambach
> Two-Time Gold Medalist, FIFA Women's World Cup Champion, and Six-Time Winner of the U.S. Soccer Athlete of the Year Award

In 2012 and 2013, I was a non-playing guest at The Michael Jordan Celebrity Invitational Golf Tournaments held at Shadow Creek Golf Club in Las Vegas. Jordan invites his friends who are sports and entertainment legends to play golf to help him raise money for charity. It was here that I was able to observe Jordan and his winning cadre of friends take actions vital to achieving excellence that seem second nature in their day-to-day lives.

Joe Morgan, considered one of the greatest second basemen of all-time won two World Series championships. Post-retirement, he chose to help Jordan raise money every year. At the tournament, Joe spoke to everyone, and everyone at Jordan's Celebrity Golf Tournament seemed to be Joe's best friend because of his kindness and consideration to everyone. I didn't know very many of the people at the event and Joe asked me if there was anyone I'd like to meet.

"Yes, there is one person I would like to meet because we have a friend in common from our past."

"Who's that?"

"Sugar Ray Leonard."

A pulsating crowd surrounded the legendary boxer who was the first boxer to earn more than 100 million dollars in purses and who had won world titles in five divisions. The crowd around the prizefighter didn't faze Joe. He said, "I'll get him right now. Sugar might leave early. You miss opportunities when you wait."[3]

Joe Morgan didn't let any opportunities pass during his career and he didn't let the opportunity for me to meet Sugar Ray pass that night even though a throng ten people deep surrounded the champ. Joe worked his way through the admirers as deftly as he did on the ball field when stealing home plate. People recognized Joe as he maneuvered his way smiling and shaking hands with everyone until he finally reached Sugar Ray and tapped him on the shoulder.

"Hey Sugar, come with me. A woman who knows somebody you knew wants to meet you."

Sugar Ray instantly emerged from the crowd smiling at Joe, happy to do whatever Joe asked. In no time flat Joe returned to me with Sugar Ray. When Joe introduced him to me, Sugar Ray looked puzzled, surveyed me up and down and said, "Who do you know that we could both possibly know?"

"Ronnie Michaels," I replied.

Sugar Ray's eyes filled with tears as he asked, "How did you know Ronnie Michaels? He was the world-renowned eye surgeon, the head of the department at Johns Hopkins who saved my eyesight two times. He was my good friend. He died unexpectedly a few years ago. He was too young to die."

"I know. He was my neighbor and friend when I was growing up. He taught me Lifesaving lessons."

"What did you say he taught you?"

"Lifesaving. But actually what he really taught me was not to give up on people even when they try to drown you — which he practically did try to drown me during the end of course test when I had to 'save him.' I weighed a third his weight back then and I had to 'save him' as he thrashed in the water and wrestled me holding me under the water! I finally got loose from his grip and swam to the side of the pool and got out as fast as I could. He was hard on everyone in the class and nearly drowned all of us. When no one would get back in the water with him, he lectured us for probably thirty minutes about how important it is not to give up – in this case on a life you could save with just a little more effort. Afterwards he asked us to get back in the pool and 'save him' again. I was the first one to get back in the pool with him and I am happy to report that I earned my Lifesaving Certificate without being drowned by Ronnie. His parents told me that Ronnie really liked you. I'd love to get a picture with you to show his family."

The only camera I had was on my iPhone — one of the early ones. The lighting was poor as the evening party was around an outdoor pool at the Aria Hotel. A bystander snapped a picture of us. Sugar Ray grabbed the iPhone to look at the photo. He shook his head "no" and gave the phone back to the person taking the photo and insisted the picture be re-taken. He did this four times until a photograph was acceptable to him. Sugar Ray, like Ronnie, didn't give up. He made sure the result he wanted matched his vision, and he persevered doing things over and over and over and over until he got the result he wanted. He didn't settle for what was easy, comfortable, or adequate. Perseverance makes the difference. Act as many times as it takes to reach the excellence you see in your mind's eye.

At an after-party later that night, I met Marcus Allen, a famous football running back and current CBS football analyst. The first thing Allen said to me was, "You're the woman who made Sugar cry. He told me upstairs about meeting you. Sugar said, 'You ain't going to believe this. Some woman just made me cry. I'm Sugar Ray and Sugar don't cry.'"

I've never heard or read that Steve Jobs cried about anything, but I did read in the *Harvard Business Review* that matching the result to vision also made a difference to Jobs. Apple engineers protested when Jobs sent them back to make circuit board chips line up to look nice even though no one would see them. Jobs chided, "I want it to be as beautiful as possible even if it's inside the box. A great carpenter isn't going to use lousy wood for the back of a cabinet, even though nobody's going to see it."[4] He told engineers they were artists and should act as artists. After the redesign, Jobs had the engineers and Macintosh team sign their names so their signatures could be engraved inside the case. "Real artists sign their work,"[5] Jobs said. Sugar Ray, Steve Jobs, and Ronnie Michaels all realized that to be a great artist in any field the final result must match the artist's vision.

The day after Jordan's welcome party, I got up early and went to the gym at the Aria Resort and afterwards to breakfast at the Shadow Creek Club house. I saw Marcus Allen and sat with him. All-American running back and wide receiver Ahmad Rashad who is now a network TV sportscaster joined us. I'd seen Rashad from a distance earlier that morning at the resort gym where we were staying and asked him how often he worked out.

"I do it every day."

Allen blurted out ribbing Rashad who was born in 1949 but doesn't look it, "Yeah and I do what he does — but one thing more!"

Joe Morgan walked over and hearing the conversation chimed in, "I do it every day, one thing more, no matter where I am!" Everybody laughed.

There are no traffic jams along the extra mile.
— Roger Staubach
NFL Hall of Fame Quarterback

Taking action every day wherever you are makes the difference. Elite achievers have relentless daily work rituals. Twyla Tharp, American dancer and choreographer, shares in her book *The Creative Habit* that every morning at 5:30 a.m. she leaves her home, hails a taxi, and goes to the gym to start her day. The most important moment she says is hailing the cab.⁶ In other words — ritual habits. It's common to find people who made it to the top in every field working to achieve and maintain excellence every day no matter where they are. Technology makes it possible to do something every day no matter where you are. Do at least three things every day to optimize results. Take persistent, consistent action and as Nike says: Just do It® every day no matter where you are. And then, like Marcus Allen, do one thing more. If the average number of sales calls you make every day is six, start making seven. Do more. No matter where you are. Winners in every field are the people who consistently take the time to do the little things that those with mediocre or little success don't do because they don't take the time and are willing to settle for less. Extra effort makes a winning difference.

ESPN's Stuart Scott, *SportsCenter* anchor, flew in late from the East Coast on the second day of Jordan's tournament and joined my daughter Win and me for dinner. Scott was cheerful and never complained about what we knew was a Herculean effort for him to be in Las Vegas. Scott had wedged his trip in between back-to-back engagements including a broadcast the night before and chemo treatments. Too sick to play golf, he said, "I can't play. I can't do everything. I do what I can. I could be here so I came."

The last time I saw Scott was when he gave the *Jimmy V Perseverance Award* acceptance speech at The ESPYS in Los Angeles in 2015. He talked about beating cancer by how he lived, why he lived, and in the manner in which he lived. He showed up for life with a winner's attitude that made the difference for himself and for others — every day — for as long as he could.

Do the best you can and take action without complaining to make a positive difference. Do what you can do. Like Scott, you do not have to do it all to make a positive impact. Combined efforts exceed the result of any lone individual. No contribution is too small when it comes to making the difference.

While in Las Vegas, a no-brainer was to seize the chance to dance with *Dancing with the Stars* contestant Jerry Rice, the former American football wide receiver who played twenty seasons in the National Football League. Rice is widely considered to be the greatest wide receiver in NFL history and one of the greatest NFL players at any position. He is the all-time NFL leader in receptions, touchdown receptions, and yards. Rice was nicknamed "World" in college because it was said there was not a ball in the world he could not catch! He proved his work ethic and dedication to personal excellence in the NFL, missing only ten regular season games in twenty seasons. In retirement, he enjoys golfing and dancing. If I were to pick a poster child for my first book, *The Dance Steps of Life*, it would be "World."

Rice has a willingness to publicly participate in areas other than that of his primary expertise. On *Dancing with the Stars* he performed before millions of viewers. He seizes joy and looks for opportunities to expand his excellence and evolve his brand in areas that are not in his primary area of expertise.

Add additional areas outside of your primary area of expertise to evolve your knowledge and skills to make the difference in your success. A willingness to evolve your areas of expertise can increase your business, add additional revenue streams, and add enjoyment to your life.

Comedians Brian Baumgartner (Kevin Malone/*The Office*), Chevy Chase (*Saturday Night Live, National Lampoon, Caddyshack*), and Kevin Nealon (*Saturday Night Live, Anger Management, Happy Gilmore*) laughed at themselves and smiled as they hit both good and bad shots throughout the Michael Jordan Celebrity Invitational. Fans related to them and did not mind that they sometimes hit their balls poorly. Fans begged for autographs and the good-humored comedians obliged.

> *Good times and riches and son of a bitches,*
> *I've seen more than I can recall ...*
> *If I couldn't laugh I just would go insane.*
>
> – Jimmy Buffett
> "Changes in Attitudes"

Power comes from a positive attitude. Your success will result from your work and your attitude. Don't take yourself too seriously. Laugh at yourself. You are responsible for your happiness. Take control of your attitude the minute you wake. Humor is one of the winner's secret weapons. A happy note at the end of a request, negotiation, or uncomfortable situation is often the reason for a win. Sara Blakely, founder of Spanx, first approached the head buyer at Neiman Marcus by mailing him a single shoe with a note that said, "Just trying to get my foot in the door; have minutes to chat?"[7]

David Remnick, author of *King of the World*, said the following in an interview with David Bianculli on NPR's "Fresh Air" about the difference Muhammad Ali's sense of humor made to his success:

> What always saved Ali, what always saved him from becoming alienated from certain publics, whether it was the bragging or the politics or the religion, there was always a sense of humor about him. He was always funny, hilarious. And finally, with time, he won over almost everybody. I mean, a few racists here and there, a few people who really felt that his stand on Vietnam was deeply, deeply wrong, a few people that, you know, still yearned for the Joe Louis model of behavior, fine. But for the most part, he won over the world so that at the 1996 Olympics, he gets up and lights this torch in the most unexpected, dramatic and moving and beautiful way. And no one's presence on this globe would've moved us more.[8]

Comedian Joan Rivers used humor to survive difficult times in her personal and professional life. Told by her agent that she was too old and not funny, she had been turned down repeatedly — auditioning seven times before she was invited as a guest on *The Johnny Carson Show*. Her ability to poke fun and laugh at herself became her trademark as she made self-deprecating remarks about her looks, aging, and sex appeal. Rivers said the following about her style of performance. "Part of my act is meant to shake you up. It looks like I'm being funny, but I'm reminding you of other things. Life is tough, darling. Life is hard. And we better laugh at everything; otherwise, we're going down the tube."[9] A sense of humor and enthusiasm makes a difference in surviving the inevitable toughness of life enabling you to move forward to reach your goals.

When times are tough — be tougher than the times.
– Robert H. Schuller
American Christian Televangelist, Pastor, Motivational Speaker and Author

American actors Gary Valentine, (Danny Heffernan on *The King of Queens*) and Richard Karn, (Al Borland in the sitcom *Home Improvement* and host of television game show *Family Feud*), agree with each other that "persistence and a willingness to try" made the difference in success. Karn said that before reaching the success he enjoys today he read "hundreds of scripts and spent my own money to travel on my own dime to go to New York and to Hollywood to read scripts."[10]

The man on top of the mountain didn't fall there.
– Vince Lombardi
Super Bowl Championship Coach and NFL Executive

In 1975, Sam Walton visited a Korean tennis ball factory where workers began their day with a company cheer to foster a good attitude. He liked the idea so much that he created a

Walmart cheer to foster a happy workplace spirit. Associates around the world now shout the Walmart cheer at the beginning of the day.

My daughter, Win, was a sports-broadcast journalist for NBC's Golf Channel when she made a well-publicized tongue slip on national television during a routine tournament update. The tongue slip was regarding Tiger Wood's withdrawal from one of his first golf tournaments after taking time off due to his widely reported indiscretions and marital woes. Win meant to say that the reason for Tiger's withdrawal was due to "a bulging 'disc' in his neck," but instead her tongue substituted a "ck" sound for an "sc" sound. She immediately corrected her error on-air and continued with her report. Win called home as soon as she was off the air. I told her, "You are human and made a mistake like all humans, and you will make more. You have to laugh at yourself when you do something like this." She started laughing and soon we were both uncontrollably howling! Win's next update was in nineteen minutes. She returned to the broadcast, her delivery flowed without a hitch, captivating viewers with her flawless performance.

Friends living in Canada and friends traveling in Barcelona heard her blooper replayed on the BBC. For several days her name and tongue slip were among the most Googled in the world. Video recordings posted on YouTube went viral. Her X-rated gaffe made the front page banner headline of the *New York Daily News* and a large photo of her — above the fold and in full color — appeared with the story, "Faux Pas Hits Tiger in the Pants."[11] Her friends were worried about how this very public slip of the tongue affected her, so she thought of a way to let them know she was okay.

Win designed a New Year's card to look like a golf scorecard. Beneath the word "Resolutions" on the front of the card were three unchecked boxes for her New Years' goals. Inside the card, beside a checked box read, "Wishing you a year bulging ... I mean bursting with joy!" Her willingness to laugh and poke fun at herself by encouraging people to laugh with her made the difference and won her praise from colleagues, friends, and acquaintances. Not all things can be laughed off but when they can, laughter is an excellent way to address what cannot be changed. Laugh at yourself and perhaps think of Eric Idle's lyrics in the Monty Python song, "Always Look on the Bright Side of Life." When you laugh at yourself, you also take power away from detractors.

> *Laugh at yourself first before anyone else can.*
> – Elsa Maxwell
> American Gossip Columnist, Author, Songwriter, Radio Personality, and Professional Hostess Renowned for Her Parties for Royalty and High Society Figures of Her Day

Forgive others when they make mistakes. At the time Win made the tongue slip she did not know Tiger Woods. Several months later she attended an event to benefit Native American youth hosted by Notah Begay, Wood's Stanford University roommate. Wood's saw Win and introduced himself. He shook her hand and said, "I saw your update and thought it was hilarious."[12] His laughing at himself and letting Win know he realized that she meant no harm made the meeting relaxed for everyone. Laugh at yourself. It will help you and those around you to be comfortable in awkward situations.

Laughter made the difference in the life of Christopher Reeve, the Superman actor paralyzed in a horseback riding accident. He told Barbara Walters in an interview for *Oprah's Master Class*, that when he was in the hospital and wanted to die that his wife told him, "If you want us to pull the plug, we'll find a way to do that. But you're still you. And we love you."[13]

Reeve was thinking about dying when a doctor entered his room and ordered him to turn over.

Reeve said, 'What?'"

The doctor said, "'I said turn over!'"

Reeve was about to call a nurse when he realized the doctor was not actually a doctor and started to laugh. It was his old pal from acting school, Robin Williams. Reeve's ability to laugh even in his darkest moments was an epiphany that he shared with Walters. Reeve told Walters, "I knew then if I could laugh, I could live."[14]

A sense of humor makes a difference in conducting your business just like it does on the golf course. It eases tension and shows that you are human. Humor creates an emotional connection not only with fans but also with family, colleagues, clients, and customers.

Some of my most memorable moments as a UNC Tar Heel have included watching my alma mater win games with Michael Jordan leading the team to victory. However, it was a serendipitous moment at Shadow Creek that made me proudest to be associated with North Carolina and Jordan.

The clubhouse was almost empty. Most of the players were on the golf course and I'd gone inside the clubhouse to get a cold drink. I walked into the dining room. A family I didn't recognize was gathered around Jordan and a young boy who looked about fourteen-years-old. I had stumbled into the granting of a boy's Make-A-Wish®. Jordan chatted with the family and then took the boy alone into a private area for some one-on-one quality time. After awhile they emerged. The boy was grinning from ear to ear. He and Jordan walked out to the putting green and putted for about fifteen minutes. Jordan is a competitor and he concentrated on every shot with the boy as much as he did when he played competitive golf. However, now he was also in coach mode, totally focusing on the boy, passing on tips about everything from the best way to hold the putter to how to read the ball's lie, and how hard to hit the ball. I started humming James Taylor's song "Carolina In My Mind" because at this moment "there ain't no doubt in no one's mind that loves the finest thing around." Carolina was in Vegas and my favorite Tar Heel had just scored more points in my heart than he ever did on the courts playing for Chapel Hill.

Use your time as well as your money to help others as they face obstacles in their human path to make a difference in the lives of others. Give your time to those who need you. People are hurting all around you. You can make the difference in the life of another with as little as fifteen minutes of your time.

Olympic Gold medalist Brandi Chastain whipped off her jersey exposing her bra after defeating China in the 1991 FIFA Women's World Cup and became the subject of one of the most famous photographs in history of a woman celebrating an athletic victory. When asked what she was thinking when she exposed her bra she said, "Momentary insanity, nothing more, nothing less. I thought, 'My God, this is the greatest moment of my life on the soccer field.' I just lost my head."[15]

I had my chance to learn more than what I'd read about Chastain when we munched burgers beside each other one night at the private Blackjack Poker event for charity held in the Aria's Deuce Lounge, where the winner of each table won a spot later that night at Jordan's poker table. The final winner's pot at Jordan's table would be given to the winner's designated favorite charity. Chastain had just lost at her blackjack table to Dallas Cowboys' DeMarco Murray. As we ate, she told me about not making her junior high school team or her freshman high school team and how her special relationship with her grandfather who had played a variety of sports with her had inspired her self-confidence and taught her the value of being a team player. She said her grandfather gave her $1.00 for every goal she made and $1.50 for every assist. She said being a strong team member made the difference in her career.[16]

I asked Chastain what she says or does to teach her young son how to be successful. She said, "Nothing really. I just live my life as an example the same way my grandfather lived his life as an example to me."[17] Her quiet leadership style was evident the next day when Chastain demonstrated living her life as an example of what she values.

I was mesmerized as I watched her from the clubhouse window while sitting inside at the table with the celebrity golfers who had finished their golf rounds. While those of us gathered inside drank, told stories, and laughed as people do at the 19th hole, Chastain was outside on the clubhouse lawn with a giant smile on her face kicking a soccer ball with a half dozen kids too young to understand the enormity of her accomplishments. She was not thinking about herself, she was actively involved giving and sharing with others — a characteristic of personal excellence that results in personal happiness.

Share your knowledge to make the difference in the excellence of others. First hand experience with excellence is the most powerful way others learn excellence. Learning is an active process. Inspire excellence as an example of personal excellence. Multiply your excellence by passing it on to others.

Michael Phelps writes in his book, *Beneath the Surface*, about an analogy his coach Bob Bowman used when coaching him. Bowman said, "When we practice long hours, we're depositing money in the bank. We need to deposit enough so that when we need to make a large withdrawal, we have enough funds to withdraw."[18] Excellence takes time to develop. No one goes immediately from point A to point Z. Take each step, deposit with consistent practice every day to develop a deep tank of personal excellence so it does not run out. "Never stop depositing. Never give up."[19]

Coach Bowman is a fan of motivational speaker Earl Nightingale's research which found that successful people all have in common the habit of doing things that unsuccessful people don't like to do. Bowman's coaching philosophy is based on that according to Phelps. "Set your goals high. Work conscientiously, every day, to achieve them … and make a habit of doing things others aren't willing to do."[20]

Successful people in every field take actions beyond acquiring technical skill and education to make the difference in their success. You can take the same actions to make your life better. You can. You do not need money, physical strength, or a high IQ to do any of these things. You merely need to act.

I stared down at the Nevada desert from the plane's window as my plane home took flight. Reflecting on the winners I'd met, interviewed, observed, and researched, I realized that Steve Jobs was right, "You can't connect the dots looking forward; you can only connect them looking backwards." For me, the answer to my question, "What makes the winning difference?" required connecting what I'd learned from many dots.

The same actions that made the winning difference for Jordan's superstars and the epic winners in this book are the same actions that made the winning difference for The Beatles. They all were born with no more inside them at birth than you and I have within us at birth — and it is all we need to reach our individual peak performances. It is only what winners do with what they have inside that makes the winning difference — no matter money, religion, hometown, ancestors or who relatives are. The winners in this book show us what actions we must take. This book details how to take the actions to reach your goals to make the winning difference in your own life. Take a look back with me as I did in flight.

The Beatles believed in themselves and did not let others derail their dreams. They kept going when they failed despite obstacles. They didn't stop with their first number one single or when they made their first million.

The Beatles were committed to the goals they set. They did what it took to achieve their goal every day no matter where they were. They took more action. They did not miss an opportunity to take action whether it was at a church festival or at a seedy bar in Germany.

The Beatles were more successful working together as a team than they ever were as individuals. Ringo's vocal range was modest but his drumbeat unique and an important factor in the group's uber success. "Come Together" with others to make the difference. Every member is important.

John, Paul, George, and Ringo maintained and used a sense of humor to relieve tension not only when performing in nightclubs, but at public performances that included the British Royal family. John broke the ice at The Royal Variety Performance in London asking the audience for their help, "Will the people in the cheaper seats clap your hands and the rest of you would you just rattle your jewelry."[21]

The Beatles constantly evolved, adding new dimensions to their repertoire with equal energy, excitement, and enthusiasm. They added instrumental influences from India, jazz, country western, rhythm and blues along with instruments including the sitar and harmonica. Their interests stretched into every aspect of selling their products and their ideas forever changed the way music is written, performed, recorded, packaged, marketed, and distributed.

The Beatles gave time not just to their families and to the development of their personal careers but to others who needed help from Milwaukee to Bangladesh. Their selfless purpose was not to increase popularity or income but the positive residual by-product of their support of others increased their popularity and success.

Within ten short years before they ceased to be a group they had made a sizeable deposit having recorded 275 songs along with passing on their ideas to create a better world to "Give Peace a Chance."

The wherewithal to add actions to make the difference to overcome seemingly insurmountable obstacles transformed four "stinky cursing leather-clad lads" performing in "sweaty stinking holes" to internationally recognized men performing before Her Majesty the Queen of England. Taking actions that made the difference maximized the sale of products, services, and ideas that created great wealth for The Beatles. Taking the same actions will also work for you. But there is something more you need to know if you are to live on as a winner.

*People do not differ in their desire to be successful;
they differ in the price they are willing to pay for success.*

– Anonymous

No matter what your work, let it be your own.
No matter what your occupation,
let what you are doing be organic.
Let it be in your bones.
In this way, you will open the door by which the
affluence of heaven and earth shall stream into you.

– Ralph Waldo Emerson

Chapter Ten

Booyah!
How To Be Memorable
And Live On Forever

The one unforgiveable sin is to be boring.

– Christopher Hitchens
English-American Author

Oprah Winfrey laughs when she tells the story about how she learned the importance of not copying others. In her early days as a news anchor in Baltimore she felt that she had to be and sound like Barbara Walters:

> I was doing a list of foreign countries. And I called Canada 'ca-NAD-a.' I got so tickled. That wasn't 'ca-NAD-a'. That was CAN-a-da. And then I started laughing. Well, it became the first real moment I ever had. And the news director later said to me, 'If you do that, then you should just keep going, you shouldn't correct yourself and let people know.' So that was, for me, the beginning of realizing, 'Oh you can laugh at yourself, and you can make a mistake and it's not the end of the world.' You don't have to be perfect — the biggest lesson for me for television.[1]

Oprah didn't copy Barbara Walters anymore. Her authenticity, her being "real" is a big reason Oprah is well-loved. Her authenticity is also why any idea or product like a book she likes becomes an enormous success. People want the real you — not an actor.

Determine your own destiny or someone else will.
– Jack Welch
Former Chairman and CEO of General Electric

Carla Harris, the Wall Street banker mentioned earlier, denied her authenticity when she started her career. Harris, not only a banker, but also a professional singer with three albums, has performed two sold-out concerts at Carnegie Hall. Harris says, "When I started in banking, I didn't want anyone to talk about my life as a singer ... I'm tough and analytical."[2] Her feelings about denying an important part of herself changed when she realized that her authenticity could help her connect with clients. My favorite story about Harris is when she presented a pitch to Burger King during its 2006 Initial Public Offering of stock to the public.

Harris knew that five other companies were also pitching to Burger King. She asked the CEO if he were going to bring back the "Have it your way" jingle and when he said "yes" she asked if both verses would be brought back. The CEO was adamant that there was only one verse. Harris insisted, there were two and then sang the entirety of both verses![3] Her uniqueness helped her to connect with the CEO, demonstrated she knew his company, and set her apart from the other five bankers. Harris won the Burger King account.

"Carlos be Carlos ... Not everyone is going to like you. You can't be everyone's golden boy," Josephina Baragrande Santana told her son when naysayers told him that unless he changed his music to sound like the current popular music he would never be a success.[4] His mother told him to play the music he loved that reflected who he was — Mexican American. He fused his music with rock, jazz, blues, salsa, Latin and African rhythms for an original and authentic sound.

Carlos Santana listened to his mother and played his original music to an audience at Woodstock that had never heard him. He became an instant hit — all before recording a single record. He embraced the lessons of his mother and a high school art teacher who told him, "There is no room for fifty percent. You must be one hundred and fifty percent in whatever you do, whether it is art, music, or anything else." Santana concluded, "I would have to be Carlos Santana and do it so well that no one would mistake me for anyone else."[5] His band's first album went triple platinum, sold more than four million copies, and remained on the *Billboard* chart for more than two years.

"What made the difference in your success?" I asked Santana when I met him having coffee in New Orleans where he was headlining Jazz Fest. "Obey your mom. She is always right."[6] He dedicates his memoir, *The Universal Tone: Bringing My Story to Light*, to his mother "for her power, patience, tenacity, unshakable faith and total conviction."[7]

Remember where you came from without losing sight of ethics and values. Let the moral compass of your roots guide your decision-making whether it's composing original music, running a business, or running plays in football. Remember, "One third of the people you know like you, one third of the people you know don't like you, and one third of the people you know don't care." Be yourself. Please yourself. Follow your dreams. Share with the world the wonderful authentic person you are — the unique person only you can be.

The most exhausting thing in life is being insincere.
— Anne Morrow Lindberg

You may not always like what your family and friends have to say, but they can inspire you to create something unique of your own choosing. John Wagner risked offending family and non-family females when he created a cartoon composite of the sassy women in his life who made irreverent comments about aging, sex, retirement, and the workplace. His decision to create an authentic character unlike any to ever grace a greeting card made a huge difference in his career and in Hallmark's™ bottom line. Over 220 million "Maxine" greeting cards have been purchased since crabby, wisecracking Maxine's debut in 1986. Maxine's originality and authenticity made her a G.O.A.T. Hallmark™ boasts, "She is the first and only greeting card character to move from the card aisle directly into popular culture. Maxine appears on everything from t-shirts to towels."[9]

Heisman Trophy winner Tim Brown was my dinner partner at the Ace Hardware Shootout at Turtle Bay in Hawaii benefiting the Children's Miracle Network. I asked him during dinner what made the difference in his success. He said that after winning the Heisman Trophy he came home and found a sign on his house his mother had made that said, "Welcome Home Timmy."

> My Mama told me, 'When you come inside you are always Timmy.' The Heisman made a difference in my life but what made the difference in my achieving the success I enjoy today is choosing to be Timmy and not doing anything different than I had been doing as Timmy. I grew up going to church. I'd spend all day and into the evening at church when I was growing up. I was around people who had values and shared the same beliefs I did.
>
> I grew up with five siblings in a two-bedroom house. I slept wherever I could find a place. One night I fell asleep on the couch. My father worked construction. He came home drunk late one night and found me asleep on the couch. He tried to kill me. I didn't want to be like that or hurt the people I love when I grew up.
>
> When I won the Heisman, I found myself in the

company of people like Magic Johnson and Whitney Houston who did a lot of partying that led to a lot of trouble that made a difference in their lives. I have an addictive personality and I knew that I couldn't do what they were doing.

When I go out to a party, I drink ginger ale. I love my wife. I love my kids. Choosing to be myself, to be Timmy, and choosing not to do what some other people are doing is what has made the difference in my success.[10]

Brown's book, *The Making of a Man*, is an inspiring discussion of the principles and priorities that made him the man he is today.

Eleven-time world record surfing champion and greatest of all-time surfer Kelly Slater, like Tim Brown, had a father who was an alcoholic. Like Brown, Slater chooses not to follow the crowd. He pursues a healthy lifestyle. I met Slater on the beach on the wild North Shore of Oahu minutes after he won the famous Volcom Pipe Pro contest. At 44 he was still at the top of the ASP (Association of Surfing Professionals) World Tour and as fit as any man I've ever seen. Slater never drinks more than one beer and credits eating a healthy diet and living a healthy lifestyle to making all the difference in his athletic ability. He says, "You'll never see a fat professional surfer."[11] After Michael Phelps' 2016 Olympic performance, Slater posted on Instagram, "When talent and desire have a common goal, everything is possible."[12]

Create an aura that makes people want to interact with you and help you realize your goals. Be yourself. Don't copy others. You may initially dazzle if you copy someone but your authentic self will eventually surface. You don't have to be perfect — you just have to be 100% you. You, your history, your uniqueness is what makes you interesting.

Ronda "Rowdy" Rousey was born with her umbilical cord wrapped around her neck resulting in a neurological speech sound disorder that required years of intense therapy. She began studying judo at age eleven. Rousey qualified for the Olympics and became the first U.S. woman to win an Olympic medal in judo in the summer Olympics in Beijing in 2008. When she returned home she found no job placement or scholarship. A high school drop out, Rousey lacked education and work experience and struggled to survive. She took bartending classes and found work as a bartender to make ends meet. It bothered her that she was one of the best fighters in the world and no one noticed, while male fighters captivated audiences and female fighters were ignored. She looked at what male fighters were doing that was different. In an interview on *Live! with Kelly and Michael* she said, "What we (women) are missing is an antagonist. Everyone is trying to be Batman and there is no Joker. So there needed to be someone to push the story line. There was no story."[13]

Rousey expanded her brand to create interest and to become un-ignorable. She pursued work in film. Rousey's credits now include acting in a reboot of *Road House, The Expendables 3, Furious 7, Entourage, and Blindspot*. Current plans include a film based on her best-selling memoir, *My Fight/Your Fight*. She has signed sponsorships with Reebok, Metro PCS, Buffalo Apparel, Carl's Jr., and Monster Energy. Taylor, a public relations agency, says, "What attracts brands to Rousey is her polarity. She can appear on *Ellen* one day and destroy her opponent the next — makes her all the more intriguing. Rousey has opened the eyes of brands everywhere that consumers look for stories to make a human connection. People want authenticity and Rousey is as authentic as it gets."[14]

Rousey at this writing has won twelve professional fights — eleven in the first round. An ESPN poll voted her "Best Female

Athlete in the World Ever." In 2015 Rousey won the ESPY for Best Female Athlete beating out Lindsey Vonn and Serena Williams. She is the first woman to ever win "Best Fighter" and is the highest paid fighter — male or female in the world. Forbes estimates her career earnings at 13 million dollars. CNNMoney calls her a "Marketing Knockout."[15]

Only four years after Dana White, President of the UFC (Ultimate Fighting Championship) said there would never be a woman in the UFC, Rousey smashed records causing White to change his mind. White now says, "She's the greatest athlete I've ever worked with. With her, it's like the Tyson era, like, how fast is she going to destroy somebody, and in what manner? Ronda's one in a million."[16]

Parisian shoe designer Christian Louboutin dreamed in 1991 of opening a shop in New York. He was frustrated because while his shoes were nice they just didn't pop. One day while working on a prototype, Louboutin noticed an assistant painting her nails red and says, "I grabbed her nail polish and painted the sole and it became my trademark."[17] The unique shiny red-lacquered soled shoes became hot items for VIPs and A-Listers who wanted to package themselves in a memorable way. Louboutin now has 93 shops and sells almost a million pairs of shoes a year. According to celebritynetworth.com, his worth is reported as $1.6 billion.

Louboutin-wearing Sarah Jessica Parker and her character, Carrie, in *Sex in the City* found unique clothing designed by Vivienne Westwood, the British fashion designer, valuable in establishing personae. A-Lister Pharrell Williams wears a signature Westwood creation that makes him memorable as "The Happy Man in the Hat." Williams' response to *CBS Sunday Morning's* Anthony Mason's question asking him about fitting in a box, "No. I just never even seen the box. It's like, what do you mean? What wall? What ceiling? What are you talking about? Hence the phrase 'Room without a Roof' you know? Limitless ... I suppose I've always had my own way."[18] Williams' decision to live his life "in a room without a roof" has certainly made the difference in his life but he says there are two things more.

Asked what changed for him after the disappointing results of his first solo album in 2006, *In My Mind*, Williams said, "It didn't turn out the way I wanted it to and I blamed everybody around me but myself ... I realized along the way that there wasn't enough purpose in my music." Williams changed his original ego-driven purpose to one that would lift up people. His song, "Happy," he says, "changed me."[19]

Williams credits others with his success as *Billboard* magazine's top producer of the past decade. He believes his success would go away without crediting those who encouraged and taught him. Williams takes time to thank his grandmother who encouraged his interest in music and every teacher by name. "You see people spin out of control like that all the time. I mean those are the most tragic stories, the most gifted people who start to believe it's really all them. It's not all you. It can't be all you. Just like you need air to fly a kite, it's not the kite. It's the air."[20]

Spinning out of control happens to many winners you wouldn't expect because they wear the biggest smiles. Fourteen-year-old Amanda Beard, the darling of the 1996 Atlanta Olympics, memorably strode onto the pool deck clutching her teddy bear, Howard, and strode off with him in addition to a gold medal and two silvers. The next year when she grew six inches and gained thirty pounds, (the normal result of going through puberty), the media called her "fat, washed up, and finished" saying that she'd never again do anything good in swimming.[21] She was devastated, became bulimic, battled depression, substance abuse, and self-mutilated before going on to prove naysayers wrong. She became a seven-time Olympic medalist, model, and TV sports broadcast personality.

Beard and I sat beside each other at lunch in 2011 before sharing the podium at The Greater Hartford Women's Conference in Connecticut. We talked not about swimming but about writing, publishing, and the critical importance of persevering to achieve in and out of the water.[22] Multiple publishers had turned down her book, *In the Water They Can't See You Cry*. She wanted to talk to me about publishing her story about her personal and professional trials and how she overcame them in hopes of helping others. Beard persisted. Touchstone, a division of Simon and Schuster, published her book the following year.

Be Memorable

We live at an accelerated pace using a variety of tools to help us compete as we strive to reach our goals. This dizzying canter forces clients, customers, family and friends to make quick decisions regarding purchases and decisions. The perception others have of you directly affects whether they will choose to form a personal or professional relationship with you. The reality of who you believe you are does not matter. The perception of who you are is the determining factor. It's not fair, but it's how it is.

What Carla Harris said is worth repeating, "Perception is the co-pilot to reality."[23] Buyers of products, services, and ideas initially will choose to have a working relationship with you based on a culmination of their perception of your physical, emotional, intellectual, social and spiritual personae. People more likely will help you win what you want if their perception of you is favorable — but only if they can remember you. The good news is, you can take actions that will affect how you are perceived and you can take actions to make yourself memorable.

Legendary Dartmouth professor John Rassias said, "Teaching is like making love. In order for your message to pass beyond the welcome mat of the brain it has to be delivered heart to heart no matter what your subject is."[24] His language teaching technique, adopted by the Peace Corps and used by teachers all over the world, involves the use of all the senses. For learning to stick, you have to first take action and use drama to catch attention, show heart to heart interest in the learner, and involve him in an active fun way. Only then can you deliver a lesson that will be remembered.

He caught the attention of students in his French literature, history, and language classes and made his lessons memorable by dressing as Molière to teach French literature and shooting off a cannon at the beginning of a lecture about the French Revolution. (The local police and fire departments showed up after that lesson). Once he brought a cabbage to class to teach the phrase "mon petit chou" meaning "my little cabbage." The first day I was a student in his Rassias Method® workshop he began by ripping off the sleeve of his blue Brooks Brother's shirt and throwing it out to the class. I caught his sleeve midair and still have it as a reminder of the energy, enthusiasm, and heart to heart display of passion that makes the difference in being a teacher whose lessons are caught and not lost forever.

Top winners are authentic and memorable for the right things. Like Rassias taught, you can't be boring. If people have to search for something interesting about you, you are boring. Brilliance when it is boring and bland is the kiss of death especially when it includes TMI — **T**oo **M**uch **I**nformation. Instead share information that is ABC — **A**rticulate **B**rief **C**lear. Share what your authentic self has to offer whether it is goods, services, or talent in an original, interesting, credible, and colorful way.

The following explains what you need to do so people won't cringe and flee when they see you coming, and ensures that you will be sought after and remembered — for the right reasons. First, let's start with the basics of being an interesting person versus being a boring person:

1. *Interesting people are dreamers and know what they want, make a plan to achieve what they want, and are driven to achieve.* Boring people let others decide their destinies and are satisfied with left-overs.

2. *Interesting people engage in conversation, are well-informed, and able to converse on a variety of topics.* Boring people avoid conversation, have little to say, and lack range and depth of topics. Boring people are not necessarily boring at their core. More often they are introverted. In a nutshell, you can't be shy. It won't kill you to talk to people.

3. *Interesting people have multiple interests and hobbies.* Boring people have few interests and hobbies. If you want to be interesting you need to have activities you enjoy and like to discuss. People will find you boring if you only have one hobby and it's one most people don't share. Diversify.

4. *Interesting people expend energy to get out of their comfort zone to experience life.* Boring people are complacent and stay in their comfort zone where they securely stay the same. If you want to be interesting, you need to be interested in exploring the world around you and the world that requires travel to places out of your comfort zone.

5. *Interesting people like variety — people, places, food, cultures, etc.* Boring people eat the same food, see the same people, go to the same places, etc.

6. *Interesting people are in motion and welcome the excitement of change.* Boring people are stagnant and afraid of change.

7. *Interesting people understand the "tennis game" of good conversation — going back and forth between conversation partners.* They engage, listen, respond, and share. Boring people control conversations, forcing others to listen to their

own voices with droning one-sided conversations.

You don't accomplish much by swimming with the mainstream. Hell, a dead fish can do that.

– Kinky Friedman
American Singer, Songwriter, Politician and Author of Several Books Including *Greenwich Killing Time* and *Elvis, Jesus and Coca-Cola*

Stuart Scott became famous as an ESPN sports broadcaster for his colorful ABC *(Articulate Brief Clear)* commentaries that added memorable magic with colorful phrases like "Booyah!" "Call him butter, he's on a roll," "He's as cool as the other side of the pillow," and "Holla at a playa when you see him in the street." Scott was educated, informed, and credible but perhaps no more than many other broadcast journalists who never make it to the top. Scott's likeability and ABC authenticity formula torpedoed him to the top to make him memorable.

Taking personal responsibility for your life and a humble, happy attitude attracts people to you. Give others credit when it is due, and be eager to lift people up not only by showing them the value they give you but the value they will find in your ability, product, service, or idea. Demonstrate genuine interest in people. Treat everyone well — even people who are not interested in what you offer including your dreams and goals.

You must make multiple impressions on those you want to remember you in order to be memorable and to build brand awareness. Repetition is in direct connection with positioning. To be remembered requires repetition. You can't say or do something once and leave it at that. Successful business people say what they want as many times as they need until they get the desired response. Would you remember a commercial if you only saw it once?

Consider the findings of Professor Andrea Ordanini of Milan's Bocconi University with the University of Southern California discussed in *The Journal of Consumer Psychology* about repetition in songs. The study found that chorus repetition in songs increases processing by the brain. Based on analysis of songs dating back to the 1950s, for each additional repeat in a song the likelihood of the song making it to the number one position increased 14.5 per cent.[25] It is no coincidence that consumers exposed to a chorus of repeated messages eventually buy music, products, services, and ideas they remember due to repetition. The Beatles' synchronized bow and comedienne Carol Burnett's tug on her ear were strategically done at the conclusion of every performance to create lasting impressions. The repetitiveness of these actions made them memorable.

Don't fool yourself or take the comfortable way out by not repeating your message after only one attempt. Telling yourself, "I don't want to bother them again or they must not want, etc. because I already asked and they never responded/did what was wanted." It is more likely they simply forgot your first message. You must ask again. And again. And again, until your message is remembered and you reap the results you want.

The number of times you need to repeat your message to be remembered is debatable but what is agreed is that the repetition does not need to be verbatim. You can repeat using a combination of messages, stories, statistics, and sound bites.

Nurture your network or it will wither and die. People are just like animals that need to be petted and fed. Follow up with the people you meet by letting those you meet know that you care about them and appreciate them. Danish comedian Victor Borge was on target when he said, "Santa Claus has the right idea. Visit people once a year."[26] Send birthday cards, sympathy notes, and letters of congratulations. Write personal notes, email, telephone, or send invitations for coffee, lunch, golf, etc. within two business days following events because people will still remember you.

Be clear and precise when extending invitations. Being clear will prevent ping-pong conversation including, "Where would you like to meet?" "What time is good for you?" Being clear will also keep you from looking weak and insecure. You'll find clarity not only is more efficient but more likely will result in the follow-up meeting you want. For example, "I'd like to invite you to the Island Café next Tuesday at noon" is far stronger than, "Let's get together sometime next week." Suggest options if you are totally wide-open and the other person is not.

To be memorable you must be smart, courteous, and valuable.

Be Smart

Be smart by recording contact information and memory joggers about people in your database so you can help others when you have a reason to help them!

Be Courteous

Instead of saying thank you with a text or email, be courteous by sending a handwritten thank you note to people who give you their business or do something for you. Handwritten letters and notes are increasingly rare. Rare is remembered.

Be Valuable

Learn about the people you meet and how you can help them. Be valuable by following up with people you meet based on their needs that you've learned about through listening. Look for ways to help people. Share articles/information you have or discover in the future that shows that you understand their interests/needs. Remember them when you find information they will find useful or enjoyable.

Share what you have that is helpful in interesting ways and when possible consider sharing information through stories. People remember and are transformed by stories because stories are more memorable than facts and figures and have the power to move hearts, minds, and feet. People tune in to stories that explain information that is helpful and generally tune out when information is presented with boring facts and numbers. Be sure not to embellish your stories with information that isn't true just to be interesting, or you'll damage your credibility causing you to be remembered for the wrong reason.

Be of value to others by being a mentor, making introductions, and recommending people you meet to others. People will be grateful and remember you.

Give gifts. Gifts are an extension of you, your company, and your brand. Take the time to make sure every touch point with others builds your brand as world class and as one the recipient values. To be memorable, gifts must make the recipient feel special and that he or she alone is thought of with the gift. Give in a way that is unmotivated in wanting anything in return. *Giving and Gifts* by Lynne Farwell White is a lively useful guide to giving the right present for every occasion. It is full of ideas for thoughtful gifts so that even the simplest gifts you give will be remembered.

Robert Cialdini in his book, *Influence: The Psychology of Persuasion*, documents numerous studies that show that giving a person something of even small value and later asking for something in return significantly increases the odds that the person will likely reciprocate. In fact, he reports that sociologists like Alvin Gouldner find that, "There is no human society that does not subscribe to this rule."[27] Our minds relate to what is visible and tangible, so choose a gift that can be seen, felt or touched and remain in front of the recipient to remind him of the positive experience with you and the value of the benefits of your relationship.

Don't overlook the opportunity to connect with the most influential or important people in your client's life — the spouse and children, when you think of a meaningful gift. If you take the time to know about who is important to your client, it will help you determine a gift that can make that person feel special.

*You can have everything in life you want,
if you will just help other people get what they want.*

– Zig Ziglar

The most priceless gift you can give is the gift of your time being kind to others. Kindness costs nothing. Whether you are rich or poor, you can give kindness. Be kind. Be kinder than necessary.

*You cannot do a kindness too soon,
for you never know how soon it will be too late.*

– Ralph Waldo Emerson

Help others first and expect nothing in return! Al Ritter writes in his book, *The 100/0 Principle: The Secret of Great Relationships*, that the most effective way to create and sustain relationships with others is the 100/0 Principle. Ritter believes the philosophy of most people who expect relationships to be 50/50 does not work. He believes instead that if you expect nothing in return you will avoid lots of disappointments because you expect nothing in return and will avoid the trap of doing things for the wrong reasons — what you expect or hope to get in return. If you take 100% responsibility for any relationship, you will need to give up judgment and your right to be right.[28]

The 100/0 Principle is a simple but life-changing concept that can dramatically improve all aspects of your life if you apply it in your interactions with everyone, including people you think don't deserve it. The paradox of this principle is that,

"When you take authentic responsibility for a relationship, more often than not, the other person quickly chooses to take responsibility as well. Consequently, the 100/0 relationship quickly transforms into something approaching 100/100. When that occurs, true breakthroughs happen for the individuals involved, their teams, their organizations and their families."[29]

Be memorable for the right reason — a good reputation. A good reputation is the result of many good deeds over a long period of time. A poor reputation is the result of only one poor deed. Do good deeds every day, over and over again. The moral quality of your actions will come back to you. Make your actions your very best and to the benefit of every person you have the privilege to meet.

The first rule of money, according to Michael Phillips, author of *The Seven Laws of Money*, is "Money will come when you are doing the right thing."[30] When asked what the most difficult thing for people to understand about money, Phillips goes back to the first rule of money, "The most difficult thing for people to understand about money is that money will come when you are doing the right thing. Money is secondary to what you are doing."[31] Do the right thing.

Be passionate about your choices. Hoi An, Vietnam — City of Lanterns, is a place to stroll on cobbled footpaths past ancient dwellings over bridges arching over the Thu Bon River. Glowing bright colored silk lanterns are everywhere adding color to the day and magic to the night. One of the most memorable elements of this place is its food. Food brings people and cultures together. Hoi An brings people and cultures together like no other ... at least it did during my visit when the city hosted the most decorated chefs on the planet at its International Food Festival. President of the Worldchefs Congress and Executive Master Chef Thomas Gugler was there wearing a sash adorned with so many medals that with a hearty chuckle he proclaimed, "I am the Christmas tree. The most decorated of all the chefs."[32] Now that's a memorable ABC comment! Gugler wears the medals to prove it. And if there is an A-List chef for the greatest winners of all time, it's Thomas Gugler. The roster of people he has cooked for includes former President of France — Francois Mitterand, German Chancellor Angela Merkel, CEOs like Conoco Phillips' James Mulva, Kings of Saudi Arabia and Jordan, Emirs of Bahrain and the UAE, Sultans and Princes, the King of Pop — Michael Jackson, Queen of Daytime TV — Oprah, mega mogul Aristotle Onassis who married Jackie Kennedy, Elton John, Madonna, Frank Sinatra, Liza Minelli, and a dizzying number of star athletes. "What made the difference in your success?" I asked Gugler in between courses at the chef's private dinner. "Passion. Loving what I do. Passionately learning about food from around the world. Passionately experimenting with food. Passionately creating my own dishes. Passionately sharing food. Passion. Passion is the one thing. Passion for what I do is the one thing that made the difference. It is why I am the Christmas tree,"[33] he said with twinkling eyes and a robust grin.

You don't have to be rich, famous, or a genius to take the actions described in this book to add abundance to your life and to make a difference in the lives of others. A participant who attended one of my programs shared what he does that helps others and adds pleasure to his life. He carries a stash of ziplock bags containing non-perishable food to share with people he sees on the roadside asking for money because they are hungry. This simple act does not bring him wealth or fame. He does not do it to make a memorable impression. However, the result of his action was evident in his face — personal happiness. Truly, you are remembered not by your words but by your actions — and kind actions you gift to others gifts you back by increasing personal happiness.

If you're afraid of being forgotten then do something.

Afterword

The Biggest Difference

Life is a long journey that quickly passes.

Muhammad Ali's friend, John Ramsey, sat ringside beside him at the 2000 Summer Olympic Games' boxing competition. The crowd began shouting "USA! USA! USA!" when the American competitor won, stepped out of the ring, and walked over to take a photo with Muhammad Ali. After the photo, Muhammad Ali whispered to Ramsey, "I want to see the loser." Ramsey told an attendant who led them to the loser's room where they found the young boxer sitting alone in a corner with a towel wrapped around his neck applying pressure to a bloody gauze patch under his eye. The vibe in the room was lowest of the low.[1]

Ali started dancing and throwing out jabs saying, "Show me what you got kid! Show me what you got!" Grabbing the now smiling kid in a bear hug Ali said, "I saw what you did out there. Man, you moving good. You going to be a champion. Don't give up." In just an instant Ali took that kid from low to high. When they left the room Ramsey said to Ali, "Muhammad, you are the greatest." Ali shot back grinning, "Tell me something I don't already know."[2]

As you walk through life, fully believe in your personal power and like Ali take time to build up others by showing you believe in the personal power of everyone. We are all worthy. As Muhammad Ali tweeted, "Service to others is the rent you pay for your room here on earth."[3]

*If you make it about yourself you will fail every time.
Honor the ones that come before you, and
leave a legacy for the ones who come after you.*

– Eric Berry
2016 AP Comeback Player of the Year
and ESPYS Best Comeback Athlete

In the end, the greatest and very likely the happiest winners on the planet are not limited to Fortune 100 CEOs, gold medal athletes, celebrities, or earners of more money than they can spend in a lifetime. They are not limited to the owners of the biggest houses on their blocks, drivers of the swankiest new cars, or members in the most exclusive clubs. The greatest winners are the ones who make the winning difference in their broader communities using the opportunities they have to make a difference in the lives of others. You can be one of the greatest winners. You now unequivocally know how.

You've now read about winners from a wide variety of faiths and careers including a Muslim boxer, a Buddhist monk, and a Jewish journalist. In closing, I share what I learned from an Episcopal Bishop named Sidney Sanders. Perhaps it will make the biggest difference in your happiness no matter your religion, profession, where you are from, who your ancestors were and your relatives are.

Sanders once told me that if I closed my eyes and remembered one of my happiest moments he could tell me three things about it. I would have rolled my eyes and politely walked away if I had not respected him. I thought of one of my happiest moments. After a minute I opened my eyes and he told me what I have never forgotten. Pause now and think of your happiest moment to determine if what makes you happiest is the same as for me. STOP reading now.

Now that you've done this, here's what he said, "You were not thinking about yourself. You were giving or sharing with someone else."[4]

True happiness results from a shift in focus from getting to giving. Happiness is about a feeling that lasts that you do not get from money, material items, sex, alcohol or drugs. Equipping yourself with skills that give you confidence frees you to forget about yourself so you can reach out to others to give and to share. When you shift from a getting mentality to a giving mentality you reach the ultimate in personal achievement — happiness. Giving makes the most profound difference in happiness. It is the easiest action to take of all the actions because you do not have to wait to land a job, make a team, get a part, or acquire money or material things in order to give. Kindness and compassion cost nothing.

Jon Bon Jovi and his wife, Dorothea, started a restaurant that allows everyone to give. JBJ Soul Kitchen is a dine-in restaurant with a menu without prices. Everyone is welcome to a well-presented nutritious meal including soup or salad, choice of entree, and freshly baked dessert. All food is fresh and local. Diners have two options. They can make a donation for their meal or they can volunteer by doing one hour of work cooking, busing tables, or waitressing for a three-course meal. A donation of $10 covers the cost of a meal. Diners who choose can donate more to cover the cost of meals for others. Bon Jovi's purpose isn't just to feed the body — it's also to nourish the community. "Friendship is our daily special."[5] Bon Jovi created an opportunity for everyone to give.

> *Mentorship is so funny because if you don't have anybody to pour back in to what's been poured in to you, then it's null and void as to what you're receiving. You gotta give back what you're receiving.*
>
> – Omari Hardwick
> American Actor

A mother once told her young son to take flowers to a shut-in neighbor. The boy returned happy to report that the neighbor was delighted with the gift. The mother told her son to smell his hands and to tell her what he smelled.

"I smell the flowers!" he chimed.

"Kindness always leaves a sweet fragrance," said the wise mother. When you give, you get. Give to get. When you get, you win. It's as easy as this.

Giving and sharing with others is not limited to your personal life. Your professional life is not separate from your personal life. The most respected, enduring businesses have employees who are happy because they feel valued, needed, and respected. Kindness demonstrated in its many forms is given and shared by their leaders and by those with whom they work. The most successful businesses are ones whose clients and customers are awarded the same.

Louis Zamperini, the American Olympian and WWII survivor whose life was the subject of a book and the movie *Unbroken* said, "To persevere is important for everybody — don't give up, don't give in."[6] Not giving up and not giving in saved Zamperini's life when he survived on a raft for 47 days after his plane was shot down and afterwards when he was sent to a series of Japanese prisoner of war camps. People at the top in every field have faced obstacles that they have persevered to overcome in order to survive and thrive at the highest levels.

The ESPY Awards presented by the sports network ESPN recognizes top individual and team athletic achievement. The ESPY capstone award is the Jim Valvano Foundation Award for Perseverance named after the famous North Carolina State University basketball coach and sports broadcast journalist. I had the privilege to attend the 22nd annual ESPY Awards ceremony that raised $6.5 million for cancer research with the Jimmy V Foundation. During the ESPY Awards ceremony, Stuart Scott was presented The Jimmy V Award. Scott gave an inspirational acceptance speech.

Scott talked about how what we do for others is worth more

in the end than what we do for ourselves. He mentioned people you might expect who supported him — doctors, nurses, and family. He also mentioned people you wouldn't expect. His bosses:

> I've got corporate executives, my bosses, this is true, who will text message me and say, 'Hey, I heard you had chemotherapy today, want me to stop by and pick you up something to eat and bring it to you?' Whose boss does that? My bosses do that.[7]

ESPN could not have purchased better publicity. Scott's bosses had not reached out to him in hopes of public recognition. They reached out to Scott because that is who they are as human beings who find time to let others know that they are valued. No wonder Stuart Scott continued to work so hard for ESPN despite surgeries and chemo treatment — in fact he'd had four surgeries in the week prior to his speech on stage at the ESPY Awards Ceremony that was broadcast live before millions of television viewers. ESPN is known for excellence in sports broadcast reporting because it fosters excellence in employees with excellent leadership. For excellent results, take time to show value, need, and respect to everyone — your family, your friends, the people you work with, the people you work for, and the people who work for you. It will make a difference in your business and in your life.

> *Wear gratitude like a cloak*
> *and it will feed every corner of your life.*
>
> – Rumi

What Steve Jobs valued will perhaps also help you when you are confused, scared, embarrassed, or anything else regarding the choices in your life:

> Remembering that I'll be dead soon is the most important tool I've ever encountered to help me make the big choices in life. Because almost everything — all external expectations, all pride, all fear of embarrassment or failure — these things just fall away in the face of death, leaving only what is truly important.[8]

Author Nicholas Sparks, inspired after the death of his sister to write *A Walk to Remember,* said what made the difference in his life was "good health."[9] Look after your health.

Vivaldi's music played while I walked down the aisle to take my seat at my older daughter's wedding. However, the words to Bon Jovi's song, "It's My Life," played in my mind as drummer Tico Torres escorted me to my seat. In this surreal moment, "my life" and my daughter's life flashed through my mind, starting with my parents who were married over fifty years. I remembered mom's toast given on their 50th wedding anniversary when she mentioned that many people had asked what made the difference in her and my father's long lasting marriage versus short failed marriages. "Commitment," she said. "Acting on your commitment every day."[10] It makes the difference in marriage as well as in business and in life.

Coach Jim Valvano was awarded the Arthur Ashe Courage and Humanitarian Award at the first ever ESPY Awards when he was dying of cancer. Valvano is remembered for many things but especially for two enormously public moments. First, for running up and down the basketball court with an expression of disbelief and looking for someone to hug after his team won the 1983 NCAA championship. And second, he is remembered for his inspirational ESPY acceptance speech given eight weeks before he died.

Valvano had thrown up on the plane during the entire flight to the ESPY Awards ceremony and was so sick that no one thought he would be able to walk on the stage, much less speak. However, he did speak, and he spoke for longer than the allotted time. A time monitoring screen started flashing indicating his speaking time was up. Valvano said to the audience:

> That screen is flashing up there 30 seconds like I care about that screen right now, huh? I got tumors all over my body. I'm worried about some guy in the back going 30 seconds? You got a lot, hey va fa Napoli, buddy. You got a lot.
>
> To me we should all do three things every day. Number one is laugh. You should laugh every day. Number two is think. You should spend some time in thought. Number three is you should have your emotions moved to tears, could be happiness or joy. But think about it. If you laugh, you think, and you cry, that's a full day. That's a heck of a day. You do that seven days a week, you're going to have something special.

The light flickered again later into his speech and he concluded:

> I know, I gotta go, I gotta go; and I got one last thing, and I said it before, and I want to say it again. Cancer can take away all my physical abilities. It cannot touch my mind, it cannot touch my heart and it cannot touch my soul. And those three things are going to carry on forever. Don't give up. Don't ever give up.[11]

Valvano died less than two months later at age 47. Life is a short journey for all of us with a one-way ticket and no return ticket. Make the most of it. Don't give up on your dreams. You are the engine — *the only engine* — that can fuel your unique dream with a winning mental mindset hellbent with passion to persistently take the actions you've learned in this book to win. Don't reach the end of your life wondering why you never won what you want. Don't give up. Make a difference in your life … and *pass it on!*

Life is short and we do not have much time to gladden the hearts of those who travel the way with us. So, be swift to love and make haste to be kind.

– Henri-Frédéric Amiel
Swiss Moral Philosopher

END

Notes

Introduction

1. Philip Galanes, "Speak Your Own Truth, On Your Own Terms," June 27, 2014, https://www.nytimes.com/2014/06/29/fashion/billie-jean-king-and-jason-collins-on-being-gay-athletes.html.

2. Michael Phelps, *Beneath the Surface* (Delaware: Skyhorse Publishing, 2012), 143.

3. Olivier Poirier-Leroy, "8 Michael Phelps Quotes to Get You Fired Up," *Swim Swam,* July 21, 2016, https://swimswam.com/8-michael-phelps-quotes-get-fired/.

4. Nick Zaccardi, "Michael Phelps Shares Goal Sheet From Young Age On *UNDENIABLE*," *NBC Sports UNDENIABLE* with Joe Buck, December 16, 2015, http://olympics.nbcsports.com/2015/12/17/michael-phelps-goal-sheet-joe-buck-undeniable-interview/.

5. Michael Phelps, *No Limits: The Will to Succeed* (New York: Free Press, 2008), 14.

6. Facebook *Sports Illustrated* Post by Michael Phelps, August 29, 2016.

Chapter One

1. Robert Lipsyte, "The Greatest," *Time*, Vol.187, No. 23, June 2016.

2. Ibid.

3. "The Beatles' Songs Are Played 50 Million Times In The First 48 Hours Of Their Music Being Available To Stream Online," *Daily Mail,* December 26, 2015, http://www.dailymail.co.uk/news/article-3375079/The-Beatles-songs-played-50-million-times-48-hours-music-available-stream-online.html#ixzz4l2cdBMv9.

4. "Weirdest Beatle Fact," *The Beatles Bible*, December 2011, https://www.beatlesbible.com/forum/yesterday-and-today/weirdest-beatle-fact/.

5. Pew Research Center, *"The Beatles Here, There, Everywhere,"* August 28, 2009, http://www.pewresearch.org/fact-tank/2009/08/28/the-beatles-here-there-everywhere/.

6. John Lennon interview, "To The Toppermost of the Poppermost." 1980, https://www.youtube.com/watch?v=GzzeaU6p4wI.

7. Tejvan Pettinger, *"Biography of John Lennon,"* Oxford, U.K. www.biographyonline.net, May 28, 2007. Updated January 15, 2018.

8. John Lennon interview, "To The Toppermost of the Poppermost." 1980, https://www.youtube.com/watch?v=GzzeaU6p4wI.

9. George Harrison Interview, "The Beatles Early Days," n.d. https://www.youtube.com/watch?v=WCUb0xGonpU&list=PLIlFmAblzeiS3X8DwX6LG_lb5pOZ3QDwq.

10. Pawan Munjal, interview with *NBC Golf Channel* at Hero World Challenge, Albany, Bahamas, December 2015.

11. Ibid.

12. Tiger Woods, interview with *NBC Golf Channel* at Hero World Challenge, Albany, Bahamas, December 2015.

13. Mark Bryan, interview with author, Myrtle Beach World Amateur Handicap Tournament, September 1, 2015.

14. Carli Lloyd, interview with Nora O'Donnell and Anthony Mason *CBS This Morning* July 7, 2015, https://www.cbsnews.com/news/womens-world-cup-usa-midfielder-carli-lloyd-epic-victory-against-japan/.

15. Sam Walton and David Glass, Historic Video Interviews Presented by and Available for Viewing at The Walmart Museum, Bentonville, Arkansas.

16. Rudy Ruettiger, interview with Winifred Joan McMurry White, Chicago, Illinois, June 23, 2014.

17. Tim Hardaway, interview with author, Oahu, Hawaii, February 4, 2014.

18. Walt Disney, The Disneyland Story (Disneyland Episode #1): October 27th, 1954, https://www.youtube.com/watch?v=k_1xsPytKJw.

19. Michael Phelps Quotes – Part 1, October 8, 2014, https://www.youtube.com/watch?v=9Ubb8ij3VkM.

20. Guy Yocom, "Sean Foley," *Golf Digest*, March 25, 2012.

21. Sean Foley, interview with author, Bay Hill, Florida, March 22, 2013.

22. Michael Phelps, *No Limits: The Will to Succeed* (New York: Free Press, 2008), 14-15.

23. Nancy Weil, "Bill Gates: In His Own Words," *Computerworld*, June 23, 2008.

24. Ben Carson, Academy of Achievement Speech, February 14, 2011, https://www.youtube.com/watch?v=sc3YJz2lBU4.

25. Tea Fani, "Judge George N. Leighton," *The Key Reporter,* Volume 78, Number 1. Spring 2013.

26. Ibid.

27. Brittany Hodak, "How Bobby Bones Became The Most Powerful Man In Country Music," *Forbes Magazine*, January 6, 2017, https://www.forbes.com/sites/brittanyhodak/2017/01/06/how-bobby-bones-became-the-most-powerful-man-in-country-music/#792e05716667.

28. Brad Schmitt, "Bobby Bones Still Feels Pain Of Mom's Addiction Death," *The Tennessean*, December 23, 2014.

29. Ibid.

30. Bobby Bones, *The Bobby Bones Show*, December 28, 2016, https://www.youtube.com/user/BobbyBonesShow.

31. Greg McKeon, "The One-Word Answer to Why Bill Gates and Warren Buffett Have Been So Successful," *Leadership & Management,* July 7, 2014, https://www.entrepreneur.com/article/240878.

32. Peter Carlisle, interview with Anderson Cooper, *60 Minutes,* December 12, 2008, http://www.cnn.com/TRANSCRIPTS/0812/12/acd.01.html.

33. Michael Phelps, interview with author, Wrightsville Beach, North Carolina, July 2013.

34. Michael Phelps, "Olympics: Michael Phelps' Glare at Rival Inspires #PhelpsFace Memes Aplenty," *The Mercury News*, August 8, 2016, https://www.mercurynews.com/2016/08/09/olympics-michael-phelps-glare-at-rival-inspires-phelpsface-memes-aplenty/.

35. Admiral Patrick Driscoll, interview with author, Bumpass, Virginia, November 2013.

36. Cyril Northcote Parkinson, *Parkinson's Law: And Other Studies in Administration*, (Boston: Houghton Mifflin Company, 1957), 2.

37. ESYPS 2016, https://www.youtube.com/watch?v=tGgP209WL8c.

38 Ibid.

Chapter Two

1. Sarah Blakely, interview with *60 Minutes*, September 1, 2013.

2. Ibid.

3. J.K. Rowling, *Harvard Gazette,* June 5, 2008.

4. Steve Jobs, *Stanford News*, June 12, 2005.

5. Ben Affleck, "Ben Affleck Oscars Speech," February 24, 2013, https://www.youtube.com/watch?v=yxIla3MDbWA

6. Lee Margulies, "Alan Thicke: Never Too Thick to Endure 'Growing Pains' Reviews," *Los Angeles Times*, October 5, 1985, http://www.latimes.com/entertainment/tv/la-et-st-alan-thicke-growing-pains-reviews-19851009-story.html.

7. Owen Thomas, "Etsy's Winning Secret: Don't Play The Blame Game!" *Business Insider,* May 15, 2012.

8. Sergey Ryazanskiy, interview with author, New Delhi, India, February 1, 2020.

9. Oprah Winfrey, "Oprah's Favorite Passage from *A Return to Love*," July 29, 2012, https://www.youtube.com/watch?v=QAmQ7MpTsTw.

10. Marianne Williamson, *A Return to Love: Reflections on the Principles of "A Course in Miracles"* (New York: Harper Collins, 1993), 165.

11. Patrick Davis, interview with author, Myrtle Beach World Amateur Handicap Tournament, September 1, 2015.

12. Michael Phelps, *No Limits: The Will to Succeed* (New York: Free Press, 2008), 6.

13. Ulysses Grant, XVIII. *Memoirs of General U.S. Grant, Complete,* Volume I, Chapter XVIII, (The Project Gutenberg EBook of *Personl Memoirs of U.S. Grant*, Complete, June 20, 2018), https://www.gutenberg.org/files/4367/4367-h/4367-h.htm#ch18.

14. Jim Stickney, "How Did Grant Succeed? "*America's Civil War*, January 2016.

15. Patrick Dennis, *Auntie Mame* (New York: Vanguard Press, 1955), https://www.youtube.com/watch?v=85pJXaiXOBU.

16. Misty Copeland, "Misty Copeland on Breaking Barriers in Ballet, Broadway Role," July 6, 2015, https://www.youtube.com/watch?v=Pe_d4jJE3AM.

17. Steve Almasy, "Muhammad Ali: Boxing Legend, Activist, and 'The Greatest' to a World of Fans," June 4, 2016, http://www.cnn.com/2016/06/04/world/muhammad-ali-obituary/index.html.

18. Richard Branson, https://quotefancy.com/quote/97772/Richard-Branson-If-somebody-offers-you-an-amazing-opportunity-but-you-are-not-sure-you.

19. Henry Wesley Hight, Sr.

20. Stefani Joanne Angelina Germanotta, "Lady Gaga On Success," *MTV News*. May 6, 2009, http://www.mtv.com/news/1610781/lady-gaga-on-success-the-turning-point-for-me-was-the-gay-community/.

21. Stefani Joanne Angelina Germanotta, Acceptance Speech at The 91st Oscars®. The Dolby® Theatre, Hollywood, California, February 24, 2019.

22. Michael Phelps, *No Limits: The Will to Succeed* (New York: Free Press: 2008), 105.

23. "Muhammad Ali," *Jet Magazine,* March 12, 1964, 57.

24. Kevin Wuzzardo, "Wilmington Man Reunited With Childhood Rival John McEnroe," April 11, 2011, https://www.wwaytv3.com/2011/04/11/only-3-wilmington-man-reunited-childhood-rival-john-mcenroe/.

25. Ibid.

26. Michael Waltrip, interview with author, Oahu, Hawaii, February 4, 2014.

27. Max Nisen, *QUARTZ*, "Job Requirements are Mostly Fiction and You Should Ignore Them," August 24, 2017, http://qz.com/255565/job-requirements-are-mostly-fiction-and-you-should-ignore-them/.

28. Gary Smith, "Forty for the Ages," *Sports Illustrated*, September 19, 1994, https://www.si.com/vault/1994/09/19/132024/40-julius-erving.

29. Julius Erving, interview with author, Oahu, Hawaii, February 4, 2014.

30. Nido Quebin, "Five Questions With Dr. Nido Quebin," *Personal Growth Magazine*, n.d., https://www.personalgrowthmagazine.com/5-questions-with-dr-nido-qubein/.

31. Tom Welling, interview with author, Chicago, Illinois, September 29, 2012.

32. Joe Girard, "Lessons from the Best Salesman in the World," March 17, 2014, https://www.youtube.com/watch?v=c0jdLhRCJRA.

33. Pat Summitt, *Sum It Up* (New York: Crown Publishing Group, 2013), 153.

34. SBC Marketing, "Put It In Writing," http://www.sbc-marketing.co.uk/put-it-in-writing/.

35. Bob Rotella, *How Champions Think* (New York: Simon & Schuster, 2015). 179.

36. Robert Lipsyte, "The Greatest," *Time*, Vol.187, No. 23, June 2016.

37. Shlomo Breznitz and Collins Hemingway, *Maximum Brainpower: Challenging the Brain for Health and Wisdom* (New York: Ballantine Books, 2012). 157.

38. Lolo Jones, "Lolo Jones on Rio Olympics," January 5, 2016, https://www.youtube.com/watch?v=XxX5hTEJkNE.

39. Lennie Rosenbluth, interview with author, February 2014.

Chapter Three

1. Brian Tracy, "The 100/0 Principle: The Secret of Great Relationships," n.d. 2011, https://www.youtube.com/watch?v=HdJkk_fOJPY&t=2s.

2. Michael Waltrip, interview with author, Oahu, Hawaii, February 4, 2014.

3. Ibid.

4. David Gregory, "David Gregory on leaving NBC and His Faith Journey," September 9, 2015, https://www.youtube.com/watch?v=_reLn72LH6U.

5. John Daly, interview with author, Myrtle Beach World Amateur Handicap Tournament, September 1, 2015.

6. Charles Simonton, M.D. interview with author, Chapel Hill, North Carolina, October 22, 2016.

7. General Robert E. Milstead, interview with author, Wrightsville Beach, North Carolina, 2016.

8. Richard Wiseman, *The Luck Factor: Change Your Luck - And Change Your Life* (New York: Hyperion, 2003), 39.

9. Ibid., 31.

10. William Nack, "Young Cassius Clay," *Sports Illustrated*, January 13, 1992.

11. Keld Jensen, "Intelligence is Overrated: What You Really Need to Succeed," *Forbes Magazine*, April 12, 2012, https://www.forbes.com/sites/keldjensen/2012/04/12/intelligence-is-overrated-what-you-really-need-to-succeed/#1326bd08b6d2.

12. Caitlin Nicholson, "Doing Business with Different Cultures," March 24, 2011, https://lingualinx.com/blog/doing-business-with-different-cultures/.

13. Sara Kehaulani Goo, "The Skills Americans Say Kids Need to Succeed in Life," February 19, 2015, http://www.pewresearch.org/fact-tank/2015/02/19/skills-for-success/.

14. Winifred "Win" Joan McMurry White, interview with author, Ponte Vedra, Florida. July 11, 2013.

15. Steve Jobs, "You've Got to Find What You Love, Jobs Says," *Stanford News*, June 14, 2005.

16. George Brett, interview with author, Blessings Golf Course in Fayetteville, Arkansas, August 21, 2015.

17. Kevin Fixler, "Shooting for Perfection," December 13, 2012, https://www.sbnation.com/longform/2012/12/13/3758698/rick-barry-underhand-free-throw-nba.

18. Peter Voogd, "Your Circle of Influence Will Either Make or Break You," August 7, 2022, https://www.facebook.com/watch/?v=1180473865861635.

19. Ibid.

20. Short Interview With The Beatles 1962, https://www.youtube.com/watch?v=EIKlcfEtgyM.

21. Steve Jobs, "Steve Jobs on *60 Minutes*," March 31, 2012, https://www.youtube.com/watch?v=pGvnJJxBAlc.

Chapter Four

1. Dawna Stone and Matt Dieter, *Winning Nice: How to Succeed in Business and Life Without Waging War* (New York: Center Street, 2007), 82.

2. Barbara Walters, "Barbara Walters Her Story 2014," May 20, 2014, https://www.youtube.com/watch?v=OaH8Pw_LDmg.

3. Ibid.

4. Steve Inskeep/National Public Radio, "Bye-Bye To Barbara Walters: A Long 'View' Of A Storied Career," May 15, 2014, http://www.npr.org/2014/05/15/312471892/bye-bye-to-baba-a-long-view-of-a-storied-career.

5. Margaret Thatcher, *The Path to Power*, (New York: HarperCollins Publishers, 1995), 294-295.

6. Patrick Sawer, "How Maggie Thatcher Was Remade," *The Telegraph*, January 8, 2012, http://www.telegraph.co.uk/news/politics/margaret-thatcher/8999746/How-Maggie-Thatcher-was-remade.html.

7. "The Handbag that Terrorised Ministers," *Daily Mail*, April 26, 2011, http://www.dailymail.co.uk/femail/article-1380065/The-handbag-terrorised-ministers-Margaret-Thatchers-famous-black-Asprey-bag-auction.html.

8. Ollie Stone-Lee, "I Was Handbagged by Mrs. Thatcher," *BBC News*, April 9, 2013, http://www.bbc.com/news/uk-politics-11518330.

9. Prince Diana's Controversial BBC Interview with Mr. Martin Bashir," November 20, 1995, https://www.youtube.com/watch?v=wRH_YJTMHoM.

10. Stewart Pearce, *Diana: The Voice of Change* (Great Britain: Shimran, 2010), 51.

11. Ibid.

12. Ryan Buxton. Katie Couric Media, "Inside Princess Diana's Confidential Image Crash Course," November 13, 2021, https://katiecouric.com/culture/princess-diana-vocal-coach-stewart-pearce.

13. Celia Rivenbark, "Helen Hayes Takes Center Stage at Retirement Home," *Star News*, April 10, 1986.

14. WLKY US, "Foreman, Holyfield Reminisce About Experiences With The Greatest," June 6, 2016, http://www.wlky.com/article/foreman-holyfield-reminisce-about-experiences-with-the-greatest/3767686.

15. "Across the Great Divide," *The Guardian,* March 7, 2009.

16. Amy Cuddy at TEDGlobal 2012, "Your Body Language May Shape Who You Are," June 2012, https://www.ted.com/talks/amy_cuddy_your_body_language_shapes_who_you_are.

17. Kristine Buenavista, "6 Ways to Make a Lasting Impression," Accessed September 23,2023, http://thesouljah.com/6-ways-to-make-a-lasting-impression.

18. Stephen C. Pelletiere, "Beatles' Motorcade Is Kept Waiting; Very Sick Girl Gets a VIP Phone Call," *The Milwaukee Journal*, September 6, 1964.

19. Belludi, Nagesh, "Want To Be More Likeable? Improve Your Customer Service? Adopt Sam Walton's 'Ten-Foot Rule," January 7, 2020, https://www.rightattitudes.com/2010/01/07/sam-walton-ten-foot-rule/.

20. Jane Templeton, "How Salesmen Can Find Out What's Really on a Customer's Mind," *Marketing Magazine*, May 6, 2015.

21. Robin Givhan, "The Handshake Will Return. It's Too Much Of Who We Are," *The Washington Post*, May 18, 2020, https://www.washingtonpost.com/lifestyle/style/handshake-greeting-germs-elbow-bump/2020/05/15/e341acb6-9465-11ea-91d7-cf4423d47683_story.html.

22. Alan Hirsch and Charles Wolf, "When We Are Judging or Trying to Deceive," Accessed September 23, 2023, http://westsidetoastmasters.com/resources/book_of_body_language/chap7.html.

23. John Lennon, "John Lennon Quotes about Elvis Presley," Accessed September 23, 2023, http://johnlennonquotes.net/john-lennon-quotes-about-elvis-presley.htm.

24. Jackie Wilson, "Graceland The Home of Elvis Presley: Quotes About Elvis," Accessed September 23, 2023, https://www.graceland.com/elvis/quotesaboutelvis.aspx.

25. Leonard Bernstein, "What They Have Said About Elvis," Accessed September 23, 2023, http://www.elvis.net/whattheysay/theysayframe.html.

26. Bob Dylan Biography, Accessed September 23, 2023, http://www.imdb.com/name/nm0001168/bio.

27. Bruce Springsteen, "Why Elvis Presley Is Called 'The King of Rock 'N' Roll," Accessed September 23, 2023, https://blog.ha.com/2014/12/elvis-presley-king-rock-roll/.

28. Brian Setzer, "What they have said about Elvis," Accessed September 23, 2023, http://www.elvis.net/whattheysay/theysayframe.html.

29. Eddie Murphy, Accessed September 23, 2023, "Graceland The Home of Elvis Presley: Quotes About Elvis," https://www.graceland.com/elvis/quotesaboutelvis.aspx.

30. David Troedson, "Remembering Elvis Presley and Muhammad Ali," June 10, 2016, https://www.elvis.com.au/presley/elvis-presley-muhammad-ali.shtml.

31. Josh Moss, "Made in Louisville: Butch Polston is 'The King Maker,'" *Louisville Magazine*, December 2015.

32. "Elvis – Fit for a King," Accessed August 30, 2023, https://www.youtube.com/watch?v=VAbVow495gE.

33. Lisa Robinson and John Lennon, "John Lennon: Our Exclusive Interview with John," *Hit Parader Magazine*, December 1975.

34. Gene Weingarten, "Pearls Before Breakfast: Can One Of The Nation's Great Musicians Cut Through The D.C. Rush Hour? Let's Find Out," *The Washington Post*, April 8, 2007, https://www.washingtonpost.com/lifestyle/magazine/pearls-before-breakfast-can-one-of-the-nations-great-musicians-cut-through-the-fog-of-a-dc-rush-hour-lets-find-out/2014/09/23/8a6d46da-4331-11e4-b47c-f5889e061e5f_story.html?utm_term=.578e65b9ddf0.

35. Carol Meyrowitz, "The CEO of TJX on How to Train First-Class Buyers," *Harvard Business Review*, May 2014.

36. Carla Harris, *Expect to Win: 10 Proven Strategies for Thriving in the Workplace* (New York: Hudson Street Press, 2009), 92-93.

37. Ibid., 93-94.

38. Ibid., 80.

39. J.A. Shapira, "Cary Grant Gentleman of Style," *Gentleman's Gazette*, Accessed October 27, 2014, https://www.gentlemansgazette.com/cary-grant-gentleman-style/.

40. Daniel Levy, "Best Wishes, Warmest Regards: A Schitt's Creek Farewell," Accessed May 20, 2020. https://www.youtube.com/watch?v=2llX_lTJcL.

41. Virginia Smith, "Best Wishes, Warmest Regards: A *Schitt's Creek* Farewell," Accessed May 20, 2020. https://www.youtube.com/watch?v=2llX_lTJcL.

42. Rachel Giese, "Best Wishes, Warmest Regards: A *Schitt's Creek* Farewell," Accessed May 20, 2020, https://www.youtube.com/watch?v=2llX_lTJcL.

43. Carol Burnett, "Best Wishes, Warmest Regards: A *Schitt's Creek* Farewell," Accessed May 20, 2020. https://www.youtube.com/watch?v=2llX_lTJcL.

44. Catherine O'Hara, "Best Wishes, Warmest Regards: A *Schitt's Creek* Farewell," Accessed May 20, 2020. https://www.youtube.com/watch?v=2llX_lTJcL.

45. Jackson Lewis, "Survey Finds Tardiness and Absenteeism Up at Workplaces That Dress Down," Accessed June 15, 2000, http://www.jacksonlewis.com/news/survey-finds-tardiness-and-absenteeism-workplaces-dress-down.

46. Alan Konopacki. "2001 Trade Show Trend: The Reversal of the 'Dress Down' Look," Accessed February 23, 2001, https://www.laboratorynetwork.com/doc/2001-trade-show-trend-the-reversal-of-the-dre-0005.

47. Shaunti Feldhahn, *The Male Factor: The Unwritten Rules, Misperceptions, and Secret Beliefs of Men in the Workplace* (New York: Crown Business, 2009), 259.

Chapter Five

1. Lewis Schiff, *Business Brilliant* (New York: Harper Collins, 2013), 51.

2. Greg Beier, interview with author, Wilmington, North Carolina, August 2015.

3. Ibid.

4. Steve Azar and Morgan Freeman, "Waitin' on Joe," Accessed August 21, 2023, https://www.youtube.com/watch?v=eCxUUK99kUU.

5. Steve Azar, interview with author, Myrtle Beach, September 1, 2015.

6. Adrian Peel, "Catching up with Steve Azar," *Entertainment,* Accessed May 18, 2013, http://www.digitaljournal.com/article/350077.

7. Michael Jordan, Shadow Creek Golf Course, Las Vegas, March 31, 2012.

8. Robert Cialdini, *Influence: The Science of Persuasion* (New York: Collins Business, 2007), 138.

9. Andrea Stenberg, "The Rule of 7," Accessed December 7, 2015, http://www.thebabyboomerentrepreneur.com/258/what-is-the-rule-of-seven-and-how-will-it-improve-your-marketing/.

10. Eric Idle and George Harrison, *Rutland Weekend,* 1975, Accessed July 11, 2023, https://www.youtube.com/watch?v=NGbRHxM4X2g.

Chapter Six

1. "Walmart Supply Chain 2020: Why It Continues to Dominate," Skubana, Accessed, January 4, 2020, https://www.skubana.com/blog/walmart-leading-way/.

2. "75 Customer Service Facts, Quotes & Statistics," Accessed, May 28, 2012, https://www.helpscout.net/75-customer-service-facts-quotes-statistics/.

3. John Robertson, "Phone Tips to Get Things Done," Accessed, September 24, 2023, http://www.streetdirectory.com/travel_guide/6309/online_business/phone_tips_to_get_things_done_professional_phone_skills.html.

4. Lisa Wirthman, "Why Businesses Should Listen To Customers on Social Media," *Forbes.com,* August 8, 2013, https://www.forbes.com/sites/ups/2013/08/08/why-businesses-should-listen-to-customers-on-social-media/#57bd6d526153.

5. Ayaz Nanji, "Email Subject Line Length: Is Brevity Better?" *MarketingProfs,* August 15, 2017, https://www.marketingprofs.com/charts/2017/32600/email-subject-line-length-is-brevity-better.

6. Guy Kawasaki, "Ten Ways to Use LinkedIn," January 4, 2007, https://guykawasaki.com/ten_ways_to_use/.

7. Nita Lelyveld, "Dishing up cheer for 50 years at Farmers Market," *Los Angeles Times,* November 13, 2013, http://articles.latimes.com/2013/nov/17/local/la-me-beat-farmers-market-longtimer-20131117.

Chapter Seven

1. Matthew Toren, "Turn Passion Into Profits? Oprah, Seinfeld and Branson Certainly Did." Entrepreneur.com, February 13, 2014, https://www.entrepreneur.com/article/231502.

2. "Concert for Bangladesh," *Dhaka Tribune,* August 1, 2016, http://www.dhakatribune.com/bangladesh/2016/08/01/concert-bangladesh-45-years/.

3. Haley Bennett, "Haley Bennett on *The Girl on the Train*," October 3, 2016, https://www.youtube.com/watch?v=riwZ8xwbZzE.

4. T.D. Jakes, "T.D. Jakes Shares 5 Simple Steps to Be Happy on the Steve Harvey Show," April 22, 2015, http://www.empoweringeverydaywomen.com/td-jakes-shares-5-steps-to-happiness-steve-harvey-eew-magazine.html.

5. Paul McCartney, "Paul on Muhammad Ali," June 4, 2016, https://www.paulmccartney.com/news-blogs/news/paul-on-muhammad-ali.

6. Dave Yearwood, interview with author, Wrightsville Beach, North Carolina, September 2013.

Chapter Eight

1. Joan Cronan, interview with author, Blessings Golf Course in Fayetteville, Arkansas, August 21, 2015.

2. *Ebony*, August 1998, 90.

3. "Top 500 Songs of All Time," *Rolling Stone Magazine,* September 15, 2021, http://www.metrolyrics.com/rolling-stone-top500-1.html.

4. "Sam's Rules for Building a Business," The Walmart Digital Museum, https://one.walmart.com/content/walmartmuseum/en_us/timeline/decades/1990/artifact/2636.html.

5. Maureen Cleave, "How Does a Beatle Live? John Lennon Lives Like This," *London Evening Standard*, March 4, 1966.

6. John Lennon, "I Apologize," Beatles Press Conference, RCA Custom Records, August 11, 1966.

7. The Beatles Bible, Accessed September 24, 2023, https://www.beatlesbible.com/people/john-lennon/biography/.

8. Nick Squires, "Vatican 'Forgives' Lennon For 'More Popular Than Jesus' Remark," *The Telegraph*, November 21, 2008, http://www.telegraph.co.uk/news/newstopics/howaboutthat/3497623/Vatican-forgives-Lennon-for-more-popular-than-Jesus-remark.html.

9. Lebron James, "I'm Returning to Cleveland Cavaliers," July 11, 2014, https://www.cbsnews.com/news/lebron-james-im-returning-to-cleveland-cavaliers/.

10. Lebron James, "I'm Coming Home," *Sports Illustrated*, July 11, 2014, https://www.si.com/nba/2014/07/11/lebron-james-cleveland-cavaliers.

11. Ibid.

12. Dan Gilbert, *Twitter*, July 11, 2014.

13. Lebron James, "I'm Coming Home," *Sports Illustrated*, July 11, 2014, https://www.si.com/nba/2014/07/11/lebron-james-cleveland-cavaliers.

Chapter Nine

1. Michael Jordan, interview with author, Medinah Country Club. September 29, 2012.

2. Jerome Bettis, interview with author, Aria Hotel, Las Vegas. March 30, 2012.

3. Joe Morgan, interview with author, Aria Hotel, Las Vegas. March 29, 2012.

4. Walter Isaacson, "The Real Leadership Lessons of Steve Jobs," *Harvard Business Review,* April 2012.

5. Ibid.

6. Twyla Tharp, *The Creative Habit* (New York: Simon & Schuster, 2003), 14.

7. Amanda Svachula, "Why A Sense of Humor Can Get You Ahead In The Workplace — And Life," katiecouric.com, March 4, 2021, https://katiecouric.com/culture/how-humor-can-boost-your-career/.

8. David Remnick, "Tracing Muhammad Ali's Rise To 'King Of The World,'" *NPR Fresh Air,* June 10, 2016, http://www.npr.org/2016/06/10/481537366/david-remnick-for-his-biography-of-muhammad-ali-king-of-the-world.

9. Andy Greene, "Joan Rivers: The Lost Rolling Stone Interview," *Rolling Stone*, September 4, 2014, http://www.rollingstone.com/tv/features/joan-rivers-the-lost-rolling-stone-interview-20140904.

10. Richard Karn, interview with author at BMW Pro-AM, Greenville, South Carolina, May 17, 2014.

11. Hank Gola and Bill Hutchinson, "Faux Pas Hits Tiger in the Pants," *New York Daily News*, May 10, 2010.

12. Tiger Woods, conversation with *NBC Golf Channel* Win McMurry White at The Notah Begay Challenge, Atunyote Golf Club at Turning Stone Resort, Verona, New York, August 28, 2012.

13. Barbara Walters, "What Christopher Reeve Taught Barbara Walters About Humor," *Oprah's Master Class*, June 29, 2014, https://www.youtube.com/watch?v=cyLyO9AeBIM.

14. Ibid.

15. Brandi Chastain, "FIFA Women's World Cup USA 1999," FIFA.com, June 19, 1999, http://www.fifa.com/womensworldcup/news/y=2007/m=3/news=fifa-women-world-cup-usa-1999-502003.html.

16. Brandi Chastain, interview with author, Aria Resort, Las Vegas, March 31, 2012.

17. Ibid.

18. Michael Phelps, *Beneath the Surface* (Delaware: Skyhorse Publishing, 2012), 122.

19. Ibid.

20. Michael Phelps, *No Limits: The Will to Succeed* (New York: Free Press: 2008), 108.

21. John Lennon, The Royal Variety Performance, November 4, 1963, https://www.youtube.com/watch?v=rvBCmY7wAAU.

Chapter Ten

1. Katherine E. Krohn, *Oprah Winfrey* (Minneapolis: Lerner Publications Company, 2005), 44.

2. Carla Harris, "Be Authentic, Take Risks and Other 'Pearls of Wisdom' from Morgan Stanley's Carla Harris," *Bizwomen The Business Journal*, October 3, 2014, https://www.bizjournals.com/bizwomen/news/profiles-strategies/2014/10/be-authentic-take-risks-and-other-pearls-of-wisdom.html?page=all.

3. Michele Drayton, *The Glass Hammer*, Accessed June 15, 2023, http://theglasshammer.com/2014/07/15/on-the-way-up-the-corporate-ladder-carry-your-pearls-advises-morgan-stanleys-carla-harris/.

4. Carlos Santana, *The Universal Tone: Bringing My Story to Light* (New York: Little, Brown, and Company, 2014), 373.

5. Ibid., 134-135.

6. Carlos Santana, interview with author, Ritz Carlton, New Orleans, April, 2014.

7. Carlos Santana, *The Universal Tone: Bringing My Story to Light* (New York: Little, Brown, and Company, 2014), v.

8. Henry Wesley Hight, Sr.

9. Maxine Greeting Card. October 11, 2016, http://www.picturecard.eu/GreetingCardTemplate/maxine-greeting-card.

10. Tim Brown, interview with author, Oahu, Hawaii, February 4, 2014.

11. Kelly Slater, interview with author, Volcom Pipe Pro, Oahu, Hawaii, February 5, 2014.

12. Kelly Slater, August 10, 2016, @kellyslater post @m_phelps00.

13. Ronda Rousey, Live! with Kelly and Michael, October 12, 2015, https://www.youtube.com/watch?v=bCXhUhC3_ws.

14. Sean Donnellly, "The Rousey Effect: Measuring Ronda Rousey's Marketing Ascension," November 13, 2015, https://taylorstrategy.com/the-rousey-effect-measuring-ronda-rouseys-marketing-ascension/.

15. Emanuella Grinberg, "Why UFC 'Best' Ronda Rousey Is Such A Big Deal," August 5, 2015, https://edition.cnn.com/2015/08/02/living/ronda-rousey-profile-feat/index.html.

16. Dana White, "Ronda Rousey: The World's Most Dangerous Woman," *RollingStone*, May 28, 2015, http://www.rollingstone.com/sports/features/ronda-rousey-the-worlds-most-dangerous-woman-20150528.

17. Christian Louboutin, "Christian Louboutin Steps Ahead With Beauty Collection," *Los Angeles Times*, August 17, 2015.

18. Pharrell Williams, "Happy and Grateful," CBS News *Sunday Morning*, August 10, 2014, https://www.cbsnews.com/news/pharrell-williams-happy-and-grateful-2/.

19. Ibid.

20. Ibid.

21. Amanda Beard, "In the Water, They Can't See You Cry," *HUFFPOST*, August 2, 2012, http://www.huffingtonpost.com/amanda-beard/amanda-beard-in-the-water-they-cant-see-you-cry-memoir_b_1397581.html.

22. Amanda Beard, interview with author, Greater Hartford Women's Conference, Hartford, Connecticut, April 27, 2011.

22. Carla Harris, *Expect to Win: 10 Proven Strategies for Thriving in the Workplace* (New York: Plume, 2009), 80.

24. John Rassias, Rassias Method® Language Teaching Workshop at Dartmouth College, 1981.

25. Andrea Ordanini, "Repetitive Pop Songs 'More Likely to be Hits," *The Telegraph*, December 28, 2014, http://www.telegraph.co.uk/news/newstopics/howaboutthat/11314624/Repetitive-pop-songs-more-likely-to-be-hits.html.

26. Victor Borge, "30 Great Christmas Quotes," *The Telegraph,* December 25, 2016, http://www.telegraph.co.uk/books/authors/30-great-christmas-quotes/30-great-christmas-quotes2/.

27. Robert Cialdini, *Influence: The Science of Persuasion* (New York: Collins Business, 2007), 18.

28. AL Ritter, *The 100/0 Principle: The Secret of Great Relationships* (Nashville: Simple Truths, 2012).

29. Ibid.

30. Michael Phillips, *The Seven Laws of Money* (Boston: Shambhala Publications, 1974), 1.

31. Ibid. 5.

32. Thomas Gugler, interview with author, International Food Festival, Hoi An, Vietnam, March 20, 2016.

33. Ibid.

Afterword

1. John Ramsey, *Eulogy for Muhammad Ali*, June 10, 2016, https://binged.it/3kAVoAU.

2. Ibid.

3. Muhammad Ali, *Twitter*, October 8, 2012.

4. Sidney Sanders, interview with author, Trinity Center, North Carolina. 1995.

5. JoKathy Jaworski, "Bon Jovi's Nonprofit Restaurant: Where 'Friendship is the Daily Special,'" *NPQ*, March 14, 2012, https://nonprofitquarterly.org/2012/03/14/bon-jovis-nonprofit-restaurant-where-friendship-is-the-daily-special/.

6. Louis Zamperini, *Unbroken*, Universal Pictures. 2014.

7. Stuart Scott, ESPYS. 2014.

8. Steve Jobs, Stanford University Commencement Speech, 2005.

9. Nicholas Sparks, interview with author, Wilmington, North Carolina, October 9, 2016.

10. Joan Williams Hight, *50th Anniversary Speech*, 1992.

11. Jim Valvano, *ESPYS Speech*, 1993.

Bibliography

Adler, Ronald B. and George Rodman. *Understanding Human Communication*. Fortworth, Texas: Holt, Rinehart and Winston, Inc., 1991.

Ailes, Roger. *You Are The Message*. New York: Doubleday, 1998.

Allesandra, Tony. *Charisma*. New York: Time Warner, 1998.

Andrusia, David and Risck Haskins. *Brand Yourself*. New York: The Ballantine Publishing Group, 2000.

Bahr, Candace. *It's More Than Money-It's Your Life: The New Money Club for Women*. New Jersey: John Wiley & Sons, Inc., 2003.

Bayan, Richard. *Words That Sell*. Chicago: Contemporary Books, 1984.

Beckwith, Harry. *Selling the Invisible*. New York: Warner Books, 1997.

Bick, Julie. *All I Really Need To Know In Business I Learned At Microsoft*. New York: Pocket Books, 1997.

Bixler, Susan and Lisa Scherrer. *Take Action!* New York: Ballantine Books, 1996.

Blair, Linda. *Straight Talking*. London: Little, Brown Book Group, 2009.

Blakely, Sara and Allison Langdon, "*60 Minutes*," June 20, 2019, https://www.youtube.com/watch?v=T6vpmIt4fck.

Bolton, Robert. *People Skills. New York*: Simon & Schuster, 1979.

Bolton, Robert and Dorothy Grover Bolton. *People Styles at Work*. New York: American Management Association, 1996.

Bones, Bobby. *Fail Until You Don't*. New York: HarperCollins, 2018.

Bowman, Daria Price and Maureen LaMarca. *Writing Notes With A Personal Touch*. New York: Michael Friedman Publishing Group, 1998.

Boyett, Joseph H. and Henry P. Conn. Workplace 2000: *The Revolution Reshaping American Business*. New York: Penguin Books, 1991.

Breznitz, Shlomo and Collins Hemingway. *Maximum Brainpower: Challenging the Brain for Health and Wisdom*. New York: Ballantine Books, 2013.

Brill, Laura. *Sales Letters That Sell.* New York: AMACON, 1997.

Brown, Charles T. and Charles Van Riper. *Speech and Man.* Englewood Cliffs, New Jersey: Prentice-Hall, Inc., 1966.

Brown, Dan. *Angels and Demons.* New York: Washington Square Press, 2000.

Brown, Steve. *How To Talk So People Will Listen.* Grand Rapids: Baker Publishing Company, 1993.

Burnett, Carol. "Best Wishes, Warmest Regards: A Schitt's Creek Farewell," May 20, 2020. https://www.youtube.com/watch?v=2llX_lTJcL.

Cardone, Grant. *Sell or Be Sold.* Austin, Texas: Greenleaf Book Group, 2012.

Carnegie, Dale. *How to Win Friends and Influence People.* Garden City, New York: Dale Carnegie and Associates, Inc., 1964.

Carter-Scott, Cherie. *If Success Is a Game, These are the Rules.* New York: Broadway Books, 2000.

Cialdini, Robert B. Influence: *The Psychology of Persuasion.* New York: Harper Collins, 2007.

Copeland, Misty. *Life in Motion: An Unlikely Ballerina.* New York: Touchstone, 2014.

Cuddy, Amy. *Presence: Bringing Your Boldest Self to Your Biggest Challenges.* New York: Little Brown & Company, 2015.

Dalio, Ray. *Principles.* New York: Simon & Schuster, 2017.

Decker, Bert. *The Art of Communicating.* Menlo Park: Crisp Publications, 1988.

Dimitrius, Jo-Ellen and Mark Mazzarella. *Reading People.* New York: Random House, 1998.

Donaldson, Les. *Conversational Magic.* Paramus, New Jersey: Prentice Hall, 1981.

Drobot, Eve. *Class Acts.* New York: VanNostrand Reinhold Company, 1982.

Dundee, Angelo. *I Only Talk Winning.* New York: McGraw Hill, 1985.

Ferraro, Gary P. *The Cultural Dimensions of International Business.* New Jersey: Prentice Hall, 1998.

Feldhahn, Shaunti. *The Male Factor: The Unwritten Rules, Misperceptions, and Secret Beliefs of Men in the Workplace.* New York: Crown Business, 2009.

Fountain, Elizabeth Haas. *The Polished Professional*. Hawthorne, New Jersey: Career Press, 1994.

Frank, Milo. *How to Get Your Point Across in 30 Seconds or Less*. New York: Simon and Schuster, 1986.

Galanes, Philip. "Speak Your Own Truth, On Your Own Terms," June 27, 2014, https://www.nytimes.com/2014/06/29/fashion/billie-jean-king-and-jason-collins-on-being-gay-athletes.html.

Gabor, Don. *Talking with Confidence for the Painfully Shy*. New York: Crown Trade Paperbacks, 1997.

Giese, Rachel. "Best Wishes, Warmest Regards: A Schitt's Creek Farewell," May 20, 2020, https://www.youtube.com/watch?v=2llX_lTJcL.

Gladwell, Malcolm. *Outliers*. New York: Little, Brown and Company, 2008.

Glass, Lillian. *Say It Right: How to Talk in Any Social or Business Situation*. New York: Perigee Books, 1992.

Goodman, Gary S. *How to Sell Like a Natural Born Sales-Person*. Holbrook, Massachusetts: Adams Media Corporation, 1998.

Grant, Ulysses S. *Memoirs of General U.S. Grant*. New York: Charles L. Webster & Company, 1885 and 1886.

Griffin, Jack. *How to Say It Best*. Paramus, New Jersey: Prentice Hall, 1994.

Hall, Edward T. *The Silent Language*. New York: Doubleday, 1981.

Harris, Carla A. *Expect to Win*. New York: Hudson Street Press, 2009.

Harris, Carla A. *Strategize to Win*. New York: Hudson Street Press, 2014.

Hill, Tim and Marie Clayton. *The Beatles: Unseen Archives*. Bath, UK: Paragon, 2009.

Hebron, Michael P. *See and Feel the Inside Move the Outside*. Smithtown, New York: Learning Golf Inc., 2007.

Hebron, Michael P. *The Art and Zen of Learning Golf*. Smithtown, New York: Learning Golf Inc., 2005.

Hoff, Ron. *Do Not Go Naked into Your Next Presentation*. Kansas City: Andrews and McMeel, 1997.

Hybels, Saundra and Richard L. Weaver, II. *Communicating Effectively*. New York: Random House, 1989.

Isaacson, Walter. *Harvard Business Review*. "The Real Leadership Lessons of Steve Jobs." April 2012.

James, LeBron as told to Lee Jenkins. *Sports Illustrated*. "I'm coming back to Cleveland." July 11, 2014.

Jeffery, Nicole. "Thorpe's Doubt of Eight Gold Sweep Spurs Phelps," *The Australian,* July 23, 2008.

Jensen, Keld. "Intelligence is Overrated: What You Really Need to Succeed," *Forbes Magazine*, April 12, 2012, https://www.forbes.com/sites/keldjensen/2012/04/12/intelligence-is-overrated-what-you-really-need-to-succeed/#1326bd08b6d2.

Jobs, Steve. *60 Minutes,* April 2, 2021, http://www.cbsnews.com/videos/steve-jobs-and-the-beatles/.

Jones, Charles. *What Makes Winners Win*. Secaucus, New Jersey: Carol Publishing Group, 1998.

Katz, Donald. *JUST DO IT*®. Holbrook, Massachusetts: Adams Media Corporation, 1994.

Khan, Adam. A*ntivirus For Your Mind: How to Strengthen Your Persistence and Determination and Feel Good More Often*. USA: YouMe Works Publishing, 2012.

Kramer, Marc. *Power Networking*. Chicago, Illinois: VGM Career Horizons, 1997.

Krohn, Katherine E. *Oprah Winfrey*. Minneapolis: Lerner Publications Company, 2005.

Larkin, Howard. *Hospitals & Health Networks* magazine. Volume 85. Number 10. October 2011.

Lavington, Camille. *You've Only Got Three Seconds*. New York: Doubleday, 1997.

Leeds, Dorothy. *Smart Questions*: *A New Strategy for Successful Managers*. New York: McGraw-Hill, 1987.

Levy, Daniel. "Best Wishes, Warmest Regards: A Schitt's Creek Farwell," May 20, 2020, https://www.youtube.com/watch?v=2llX_lTJcLw.

Lipsyte, Robert. "Ali: Champion. Outcast. Hero. Legend." *Time*. Vol. 187. No.23. 2016

Lowndes, Leil. *How to Be a People Magnet.* Chicago: Contemporary Books, 2001.

Martinet, Jeanne. *The Art of Mingling.* New York: Thorsons, 1992.

McCormack, Mark. *Staying Street Smart in the Internet Age.* New York: Viking, 2000.

McKeown, Les. *Predictable Success.* Austin, Texas: Greenleaf Book Group, 2010.

McMurry, Jane Hight. *The Dance Steps of Life.* USA: Stellar Publishing, 2002.

McMurry, Jane Hight. *The Etiquette Advantage®.* USA: Stellar Publishing, 2002.

McMurry, Jane Hight. *Navigating the Lipstick Jungle.* USA: Stellar Publishing, 2012.

Meyrowitz, Carol. "The CEO of TJX on How to Train First-Class Buyers," Boston: *The Harvard Business Review*, May 2014.

Michelli, Dena and Alison Straw. *Successful Networking.* Hong Kong: Barron's, 1997.

Mindell, Phyllis. *A Woman's Guide to the Language of Success.* Paramus, New Jersey: Prentice Hall, 1995.

Mochlinski, Kaz. "Ian Thorpe happy to have been proved wrong by Michael Phelps." London: *The Daily Telegraph*, August 20, 2008.

Mohr, Tara Sophia. "Why Women Don't Apply for Jobs Unless They're 100% Qualified." *The Harvard Business Review*, August, 25, 2014, http://blogs.hbr.org/2014/08/why-women-dont-apply-for-jobs-unless-theyre-100-qualified/.

Molloy, John T. *New Women's Dress for Success.* New York: Warner Books, Inc. 1996.

Myers, Marc. *How To Make Luck.* Los Angeles: Renaissance Books, 1999.

Nisen, Max. *QUARTZ*, "Job Requirements are Mostly Fiction and You Should Ignore Them," August 27, 2014, http://qz.com/255565/job-requirements-are-mostly-fiction-and-you-should-ignore-them/.

O'Hara, Catherine. "Best Wishes, Warmest Regards: A Schitt's Creek Farewell," May 20, 2020, https://www.youtube.com/watch?v=2llX_lTJcL.

Parker, Sam. 212: *The Extra Degree*. USA: The Walk the Talk Company, 2005.

Parkinson, Cyril Northcote. *Parkinson's Law: And Other Studies in Administration*. Boston: Houghton Mifflin Company, 1957.

Pausch, Randy. *The Last Lecture*. New York: Hyperion, 2008.

Peacher, Georgiana. *Speak To Win*. New York: Bell Publishing Company, 1985.

Pearce, Stewart. *Diana: The Voice of Change*. United Kingdom: Shimran, 2020.

Pitino, Rick. *Success is a Choice*. New York: Broadway Books, 1997.

Phelps, Michael with Alan Abrahamson. *No Limits: The Will to Succeed*. Simon and Schuster, 2008.

Phelps, Michael with Brian Cazeneuve and Bob Costas. *Beneath the Surface*. Delaware: Skyhorse Publishing, 2012.

Phelps, Michael with Ward Jenkins. *How to Train with a T. Rex and Win 8 Gold Medals*. New York: Simon & Schuster, 2009.

Phillips, Michael. *The Seven Laws of Money*. San Francisco: Clear Glass Publishing, 1974.

Remnick, David. *King of the World*. New York: First Vintage Books, 1998.

Ritter, Al. *The 100/0 Principle: The Secret of Great Relationships*. USA: Simple Truths, 2010.

Rivenbark, Celia. "Helen Hayes Takes Center Stage at Retirement Home." *Star News*, April 10, 1986.

Rotella, Bob. *How Champions Think*. New York: Simon & Schuster, 2015.

Schiff, Lewis. *Business Brilliance: Surprising Lessons from the Greatest Self-Made Business Icons*. New York: HarperCollins Publishers, 2013.

Schmitt, Brad. "Bobby Bones Still Feels Pain of Mom's Addiction, Death." *THE TENNESSEAN*, December 20, 1014. http://www.tennessean.com/story/entertainment/2014/12/21/bobby-bones/20607287/.

Stephens, Nancy J. *Streetwise Customer-Focused Selling*. Holbrook, Massachusetts: Adams Media Corporation, 1998.

Silverstein, Shel. *Where the Sidewalk Ends*. New York: HarperCollins Publishers, 1974.

Smith, Virginia. "Best Wishes, Warmest Regards: A Schitt's Creek Farewell," May 20, 2020, https://www.youtube.com/watch?v=2llX_lTJcL.

Stone, Dawna and Matt Dieter. *Winning Nice: How to Succeed in Business and Life Without Waging War*. New York: Center Street, 2007.

Summit, Pat Head. *Reach for the Summit*. New York: Broadway Books, 1998.

Summit, Pat Head. *Sum it Up: A Thousand and Ninety-Eight Victories, A Couple Of Irrelevant Losses, And A Life In Perspective*. New York: Crown Publishing Group, 2013.

Tannen, Deborah. *Talking From 9 To 5*. New York: William Morrow and Company, Inc., 1994.

Tharp, Twyla. *The Creative Habit*. New York: Simon & Schuster, 2003.

Thatcher, Margaret. *The Path to Power*. New York: HarperCollins Publishers, 1995.

Vujicic, Nicholas James. *Life without Limits*. New York: Doubleday Religion, 2010.

Waltrip, Michael. *In The Blink of An Eye*. New York: Hyperion, 2011.

WAAY TV 3 ABC: http://www.wwaytv3.com/2011/04/10/only-3-wilmington-man-reunited-childhood-rival-john-mcenroe.

Weinstock, Matthew. "Hospitals & Health." *Networks* magazine. Volume 83. No. 8. August 2009.

Westmoreland, Rose. *Building Self-Esteem*. Torrance, California: Frank Schaffer Publication, Inc., 1994.

White, Lynne Farwell. *Giving and Gifts*. United States of America: Givery, 2017.

Williams, Jennifer. *Staying In Touch*. New York: Hearst Books, 1998.

Williams, Pat with Michael Weinreb. *How To Be Like Mike*. Deerfield Beach, Florida: Health Communications, Inc., 2001.

Willingham, Ron. *The Best Seller!* Englewood Cliffs, New Jersey: Prentice-Hall, 1984.

Williamson, Marianne. *A Return To Love*. New York: Harper Collins, 1992.

Williamson, Marianne and Winfrey, Oprah: *Super Soul Sunday*. OWN TV. https://www.youtube.com/watch?v=QAmQ7MpTsTw.

Wiseman, Richard. *The Luck Factor*. New York: Hyperion, 2003.

Index

A

Abbey Road Studios 141
ABC Evening News 149
ABC News 148
ABC with Harry Reasoner 148
Abe's Bar-B-Q 204
Academy Awards 54, 55
Academy of Achievement 40
Ace Hardware Shootout 282
"Across the Universe" 24
Affleck, Ben ix, 54
Africa 114, 157, 239, 254
Agassi, Andre 237
Albert Schweitzer Medal 155
Albright, Madeleine K. ix, 182
Ali, Muhammad ix, 21, 23, 24, 28, 32, 47, 67, 68, 69, 73, 83, 87, 102, 153, 157, 183, 184, 185, 240, 258, 268, 297, 318
Allen, Belinda Judkins ix
Allen, Marcus 264, 265, 266
Alternatives to Shaking Hands 175
"Always Look on the Bright Side of Life" 271
America's Funniest Home Videos 143
American Ballet Theatre 67
American Bar Association 42
Ames, Stephen 36
Amiel, Henri-Frederic 304
Angels and Demons 214
Anger Management 267
Apologize Album 254
Apple Inc. 54, 89, 113, 142, 264
Aria Resort 265
Aristotle 85
Art and Zen of Learning Golf 37
Ashe, Arthur ix, 302

Ash, Mary Kay 246
Asia 89, 138, 197, 217
ASP (Association of Professional Surfers) 283
Auditory Oriented 124
Auntie Mame 66, 67
Australia 89
Autocratic Leadership 191
Azalea Festival Tennis Challenge 73
Azar, Steve ix, 203, 204

B

Badfinger 238
Bahamas, Albany 30
Baltimore 279
Bangladesh 238, 276
Bangladesh Concert, The 239
Baragrande, Josephina 280
Barcelona 17, 270
Barnum, P.T. 148
Barry, Rick 140
Baruch, Bernard M. 200
Baumgartner, Brian ix, 267
Bay Hill Golf Club 36
BBC 209, 270
Beard, Amanda ix, 286
Beatles, The ix, 21, 23, 24, 25, 26, 27, 28, 31, 39, 79, 142, 169, 183, 184, 185, 209, 232, 233, 237, 238, 253, 254, 275, 276, 277, 291
Begay, Notah 271
Beier, Gregory 201
Beijing Olympics 16, 73, 284
Bell, Joshua ix, 186
Beneath the Surface 274
Bernstein, Leonard 183
Berra, Yogi 66

Berry, Eric 298
Best Actress 55
Best Fighter 285
Bettis, Jerome "The Bus" 261
Bianculli, David 24, 238, 281, 286
Biden, Jr., Jospeh "Joe" Robinette 94
Billboard 24, 238, 281, 286
Bills, DDS, Jeri, ix
Billings, Josh 156
Bird, Larry 50
Blair, Linda 162
Blakely, Sara ix, 52, 71, 75, 268
Blameless Postmortem 56
Blessings Golf Club 245
Blue Angels 46
Bocconi University 291
Body language 116, 117, 118, 122, 133, 161, 162, 165, 170, 175, 176, 179, 184, 188, 208, 218, 227, 248
Body Language
  Alternatives to Shaking Hands 175, 176
  Chewing Gum 178, 218
  Chin Rubbing 176
  Covering the Mouth 176
  Duchess Slant 167
  Ear Pulling 176
  Eye Contact 178
  Eyeglasses 176
  Eye Rubbing 176
  Feet Placement 167
  Grooming 169, 195
  Hands 248
  Handshakes 172, 173, 174
  Jiggling Foot 178
  Leaning Forward 166
  Legs 164, 167, 178
  Manspreading 167
  Nodding 129, 170, 260
  Nose Rubbing 176
  Physically Challenged 174
  Pointing 176
  Posture 98, 122, 162, 164, 165, 166, 173, 178, 207
  Sitting 166, 167, 168
  Smiling 129, 135, 169
  Standing Up 166
  Steepling 178
  Stroking a Scarf 178
  Stroking Chin 177
  Tilting the Head 179
  Touching 172
  Touching Hair 177
  Tugging the Collar 178
  Walking 172
  Wedding Band 171
Bones, Bobby ix, 43
Bongiovi, Dorothea 299
Bongiovi, John Francis, Jr. (aka Jon Bon Jovi) 299
Bon Jovi ix, 299, 302
Borge, Victor 291
Borland, Al ix, 269
Boston Symphony Hall 186
Bowman, Bob 56, 274
Boys & Girls Club 255
Branson, Richard 15, 53, 68
Brett, George ix, 139
Breznitz, Shlomo 83
Briefcases 193, 194
Brilliant, Ashleigh 157
Brophy, Mary 158
Brown, Dan 214
Brown, H. Jackson 66
Brown, Timothy "Tim" Donnel ix, 282, 283
Bryan, Mark ix, 32
Bryant, Kobe 48
Buck, Joe 18
Buddha 249
Buffett, Jimmy ix, 268
Buffett, Warren ix, 44, 237
Burger King 280
Burnett, Carol 189, 291
Bush, George H.W. 182
Business and Professional Women 95
Business Attire 190, 195, 198

Business Cards 130, 137, 138
Business Casual 195
Business Cultures 191, 193, 194, 195, 197
Business Introductions 101, 138
Business Owners Council 201
BuzzStream 101
"By A Hundredth" 16
Byrne, Rhonda 81

C

Caddyshack 267
Canada 158, 217, 270, 279
Captioning 121
Carlisle, Peter 45
Carlyle, Thomas 54
Carnegie, Dale 154, 168
Carnegie Hall 280
Carnegie Institute of Technology 108
"Carolina In My Mind" 272
Carroll, Lewis 237
Carson, Ben 39, 40
Carson, Sonya 39
Cash, Johnny 159
Casual Wear 197
CBS Sunday Morning 285
CBS This Morning 33
Celebritynetworth.com 285
Cell Phone 220, 222
Chamberlain, Wilt 85
Chapel Hill, North Carolina 42, 109, 112, 259, 272
Charles, Nick 68
Charleston, Mississippi 204
Chase, Chevy ix, 267
Chastain, Brandi ix, 273
Chiang Mai 29
Chicago 42, 77, 82, 104, 201, 259
Children's Miracle Network 282
Churchill, Winston 66
Cialdini, Robert 205, 293
Cisco 89
Citigroup 89

Clapton, Eric 158, 238
Clay, Jr., Cassius Marcellus 22, 68, 102
Cleveland Cavaliers 255
Clinton, President Bill 177
Clothing 92, 93, 123, 150, 170, 182, 185, 187, 188, 189, 190, 192, 193, 194, 195, 196, 198, 285
CNN 18, 68
Cobb, Ty 65
Coleman, Vince 82
Compliments 92
Conservative Business Culture 191
Conversation Bait 98, 100, 102, 129, 174
Conversations 97, 109, 110, 111, 114, 117, 120, 124, 129, 135, 144, 172, 188, 206, 220, 290
Conway, Daniel 150
Cooper, Anderson 45
Cooper, Bradley 55
Copeland, Misty ix, 67
Cordell, Allison McMurry ix, 179
Correspondence 227, 231, 232
Costello, Elvis 204
Covey, Steven 144
Creative Habit, The 265
Credit Suisse 57
Cronan, Joan ix, 245
Cuddy, Amy 165
Curry, Bishop Michael 101
Cutler, Christine 169

D

Daily Mail 305, 312
Dalio, Ray 62
Dallas Cowboys 273
Daly, John ix, 94
Dance Steps of Life, The 267
Dancing with the Stars 267
Dartmouth College 320
Darwin, Charles 179
Davis, Patrick ix, 60
Daytona 500 74

DeGeneres, Ellen ix, 237, 238
Detroit 39, 79
Deuce Lounge 273
Dewey, John 246
Diana, Princess 151, 152
Diana: The Voice of Change 151
Dickerson, Chad ix, 56
Diction 123
Diff'rent Strokes 55
Dior 55
Disengaging from Conversations 135
Disney, Walt 35
Disney World 35
Doucette, Gene 184
Draper, Don 62
Driscoll, Rear Admiral Patrick ix, 46
Dr. Phil 237
Duke University 80
Dundee, Angelo 102
Durham College 21, 42, 68
Dworsky, Frank ix, 38
Dyer, Wayne ix, 71
Dylan, Bob 183, 238

E

East Pakistan 238
eBay 18
Ebony 246
Edison, Thomas 43, 76
Einstein, Albert 33, 47
Ellen DeGeneres Show, The 238
El Salvador 242
Elvis 39, 158, 183, 184, 255
Email 132, 136, 225, 226, 227, 228, 229, 231, 235, 249, 291, 292
Emerson, Ralph Waldo 17, 26, 27, 99, 161, 164, 278, 294
Eminem 17
Emmy 155, 189
Emotional Control 247
Enright, Anne 141
Epstein, Brian 28, 31, 184, 185, 254
Ernst, Bob 38
Erving, Julius "Dr. J" ix, 75
ESPN 48, 78, 116, 266, 285, 290

ESPY 48, 285
Etiquette Advantage®, The 161
Etsy 56
Europe 181
Executive Women International 95
Eye Contact 169, 170, 173, 175, 178, 199

F

Facebook 19, 70, 228, 305
Facts of Life, The 55
Fail Until You Don't 44
Family Feud 269
Feldhahn, Shaunti 196
Ferdowski, Bob 193
Fidget 213
FIFA 33, 160, 262, 273
First Tee, The 245
Fischer, Newton 259
Fly Away Home 159
Foley, Sean 36, 37
Forbes Magazine 43
Ford, Henry 71, 89
Foreman, George 157
Forms of Address 102
Fortress Investment Group 90
France 119, 296
Franklin, Aretha 246
Franklin, Benjamin 248
Frazier, Joe 261
Freeman, Morgan 203, 204
Fresh Air, NPR 268
Fresh Prince of Bel-Air 143
Freud, Sigmund 246
Friedman, Kinky 290

G

Garcia, Eddie 43
Gates, Bill ix, 237
General Mills 245
Georgetown Hoyas 259
Germanotta, Stefani Joanne Angelina 70
Gestures 91, 99, 156, 162, 163, 178,

208, 217, 227, 235, 242, 250
Giese, Rachel 189
Gilbert, Dan 255, 256
Giordano's 77
Girard, Joe 79
Girl on the Train, The 239
Give Peace a Chance 276
Giving and Gifts 293
Glass, David 33
Goethe 78
Gold Glove Award 139
Golf Channel 270
Gone with the Wind 53
Good Will Hunting 54
Gossip 248
Gouldner, Alvin 293
Grant, Cary 189
Grant, General Ulysses S. 63, 65
Gratitude Campaign 235
Great Britain 142, 253
Great Harvest Bread Company 76
Great Smoky Mountains 240, 241
Great Wall of China 79
Gregory, David 94
Gretzky, Wayne ix, 37
Growing Pains 55
Gugler, Thomas ix, 295

H

Hallmark 282
Handbagging 150
Handbags 193
Handshakes 97, 99, 174
Hansen, Mark Victor 31
"Happy" 286
Happy Gilmore 267
Hardaway, Tim ix, 34, 35
Hard Rock Café, The 158
Hardwick, Omari 299
Harris, Carla A. ix, 72, 187, 188, 280, 287
Harris, Johnny 90
Harrison, George 26, 27, 209, 238, 239

Harris, Colonel Thomas 64
Harry Potter 53, 54
Harvard Business Review, The 74, 187, 264
Hawk, Anthony "Tony" Frank 222, 223
Hayes, Helen ix, 155, 156
Haywood, Terri ix
Head, Richard 48
Hebron, Michael 37
Heffernan, Danny 269
Heisman Trophy 282
Help, The 239
Hemingway, Collins 83
Hero MotoCorp Ltd 29, 30
Hertz 223
Hewlett Packard 18, 74
High Point University 76
Hight, Henry Wesley, Sr. viii, ix, 61
Hight, Joan Williams viii, ix, 47, 147, 191
Hill, Grant 80, 81
Hirsch, Alan 177
Hitchens, Alex *"Hitch"*/Will Smith, Movie *Hitch* 162
Hitchens, Christopher 279
Hogan, Ben 261
Hoi An, Vietman 295
HomeGoods 187
Home Improvement 269
Honorifics 101
Hootie & The Blowfish 32
Horatio Alger Award 57
Hospitality House 110
Houston, Whitney 283
How Champions Think 82
How Salesmen Can Find Out What's Really on a Customer's Mind 171
How To Be A No-Limit Person 71
Hubbard, Elbert 235
Humor 268, 272, 276
Hussein, Saddam 182
Huxley, Thomas Henry 46

I

IBM 26, 89
Icon Award 48
Idle, Eric 209, 271
iHeart Radio 43
"Imagine" 35
IM (Instant Messaging) 221
Incomm Center for Research and Sales Training 195
Influence; The Psychology of Persuassion 205, 293
"In My Mind" 286
Inskeep, Steve 149
Interpersonal Zone 181
Interrupting 208, 252
In The Blink of An Eye 113
In the Water They Can't See You Cry 287
Introductions 97, 101, 103, 104, 105, 138, 242, 293
Invitations 232, 291
"It's My Life" 302

J

Jackman, Hugh 55
Jackson Lewis Law Firm 195
Jackson, Michael 296
Jackson, Phil 36, 37
Jakes, T.D. 239
James, LeBron ix, 255, 257
James, William 199
JBJ Soul Kitchen 299
Jenkins, Lee 255
Jensen, Keld 311, 326
Jewel 60
Jewelry 182, 276
Jimmy V Perseverance Award 266
Jobs, Steve 54, 113, 142, 264, 265, 275
John, Elton 296
Johnny Carson Show, The 269
Johns Hopkins Hospital 39
Johnson & Johnson 89
Johnson, Magic 283
Jones, Lolo ix, 84
Jordan, Michael ix, 31, 36, 57, 73, 81, 204, 212, 259, 262, 267, 272
Journal of Consumer Psychology, The 291
Judo 284

K

Kansas City Royals 33, 139
Kansas Jayhawks 85
Karma 238, 239
Karn, Richard 269
Kaufmann, Rob ix, 114
Kearns, Tommy 86
Kendrick Ph.d., Dar ix
Kennedy, Jackie 296
Khrushchev, Nikita 167
Kinesthetic Sub-Modalities 37
King, B.B. 158
King, Billie Jean 17
King, Gayle 84
King, Larry 200
King, Martin Luther 255
King of Queens, The 269
King of the World 268
Kiwanis International 95
Knight, Phil 142
Krzyzewski, Mike 80, 81
Ku Klux Klan 254

L

Lady Antebellum 59
Lady Gaga ix, 51, 70
Laettner, Christian 80, 81
Langdon, Allison 52
L.A.S.T. Technique 249
Las Vegas 36, 204, 262, 266, 267
Lawrence, Jennifer ix, 55
La-Z-Boy Corporation 76
Leach, Archibald 188

Le Clos, Chad 45
Leighton, George N. 42
L'Enfant Plaza 186
Lennon, John 21, 26, 35, 60, 142, 183, 185, 253, 254
Leonard, Sugar Ray ix, 183, 262
Levy, Daniel 189
Lewis, Carl 49
Life in Motion 67
Life Without Limits 78
Lincoln, Abraham 65
Lindberg, Anne Morrow 281
Linett, Larry 73, 74
LinkedIn 111, 229
Lions Club International 95
Lipsyte, Robert 23
Listening 34, 118, 135, 155, 164, 168, 179, 199, 200, 206, 207, 209, 210, 212, 252, 255, 292
Liston, Sonny 23, 67, 185
Live! with Kelly and Michael 284
Lloyd, Carli ix, 33
Lockwood, Jess 38
Loire Valley 119
Lombardi, Vince 269
Lopez, Gerry 144
Los Angeles Farmers Market 232
Los Angeles Times 55
Louboutin, Christian 285
Loughborough University 150
Louisville Magazine 184

M

Macintosh 265
Mack, John 57
Madonna 296
Madrid 167
Magee's House of Nuts 232
"Magic" 236
Mahan, Hunter 36
Major League Baseball Hall of Fame 139
Make-A-Wish® 272

Makeup 192, 193, 194, 197
Making of a Man, The 283
Male Factor: The Unwritten Rules, The 196
Malkiel, Burton 60
Malraux, Andre 70
Manners 98, 99, 154, 161, 167, 171
Manning, Peyton 47
Manspreading 167
Marshalls 187
Martin, Joe 22
Masks 194
Maslow, Abraham 246
Mason, Anthony 285
Maximum Brainpower 83
Maxine 282
May, Paul 101
McCartney, Paul 26, 158, 169, 240
McCuller, Carson 158
McEnroe, John 73, 74
McGee, Frank 148
McNaught, Judith 36
Medinah Country Club 259
Meeting and Greeting 99, 101
Meet the Press 94
Melville, Herman 65
Member of the Wedding, The 158
Memoirs of General U.S. Grant 64
Merkel, Angela 296
Meyrowitz, Carol ix, 187
Miami Heat 34, 255, 256
Michaelangelo 18
Michaels, Ronnie 263, 265
Michael Waltrip Racing 90, 91
Microsoft 39, 89
Mills, Mike 257
Milstead, Jr., General Robert E. ix, 94
Milwaukee Journal 169
Minelli, Liza 296
Mirroring 122
Mitchell, Margaret 53, 72
Mitterand, Francois 296
Modern Business Culture 193
Mohawk Guy 193

Molière 251, 288
Montana State University 188
Monty Python 271
Morgan, Joe ix, 78, 262, 263, 265
Morgan, M.D., Richard Earl ix
Morgan Stanley 57, 187
Morse Code 162, 163
MTV News 70
Muhammad Ali Health and Physical Education Building 68
Mulva, James 296
Munjal, Pawan 29, 30
Murdock, Mike 244
Murphy, Eddie 184
Murray, DeMarco 273
Musk, Elon 83
Myrtle Beach, SC 158, 203
My Fight/Your Fight 284
"My Sweet Lord" 209

N

NASA 24, 193
NASCAR 113
Nash, Odgen 257
National Football League 267
National Lampoon 267
National Public Radio (NPR) 149
Navigating the Lipstick Jungle 132, 216, 343
NBA 34, 50, 75, 82, 140, 255, 256
NBC Golf Channel 270
NBC Hospitality Tent 259
NBC TODAY 148
NCAA (National Collegiate Athletic Association) 79, 80, 85, 116, 140, 259, 302
Nealon, Kevin ix, 267
Negative People 139
Negotiation 268
Neiman Marcus 75
Nelson, Steve ix
Networking 94, 95, 111, 118, 129, 130, 131, 132, 133, 172, 218, 229

Neuro-Linguistic Programming 37
New York Daily News 270
New York Times 17, 113, 167
New York Times Best Seller List 113
NFL 265, 267
Nicaragua 242
Nicklaus, Barbara ix, 111, 112
Nicklaus, Jack ix, 111, 112
Nicknames 121, 122
Nicks, Linda 109, 110
Nightingale, Earl 274
Nike 142, 266
Nixon, Richard 167
Nonverbal Communication 99, 178, 188, 190
North America 169, 179, 181
North Carolina Memorial Hospital 259
North Carolina State University 300
Northwestern University 201
Novant Health 201
NPR (National Public Radio) 149, 268

O

Octagon Sports Agency 45
Office, The 175, 267
O'Hair, Sean 36
O'Hara, Catherine 190
Olivier, Laurence 151
Onassis, Aristotle 296
Open-Ended Questions 114, 128
Oppenheimer, J. Robert 19
Opportunity Words 210
Oprah ix, 28, 58, 77, 237, 238, 239, 271, 279, 296
Oprah's Master Class 271
Oprah Winfrey Show 238
Ordanini, Andrea 291
O'Reilly, Tim 243
Oscar 54, 71, 155
Oxford University 24, 343

P

Palmer, Arnold ix, 36
Panama 242
Paquin, Anna ix, 158
Pareto Principle 47
Pareto, Vilfredo 47
Parker, Sarah Jessica 285
Parkinson, Cyril Northcote 46
Parkinson's Law 46
Parton, Dolly 237
Pasteur, Louis 113
Patton, General George S. 53
Path to Power, The 150
Pauses 136
Peale, Norman Vincent 147
Pearce, Stewart 151, 152
Pentagon 217
Perfume 192, 193, 194
Perseverance 147, 204
Pew Research Center 24, 109
PGA Championship 94
PhelpsFace 45
Phelps, Michael ix, 15, 16, 17, 18, 19, 23, 28, 36, 38, 45, 57, 63, 73, 79, 274, 283
Phillips, Michael 295
Piano, The 158
Pipeline 144
"Pirate Song" 209
Plant, Robert 204
Politeness 156
Polston, Butch 184
Positive Attitude 108, 116, 138, 169, 253, 268
Power of Positive Thinking, The 147
Presence 165
Presidential Medal of Freedom 40, 155
Preston, Billy 238
Prince Charles 151
Protocol 101, 138, 172
Proxemics 181

Q

Quartz 74
Quebin, Nido 41, 76
Queen Elizabeth 277

R

Raging Idiots, The 43
Ramsey, John 297
Rapport Building 120
Rashad, Ahmad ix, 265
Rassias, John ix, 288
"Read My Pins" 182
Reasoner, Harry 148
Receiving Lines 99
Redding, Otis 246
Reese, Gordon 150
Reeve, Christopher 271, 272
Remembering Names 106, 107
Remnick, David 268
"R-E-S-P-E-C-T" 246, 249
Resurreccion, Rex 94
Return to Love, A 58
Rhythm and Blues 246
Ribeiro, Alfonso 143
Rice, Jerry ix, 267
Ritter, Al 294
Rivenbark, Celia 155
Rivers, Joan 269
Robison, Maryann 110
Rock and Roll 158, 159, 183, 253, 255
Rockefeller, John D. 108
Rohn, John 31
Rolling Stone 246
'Room without a Roof' 286
Roosevelt, Eleanor 114
Roosevelt, Theodore 68
Rose, Justin 36
Rosenbluth, Lennie 85
Rosolino, Massi 17
Rotary International 95
ROTC 171
Rotella, Bob 82

Rousey, Ronda "Rowdy" 284
Rowling, J.K. 53, 72
Royal Academy of Dramatic Art 184
Royal National Theatre 151
Rucker, Darius 32, 60
Ruettiger, Daniel "Rudy" 34, 60
Rule of Three, The 131
Rumi 139, 301
Rusling, Colonel James 65
Russell, Leon 238
Rutland Weekend Television 209
Ryder Cup 259
Ryazanskiy, Sergey 58

S

Sacred Hoops 37
Sandburg, Carl 197
Sanders, Sidney ix, 298
Sanskrit Advice 46
Santana, Carlos ix, 31, 158, 280
Saturday Night Live 267
Scabbard and Blade 171
Schiff, Lewis 201
Schitt's Creek 189
Schuller, Robert H. 269
Schwartzenegger, Arnold 75
Scott, Stuart ix, 266, 290
See and Feel The Inside Move the Outside 37
Secret of Great Relationships, The 294
Secret, The 81
Seneca, Lucius Annaeus 20, 29
Setzer, Brian 183
Seven Laws of Money, The 295
Sex in the City 285
Shadow Creek Golf Club 36, 262
Shakespeare, William 92, 135
Shankar, Ravi 238
Sherman, William T. 65
Silver Linings Playbook 55
Silverstein, Shel 236
Simon, Paul 204

Simonton, M.D., Charles 95
Sinatra, Frank 296
Sinek, Simon 41
Sixty (60) Minutes 45, 52, 77, 142
Skywalker, Anakin 45
Slater, Robert Kelly ix, 283
Slim Shady 45
Small Talk 103, 105, 118, 119, 126, 128, 259
Smallville 77
Smell Orientation 125
Smiling 97, 129, 135, 168, 263, 297
Smith, Dean 82
Smith, Ozzie 82
Smith, Virginia 189
Smith, Will 143, 162
Snow, C.P. 215
Social Cards 136
Social Introductions 101
Spanx 268
Sparks, Nicholas 302
Spatial Distance 181
Spencer, Stuart 259
Sochi Olympics 58
SportsCenter 266
Sports Hall of Fame Administrator of the Year 43, 245
Sports Illustrated 19, 75, 255, 305
Springsteen, Bruce 183
Stanford University 54, 113, 271
Starr, Ringo 238
Staubach, Roger 265
Stein, Gertrude 230
St. Francis Hospital 169
"Stick Talk" 45
Stone, W. Clement 143, 246
Stradivarius 186
Streisand, Barbara 237
Subliminal Rapport 122, 123, 126, 127, 191
Summitt, Pat 43, 48, 79, 80, 88, 245

T

Tafoya, Michelle 45
Tap Dance Kid, The 143
Tar Heels 112, 259
Taste Orientation 126
Taylor, James 239, 272, 284
Taylor, Tate 239
Technology 108, 214, 215, 217, 221, 266
Ted Turner 188
Telephone 31, 97, 102, 109, 118, 136, 169, 218, 220, 223, 227, 234, 249, 291
Templeton, Jane 171
Tennessean, The 43
Texting 221
Thanking People 232
Thank You Notes 231, 232
Tharp, Twyla 264, 265
Thatcher, Margaret 149, 150, 151
The 100/0 Principle 294
Thicke, Alan ix, 55
Thorpe, Ian "Thorpedo" 72
Thu Bon River 295
Timberlake, Justin 47
Time Management 47, 132
T.J. Maxx 187
TODAY 148
TOMS Shoes 243
Tone 151, 162, 193, 208, 217, 218, 227, 228, 247, 250
Torres, Tico ix, 302
Touching 167, 171, 175, 177, 222
Tracy, Brian 89
Truitt, Scott 235
Turner, Ted 188
Turtle Bay 282
Twain, Mark 19, 190
Twain, Shania 204
Twitter 222, 224

U

UFC (Ultimate Fighting Championship) 285
Unbroken 300
UNC 82, 259, 272
Undeniable 18
"Underdog, The" 204
UNICEF 239
United States Bureau of Hiring and Training Management 108
Universal Tone: Bringing My Story to Light, The 281
University of Chicago 201
University of Hertfordshire 97
University of Kansas 85
University of Kentucky 80
University of Missouri 171
University of North Carolina at Chapel Hill 112, 259
University of Notre Dame 34
University of South Carolina 32
University of Southern California 291
University of Tennessee 79, 245
University of Virginia 180
Unstructured Business Culture 193
Unwritten Rules, Misperceptions, and Secret Beliefs of Men in the Workplace 196
Utech, Mary Kay 245

V

Valentine, Gary 269
Valvano, Jim ix, 30, 300, 302, 303
Vatican 254, 255
Vena, Jocelyn 70
Virgin Group 53
Visual Orientation 124
Vogue Magazine 189
Voice 37, 60, 118, 123, 151, 162, 183, 199, 209, 217, 220, 221, 227, 247, 249
Volcom 144, 283

Vonn, Lindsey 285
Voogd, Peter 141
Vujicic, Nick 77, 79

W

Wagner, John 281
"Waitin' on Joe" 203, 204
Walk to Remember, A 302
Walmart 33, 170, 216, 251, 270, 306
Walters, Barbara ix, 31, 148, 271, 272, 279
Walton, Bill 86
Walton, Sam ix, 31, 33, 43, 170, 171, 216, 251, 252, 269
Waltrip, Michael ix, 74, 75, 90, 95, 113
Wambach, Abby 48, 160, 262
Washington, D.C 186
Washington, D.C. Metro 186
Washington, Denzel 38, 172, 186, 187, 237
Washington Post 172, 186, 187
Watson, Thomas J. 26
Wayne, John 37, 71, 149, 201
Welch, Jack 280
Welling, Tom ix, 77
West, Mae 146
Westwood, Lee 36
Westwood, Vivienne 285
Wheel of Fortune 55
White, Lynne Farwell 293
White, Winifred "Win" McMurry ix, 14, 34, 41, 111, 114, 158, 222, 226, 270
White, Dana 285
Whitman, Meg 18
Whittingdale, John 150
William Arthur Stationery 231
Williams, Armstrong 109
Williamson, Marianne 58
Williams, Pharrell ix, 139, 285
Williams, Robin 272
Williams, Serena 285

Wilmington, NC 73, 103, 155, 222
Wilson, Brian 158
Wilson, Jackie 183
Winfrey, Oprah 58, 238, 279
Wiseman, Richard 96
Wolf, Charles 177
Wooden, John 14
Woods, Tiger 30, 36, 271
Woodstock 280
World Anti-Doping Agency (WADA) 16
Worldchefs Congress 295
World Series 139, 262
World War II 142, 182
Wrightsville Beach, North Carolina 15, 16
Written Correspondence 230

X

X 222, 224, 225
X-Men: First Class 55
XTRA 189

Y

Yearwood, Dave 241
Yearwood Surfboards 241, 242
YouTube 44, 77, 151, 239, 270

Z

Zamperini, Louis 300, 321
Zappa, Frank 27
Zen 36
Ziglar, Zig 44, 53, 61, 96, 294
Zuckerberg, Mark 237

About the Author

Jane Hight is the founder of Effective Business Communication, a training and professional speaking company focused on actions beyond education and technical skills that drive success. She is the author of several books, including bestselling *Navigating the Lipstick Jungle*.

Her curiosity about what makes the winning difference began when she left home as a young student to study at Oxford University. It was in England that she first noticed that it was not simply education. Learning the definitive answer to her question came later through face-to-face encounters with many of the most legendary winners on the planet with a chance to ask what others with only theories had not: "What made the winning difference to your success?" Not a single superstar mentioned education, technical skill, talent, luck, body-build, or money.

Jane Hight weaves winners' secrets and stories with in-depth research to provide a lodestar guide to peak performance that is indispensable for anyone who wants to win.

Visit **www.janehight.com** for information about having the author speak at your conference, meeting, or event.

www.ingramcontent.com/pod-product-compliance
Lightning Source LLC
Chambersburg PA
CBHW062108290426
44110CB00023B/2747